Following

LIVING A
BALANCED
FINANCIAL
LIFE

LIVING A
BALANCED
FINANCIAL
LIFE

A Bible Study by

DEBORAH NAYROCKER

Advancing the Ministries of the Gospel
 AMG Publishers

God's Word to you is our highest calling.

Following God

LIVING A BALANCED FINANCIAL LIFE

First Printing, 2007

ISBN 10: 0-89957-246-8
ISBN 13: 978-0-89957-246-4

Cover design by ImageWright Marketing and Design, Chattanooga, TN
Layout by Jennifer Ross and Rick Steele
Editing by Rick Steele

Printed in Canada
11 10 09 08 07 –T– 5 4 3 2 1

This book is dedicated to my parents,

Samuel and Eleanor

Thank you for your
unconditional love
and genuine encouragement.

Acknowledgments

I am grateful to my parents, Samuel and Eleanor Ross, for being examples of what it means to follow God's leading in our everyday lives. Their desire to know God and to serve Him has been evidenced throughout their lives. It was they who first gave me a glimpse of what God's great love is like. My father, a seminary graduate, was a Bible college professor, church planter, pastor, and missionary. He was always ready with a wise answer about God's Word. He is an example of one who ministered faithfully to others. My mother, a Bible college graduate and missionary, naturally shared her faith and encouraged others. I am truly grateful for parents who loved God and "walked their talk."

References consulted for the lessons include Strong's Hebrew and Greek Dictionaries, Albert Barnes' Notes on the Bible, Adam Clarke's Commentary on the Bible, Matthew Henry's Commentary on the Whole Bible, all provided in electronic format via e-Sword, © 2005, Rick Meyers; the Key Word Study Bible by Spiros Zodhiates, from AMG Publishers; and the Funk & Wagnalls Standard Desk Dictionary. I am grateful for everyone at AMG Publishers who publish good books that help readers grow in their knowledge of God. I also want to give thanks for the diligent work of Rick Steele and others of the editing team at AMG Publishers.

 DEBORAH NAYROCKER

About the Author

Deborah Nayrocker graduated with honors from Bethel College in Mishawaka, Indiana, and holds a Masters degree from Indiana University. She has been an educator for over twenty-five years. Her articles on Christian living and personal finance have been published in various magazines and other publications. She is the author of *The Art of Debt-Free Living—Living Large on Less Than You Earn* (Enumclaw, Washington: Pleasant Word). She and her husband make their home in northern Indiana, and have two adult children.

About the Following God Series

Three authors and fellow ministers, Wayne Barber, Eddie Rasnake, and Rick Shepherd, teamed up in 1998 to write a character-based Bible study for AMG Publishers. Their collaboration developed into the title, *Life Principles from the Old Testament*. Since 1998 these same authors and AMG Publishers have produced six more **character-based** studies—each consisting of twelve lessons geared around a five-day study of a particular Bible personality. In 2004, AMG Publishers launched a series of topical studies called the **Following God™ Christian Living Series,** and this release of *Living a Balanced Financial Life* by Deborah Nayrocker becomes the fifth title released in this format. Though new studies and authors are being introduced, the interactive study format that readers have come to love remains constant with each new Following God™ release. As new titles and categories are being planned, our focus remains the same: to provide excellent Bible study materials that point people to God's Word in ways that allow them to apply truths to their own lives. More information on this groundbreaking series can be found on the following web page:

www.amgpublishers.com

Preface

If we look more closely at the stories and accounts in the Old and New Testaments, we will find they reveal many truths and principles for us today. Hundreds of verses are found in the Bible relating specifically to money and our possessions. Two-thirds of the parables Christ told us deal directly with money. Come along as we explore basic biblical financial principles.

Research for my book *The Art of Debt-Free Living—Living Large on Less Than You Earn* and this Bible study showed me that we need more biblical guidance in the area of personal finance. As we learn more from the lessons in the Bible, we will have a better understanding of how God wants us to live our lives to the fullest.

Throughout this study, I quote from the New International Version of the Bible. It will be easiest to use this translation when studying the passages and answering the questions. This study has twelve weekly lessons with five lesson segments for each week.

Join me as we take an in-depth look at our core values and beliefs and how they affect the way we manage our money and possessions. This Bible study on money management not only will provide principles and guidelines to help you along life's journey. It will also help you focus on developing a growing relationship with our great and loving God.

Following Christ,

Deborah Nayrocker

Table of Contents

God Owns Everything:
He Is Master of All 1

We Are God's Stewards:
How to Be Faithful Managers 15

God's Commands
Protect Us from Indebtedness 29

Virtues that Help
Keep Debt at Bay 45

Principles for Learning God's Will
in Our Lives 61

Evaluating Our Life-Goals:
Desiring to Please God 77

Faithfulness in Handling Our Money 93

Getting Our Finances in Order
With a Spending Plan 109

Borrowing and Credit:
Understanding Biblical Principles......................125

Saving and Planning for Future Needs 141

Being Content with God's Provision 157

Exploring Our Riches as Believers:
Recognizing God's Blessings 173

GOD OWNS EVERYTHING.
HE IS MASTER OF ALL

Welcome to our Bible study, *Living a Balanced Financial Life*. God cares about each one of us. He wants to bless us with His wisdom, and His Word can serve as a guide for our daily lives. It is our choice to learn more about God's Word and to accept it. In order to get our personal and financial lives more into balance, this Bible study book:

helps us examine our purpose in life, our walk with God, and our commitment to God

provides a practical step-by-step guide for getting on the right track financially, based on God's Word

helps us to understand our real needs

focuses on the deeper issues of why we make our lifestyle choices and remain in debt or in tough financial situations

encourages us to examine our spending habits and look at positive and negative consequences

suggests a new perspective on enjoying life without having to live a life of consumerism

challenges us to consistently maintain fiscal responsibility

encourages us to experience positive life changes through Bible study and pertinent discussion questions.

Many of us today are looking for prosperity, believing that "the good life" is defined in the happiness that our possessions bring us. We have come to believe that we can't be happy unless we have what we desire, whatever that may be. We may find it hard to wait for those things we desire. We jump to financial decisions, which are in hindsight poor choices. And when we do

Many of us are looking for prosperity, believing that "the good life" is defined in the happiness that our possessions bring us.

receive what we want, we may still find ourselves unhappy. We may discover other new problems that we need to deal with.

Life doesn't come without problems. Our own foolish decisions and not-so-wise choices have brought on some of these problems. Or we may have no control over some of our circumstances. How we look at our lives and circumstances can play an important part in our happiness and contentedness in life.

Throughout this study we will explore the following areas:

What did God say about our money, possessions, and riches?

What did others in the Bible say and do about it?

What did Jesus say about money?

God has given us financial principles from His Word because He knows what is best for us. These principles, parables, and stories were given to us so we could learn from them. Through these, God desires that we trust Him and listen to His words of financial wisdom.

Through these lessons, we can strive to:

discover God's truths about money and possessions and other important biblical concepts

understand God's truths and biblical wisdom on money

apply God's truths and money principles

share God's truths

God Owns Everything

DAY ONE

GOD MADE US, AND HE KNOWS WHAT'S GOING ON

In today's lesson we will look at the life of a man who had everything a man could desire. He had a lovely wife, and his family was complete with seven responsible sons and three beautiful daughters. His next-door neighbors and people from all around the land of Uz (in the Middle East) knew him to be a very wealthy man. When he was able to get away from managing his assets, he would spend some time with his three closest friends, also prosperous, respected, and well-known throughout the land. This rich man's name is Job.

In the book of Job 1:3 we read, *"And he owned seven thousand sheep, three thousand camels, five hundred yoke of oxen and five hundred donkeys, and had a large number of servants. He was the greatest man among all the people of the East."* We know that Job was an upright man who feared God and hated evil. He desired to live a blameless life before God.

One day, however, tragedy unexpectedly hit Job's household. All of his flocks and herds were lost. Almost all of his trusted servants were killed. And before the sun had set, Job's beloved sons and daughters died in an instant when the roof of the house they were in collapsed. Mourning and filled with despair, Job responded by saying, *"The LORD gave and the LORD has taken away; may the name of the LORD be praised"* (Job 1:21).

To make matters worse, the very next day he was afflicted with a horrible skin disease. He was covered with sores from his head to his feet. They were terribly unpleasant to look at and equally painful. Job grieved. He knew deep down that he didn't deserve what had happened to him. Yet he was convinced there *must* be an explanation for all that had happened.

When his wife asked him how he could still hold on to his integrity with the loss of his great wealth and his health he answered, *"Shall we accept good from God, and not trouble?"* (Job 2:10). News traveled fast, and Job's three closest friends quickly packed their bags, left their homes, and decided to see what they could do to help their friend. We read that, in the end, Job received little encouragement from his friends.

Job went through more pain and despair in a short amount of time than many people go through in a lifetime. Yet he did not lose his trust in God. Job held onto his strong desire to obey God and to trust in Him.

Job turned to the only One who could give him the answers and strength he most desperately needed. In the silence, He longed to speak with God and have God reveal Himself to him. After what must have seemed like years of silence, one day God answered Job. The Almighty God told him it was His turn to ask the questions, now. The beginning of His reply was more like a nature lesson. God began with a beautiful discourse on His creation.

📖 Read Job 38:1–14 for God's response to Job.

Who laid the foundations of the earth (Job 38:4)?

_____

📖 Read Job 38:15–41. What message is God desiring to show Job (and us) through his reply?

_____

_____

_____

📖 According to Proverbs 22:2, what do the rich and poor have in common?

_____

_____

> **"The heavens declare the glory of God; the skies proclaim the work of his hands."**
>
> **Psalm 19:1**

When we think of God's greatness, we are in awe of *Yahweh,* our Creator. The revelation of God in His creation is self-evident. What a vast difference between our puny humanity and the God of all creation! God knows what is going on in our lives. He is watching over us and is with us at all times. From the beginning of time His love has always existed for us. We can walk freely in the knowledge that God will take care of us.

🛑 APPLY Write a prayer of thanks to God for His creation. What wonders of our Father's creation stand out to you as signs of His greatness?

_____

_____

_____

God Owns Everything

DAY TWO

📖 Read the end of the Job's story in chapter 42, verses 7–16.

What impresses you most about the story of Job?

_____

_____

_____

_____

 God has promised that He will be with us. But how we relate to God in our obedience, love, and faith plays a major role in the depth that we can experience His daily presence. In what areas of our life can we draw closer to God?

GOD'S CONTROL OF HIS CREATION

Yesterday we read God's majestic reply to Job. His long awaited response resembled a nature lesson describing the intricate details of His creation.

📖 Read Psalm 33:6–9. Fill in the blanks according to verse 9.

"For he _____, and it came to be; he _____, and it _____ _____."

Not only did God create the world and everything in it, but He is also still in control of His creation. He didn't create the world and walk away from it. He founded the world and still remains in authority. He continues to sustain the world and remains sovereign. The word "sovereign" refers to "a person or governing body in whom the supreme power or authority is vested; ruler."[1] God is the Supreme Ruler over all; He triumphs over all.

The name *Adonai* (Hebrew), means "Lord" in the sense of one being master, owner, or in authority. In this lesson we'll focus on God as *Adonai*.

📖 Read Psalm 24, a psalm King David wrote about God's authority.

To whom does the earth and everything in it belong (verses 1–2)?

_____

Who may stand in the holy place of the Lord (verses 3–4)?

_____

According to Psalm 24:5, what will the pure in heart receive?

_____

Throughout the first thirty-nine chapters of Isaiah, the prophet Isaiah has harsh words of judgment for the Israelites. Then in chapter forty he offers words of hope and comfort to them.

📖 Read of God's sovereignty in Isaiah 40:12–31. As you read these verses, note Isaiah's amazing insights into God's creation.

_____

_____

_____

_____

_____

What verses that reflect God's glory and authority stand out to you? Make a note of the verses that have special meaning to you.

_____

_____

_____

God is in control of His creation including humanity. He is in control of our lives and of our circumstances. The Bible has many examples of how God worked in people's lives. We will look at the life of a woman named Hannah, who had a simple faith in her great God.

Hannah, a Woman of Faith

Hannah was a barren woman who longed to have a child. Elkanah, her loving husband, would try to comfort and encourage her, year after year. Yet this woman continued to grieve, childless and scorned by others. The time came when Hannah made her yearly pilgrimage to the tabernacle in Shiloh to worship God and make an offering. Weeping in anguish, she prayed earnestly to God, asking Him not to forget her heart's desire. She made a vow that if God would give her a male child, then she would give him back to God.

Eli the priest saw her lips moving as she wept and prayed quietly. Asking if she was drunk, she replied, *"I am a woman who is deeply troubled. . . . I was pouring out my soul to the LORD. Do not take your servant for a wicked woman; I have been praying here out of my great anguish and grief"* (1 Samuel 1:15–16). Then Eli told her, *"Go in peace, and may the God of Israel grant you what you have asked of Him."* She responded, *"May your servant find favor in your eyes."* So Hannah left and was no longer sorrowful, but reassured and full of hope (1 Samuel 1:17–18).

God answered Hannah's earnest request and gave her a son whom she named Samuel. Delighted to be a mother, Hannah knew that when Samuel was weaned and old enough to remain at the temple, he would serve God in the Temple with Eli the priest.

The day came for Hannah to take her only son, Samuel to the temple. She lovingly dedicated him there, giving a heartfelt prayer of thanks to God and acknowledging His authority in her life. Hannah's prayer is filled with honor and praise for the Lord. In this passage, she expresses her reverence and sense of awe of God in her prayer.

Read Hannah's prayer of thanksgiving in 1 Samuel 2:1–10.

In 1 Samuel 2:2, what is God compared to?

_____

According to 1 Samuel 2:7, what does God do?

_____

> **"The LORD sends poverty and wealth; he humbles and he exalts."**
>
> **I Samuel 2:7**

God Owns Everything

> **"For the foundations of the earth are the LORD'S; upon them he has set the world. He will guard the feet of his saints, but the wicked will be silenced in darkness."**
>
> **I Samuel 2:8–9.**

Fill in the blanks according to verse 8.

"He _____ the poor from the dust and _____ the needy from the ash heap; he _____ them with the princes and has them _____ a throne of honor."

Note—There are several other barren women in the Bible whom God miraculously helped. In the Old Testament we read of Sarah (Genesis 11:30), Rebekah (Genesis 25:21) and Rachel (Genesis 30:22–23). In the New Testament, Elizabeth had a child in her older years (Luke 1:7, 13).

GOD'S PROVISION

God is the supplier and provider of our needs. In today's study section we will look at an example of how God made provisions for His people in the Old Testament.

The Israelites lived for many years on the Sinai Peninsula, a harsh land, and a difficult place to live. God supplied daily food and water for them in the desert. They had to rely on God for their daily sustenance.

In the book of Deuteronomy, the great leader Moses delivers three long talks to his people, the Israelites. He talks to his people as a father, retelling his life's story and communicating again his desire for them to not forget God's laws he had taught them. Although at times he reprimands them, his love and concern for them also shine through.

Moses had changed since his earlier days when he pleaded with God, asking God that he not be the one to speak to the Israelites for Him. After his life-changing experiences of over forty years in the desert, Moses had become eloquent and desired to share his heart with the Israelites before he was to leave them.

God had made it clear to Moses that he would not be entering the Promised Land with the Israelites. Living along the banks of the Jordan River, about to enter Canaan, Moses probably wondered how well the people would follow God's instructions when they were on their own. They had lived in the desert for many years, many of them born there. They were about to enter a land of plenty. Would they still remember their hard experiences in the desert? Would they soon forget how God had provided for them in so many ways?

Would they follow God's laws as they had been taught or would they be enticed by what they found in the new land? Moses' second and longest speech is recorded in Deuteronomy, chapters 4—26. Here Moses carefully reviews their civil and moral decrees. His parting words were intended as reminders of how God had provided for them in the past.

📖 Read Deuteronomy 8:1–18.

How did God provide for the Israelites' clothing in the desert (verse 4)?

_____

_____

What command did Moses give to his people? (verse 6)?

_____

_____

_____

What were the Israelites to do when they had eaten and were satisfied (Deuteronomy 8:10)?

_____

_____

_____

In Deuteronomy 8:18, what does Moses say about wealth?

_____

_____

_____

APPLY How does this passage in Deuteronomy 8 apply to our lives today? What does it teach us?

_____

_____

_____

_____

_____

There are many examples in the New Testament of God's miraculous provision. We read in Luke 5 about Simon, a fisherman by trade, who had been fishing all night. The next day, people followed Jesus to the Lake of Gennesaret, and they crowded around him. At the shore's edge, Jesus saw Simon's boat nearby and sat in it, talking to the people that were eager to listen to His words.

📖 Read Luke 5:1–11.

According to Luke 5:5, why did Simon Peter decide to cast down the nets again?

_____

_____

What was the result (verse 6)?

_____

_____

God is Yahweh-Yireh, meaning, "Yahweh will provide."

APPLY Think about the different ways God has provided for you and your needs. Fill in the following chart.

Situation	How God Provided

We'll conclude today by focusing on God's most important provision for us. Without a doubt, God's best provision to all of us is His one and only Son, Jesus Christ. God's Son satisfies His anger against our sins. Romans 6:23 states: *"For the wages of sin is death, but the gift of God is eternal life in Christ Jesus our Lord."*

We read in Hebrews 2:14–15, and 17 how Jesus became one of us:

> *"He too shared in their humanity so that by his death he might destroy him who holds the power of death—that is, the devil—and free those who all their lives were held in slavery by their fear of death. . . . For this reason he had to be made like his brothers in every way, in order that he might become a merciful and faithful high priest in service to God, and that he might make atonement for the sins of the people."*

Today we can enjoy the free gift of salvation. Paul reminds us that since we have so great a gift of salvation, will God not also graciously give us more? *"He who did not spare his own Son, but gave him up for us all—how will he not also, along with him, graciously give us all things?"* (Romans 8:32).

God Owns Everything

DAY FOUR

As we seek more of God, he will provide us with many other gifts. "But seek first his kingdom and his righteousness, and all these things will be given to you as well."

Matthew 6:33

GOD'S POWER

God is all-powerful. He has shown Himself in countless ways over the ages and generations. God's power may not always be visible, but those who believe in God know He is at work. His power is evidenced through extraordinary events, not only in the past, but today, as well. Because God is an omnipotent God, we can know that *"with God all things are possible"* (Matthew 19:26).

We can recount many stories in the Bible revealing God's power. They illustrate how God can intervene when people do not see a way out and when there seems to be no hope. King David is an example of someone who had seen God's power from the time he was a young shepherd boy. His life's story shows God's intervention and might.

For years King David's greatest desire was to build an immense and beautiful temple where his people could worship and serve God. The Temple was also to be the designated resting place for the Ark of the Covenant. The Lord God, the Master Architect, gave the king clear instructions on all of the intricate details for the great Temple's building plans.

In 1 Chronicles 29:1–20, King David spoke to the whole assembly before the beginning of the Temple construction. He rejoiced that the many materials needed for the building of the Temple had been gathered. He knew that his young son Solomon would be in charge of building the Temple. Actually, Solomon would become king the very next day. David's prayer, spoken with everyone assembled, reveals that he wanted all the glory to go to God in this huge undertaking. In essence, this is the dedication service of the new temple.

📖 Read David's prayer in 1 Chronicles 29:10–13. Although he was a man of great wealth and many achievements, David wanted God to receive the honor for everything.

What is God's (verse 11)?

_____

Fill in the blanks according to verse 12.

"_____ and _____ come from you; you are the _____ of all things."

What are in God's hands (verse 12)?

_____

How did King David end his prayer (verse 13)?

_____

_____

In 1 Chronicles 29:16 King David emphasizes again how the abundance of their resources came from God's hand and all of it belonged to Him.

📖 In Exodus 15:11, how is the Lord God's power described?

_____

_____

In the apostle Paul's letter to the Colossians, Paul writes to the church in the first–century town of Colosse. In this letter, Paul informs his readers that he is aware of the early Christian converts being affected by deceptive philosophies, false religious ideas, and cultic beliefs. But Paul reiterates that "Christ is enough" and alludes to the possibility that they may have included Greek mythology and philosophy or legalism into their beliefs.

Paul writes eloquently about the supremacy of Christ in Chapter 1 of Colossians. One can sense God's awesome power in these words:

> "He is the image of the invisible God, the firstborn over all creation. For by him all things were created; things in heaven and on earth, visible and invisible, whether thrones or powers or rulers or authorities; all things were created by him and for him. He is before all things, and in him all things hold together. And he is the head of the body, the church; he is the beginning and the firstborn from among the dead, so that in everything he might have the supremacy." (Colossians 1:15–18)

Paul encouraged the believers to experience the fullness of God. He writes:

> "That you may live a life worthy of the Lord and may please him in every way: bearing fruit in every good work, growing in the knowledge of God, being strengthened with all power according to His glorious might so that you may have great endurance and patience. (Colossians 1:10–11)

Let's look at the following words found in Colossians 1:11: "strengthened with all power according to His glorious might."

strengthened—from the Greek word dunamoo, meaning "to grow strong, of moral strengthening"[2]

glorious—from the Greek work doxa, meaning "as very apparent as in honor, praise, worship"[3]

might—from the Greek word dunamis, meaning "force, miraculous power, wonderful work"[4]

"And my God will meet all your needs according to his glorious riches in Christ Jesus."

Philippians 4:19

God is all-powerful. God is El-Shaddai, or "Lord Almighty."

It's exciting to know that the fullness of God (*Yahweh*) in the Old Testament was made alive in the Person of Jesus Christ, who lived on this earth, died, and rose again. Through Jesus Christ and His Holy Spirit, we, too, are enabled by God to walk in His ways. We are enabled through His power to "live a life worthy of the Lord."

When we receive the gift of salvation and new life in Christ, God's Holy Spirit gives us the power to live that new life. God wants us to fully utilize that power to live for Him. The all-powerful God can and will continue to prove Himself in our daily walk with God. God is *El-Shaddai*, the One who shows Himself still today.

APPLY Write a journal entry of how you have seen God's intervention and power in your life. How has He enabled you through His power?

_____

_____

_____

_____

_____

God Owns Everything

"Wealth and honor come from you; you are the ruler of all things."

I Chronicles 29:12

TRUSTING IN GOD, OUR CREATOR

In what or whom do we put our trust? Do we trust in our religious heritage, family name, good works, or our strict adherence to particular rules or laws? Do we put our trust in other people's promises, knowledge, or teachings? Or maybe we find that we lean on and trust in our possessions and bank accounts to get us through life. Have we thought about whether we have a substitute for God? We read many examples in God's Word of those who chose *not* to put their trust in God.

The Rise and Fall of Solomon
One privileged man who knew much wealth was Solomon, the king of Israel. The son of King David and Queen Bathsheba, Solomon was raised as a prince, having luxuries at his command. From a young age he was known for his songwriting ability and his knack for expressing truth about life. He composed thousands of proverbs, three thousand of them recorded in the book of Proverbs. He was known to be the wisest and most prosperous man in the world during his lifetime.

As his father David had requested, Solomon oversaw the construction of the ornately beautiful temple of God in Jerusalem. Over two hundred thousand builders, artisans, and craftsmen were involved in the seven years it took to build this famous building.

📖 Read 1 Kings 10:14–29 for an account of his wealth.

📖 In Deuteronomy, Moses lists the qualifications required of the kings of Israel. Read Deuteronomy 17:14–20 to find out what these were. Based on your knowledge of King Solomon, compare his qualities and characteristics as king with those qualities Moses described.

The people of Israel began to look to King Solomon, their leader, for guidance and religious leadership. However, he became a king of excess, hoarding huge amounts of silver and gold. He lived with seven hundred wives and three hundred concubines. When Solomon no longer devoted his heart to the Lord God and disobeyed God's laws, turning to other gods, God warned him that his kingdom would be taken away from him. The story of Solomon reminds us that we must not stray from the one true God. As we obey God's commands and trust Him and put our faith in Him, God will prosper us.

APPLY Although Solomon began his reign with good intentions, he lost focus on God, his source of wisdom. Are there any ways that you have lost focus of God in your life? What ways can you think of where your attention and affections have turned away from God?

_____

_____

_____

_____

_____

_____

_____

In his earlier years, Solomon knew what it was like to walk with God. In Proverbs 3:5–6 he writes about living closely to God:

"If you want favor with both God and man, and a reputation for good judgment and common sense, then trust the Lord completely; don't ever trust yourself. In everything you do, put God first, and he will direct you and crown your efforts with success." (LB)

Whom Do We Trust?

When we trust in God, we have faith in God and reliance on Him. The prophet Jeremiah talked about the dilemma of trusting in man or trusting in God. Who is one to trust? God's Word says:

"This is what the LORD says: 'Cursed is the one who trusts in man, who depends on flesh for his strength and whose heart turns away from the LORD. He will be like a bush in the wastelands; he will not see prosperity when it comes. He will dwell in the parched places of the desert, in a salt land where no one lives. But blessed is the man who trusts in the LORD, whose confidence is in him. He will be like a tree planted by the water that sends out its roots by the stream. It does not fear when heat comes; its leaves are always green. It has no worries in a year of drought and never fails to bear fruit.' " (Jeremiah 17:5–8)

Describe the person who trusts in man (Jeremiah 17:5–6). Describe the person who trusts in God (Jeremiah 17:7–8).

_____

_____

_____

_____

_____

_____

"Who among the gods is like you, O LORD? Who is like you—majestic in holiness, awesome in glory, working wonders?"

Exodus 15:11

> "My grace is sufficient for you, for my power is made perfect in weakness."
>
> 2 Corinthians 12:9

We note that people who trust in men or women will be like a dry and fruitless bush. But those who choose to trust in God will be like a tree whose leaves stay green and continue producing fruit.

Lord God, thank you for showing yourself through your creation. You are *Yahweh*, my Creator. Your greatness is matchless. I praise You that You are sovereign. You are *Adonai*, the One in authority over me. May I always be willing to yield to You. I recognize Your care and love for me. I thank You that You are the provider of my needs. You are *Yahweh-Yireh*, who will provide. Help me to trust You more for my needs. You are the Lord Almighty, *El-Shaddai*. Your mighty power has been evidenced throughout the generations. I pray for Your strength in my life and the continuation of Your wonderful work. I believe and trust in You, Lord God. In Jesus' name I pray. Amen.

Write your prayer expressing your thankfulness to God for who He is.

_____

_____

_____

_____

_____

_____

_____

_____

NOTES

1. *Funk & Wagnalls Standard Desk Dictionary*, Vol. 2, (USA: Harper & Row Publishers, Inc. 1984), 644.

2. Spiros Zodhiates, *Hebrew-Greek Key Word Study Bible*, (Chattanooga:AMG Publishers, 1990), 1827.

3. Strong's *Hebrew and Greek Dictionaries*, In e-Sword Bible software database, 2005, Rick Meyers.

4. Ibid.

Notes

Notes

WE ARE GOD'S STEWARDS: HOW TO BE FAITHFUL MANAGERS

The term "stewardship" is not often used in our everyday vocabulary. Yet most of us are acutely aware of the importance of being good stewards in the different compartments and areas of our lives. Stewardship is defined as "management and accountability for something that belongs to someone else; especially human stewardship of God's gifts."[1] In this lesson we will look at the various ways we are accountable to God and to others in our everyday lives.

When we first think of the term "stewardship," we may think of giving to the church or to other ministries. We may think of giving a portion of our income to charity. In 2 Corinthians 9:7 we read: *"Each man should give what he has decided in his heart to give, not reluctantly or under compulsion, for God loves a cheerful giver."* Yet stewardship encompasses more than this. It is not so much that God needs our money, but He wants our lives and our commitment to Him.

Even our breath is because of God. God knows how long we will live on this earth. The hours we are given each day to accomplish our tasks are finite. How we use our time affects the progress of our spiritual growth. Moses' prayer in Psalm 90 states: *"Teach us to number our days, that we may gain a heart of wisdom"* (verse 12, NKJV).

In this lesson we will look at the various ways we are accountable to God and to others in our everyday lives.

Stewardship is defined as "management and accountability for something that belongs to someone else; especially human stewardship of God's gifts."

(The Student Bible, New International Version [Grand Rapids, MI: Zondervan, 1996], 1396)

WHAT IS STEWARDSHIP?

How we live on this earth plays a part in both our spiritual and general health. Those who live immoral lives and practice the works of the flesh are not wise stewards. Our bodies are the temples of the Holy Spirit. In 1 Corinthians 3:16 we read, *"Don't you know that you yourselves are God's temple and that God's Spirit lives in you?"* In the Old Testament, God spoke to His people saying, *"Come out from them and be separate, says the Lord. Touch no unclean thing, and I will receive you. I will be a Father to you, and you will be my sons and daughters, says the Lord Almighty"* (2 Corinthians 6:17–18). God wants to use us, His children and His people.

📖 Read 1 Corinthians 6:19–20. According to these verses, to whom do we belong?

Write 1 Corinthians 6:20 on the lines below:

_____

_____

_____

_____

When we are willing to give God every part of our lives, He will be able to use us more effectively.

God has given us many spiritual blessings. Because we believe that Jesus Christ is Lord, we are to be stewards of God's grace and of His Word, wherever our lives may take us or whatever we may do.

God has blessed us materially. We are accountable to Him to be good managers of the resources He has given to us. When we allow God to lead in our lives, we acknowledge and obey His financial wisdom. The Bible has more than sixteen hundred verses on money and possessions. As we learn more about these biblical money principles, we are able to make wiser choices in our lives. We can honor Him with our material possessions.

Throughout the Bible, we read of the importance God places on the faithfulness of His people. As stewards we are expected to have the quality of faithfulness. Jesus used parables to teach important lessons and concepts to His disciples and to others who hear the Word of God.

In Luke 12:42–48, we read Jesus' parable of the faithful and wise servant. Jesus had just told the parable of the watchful servants. In this parable, the watchful servants are keeping their lamps burning and waiting in anticipation of their master's return from a late-night wedding. Peter then asked Jesus if this parable was just for them or for everyone. Jesus answered by telling this next parable in Luke 12. Read the words of Jesus in Luke 12:42–48:

> *"I'm talking to any faithful, sensible man whose master gives him the responsibility of feeding the other servants. If his master returns and finds that he has done a good job, there will be a reward—his master will put him in charge of all he owns.*

"But if the man begins to think, 'My Lord won't be back for a long time,' and begins to whip the men and women he is supposed to protect, and to spend his time at drinking parties and in drunkenness—well, his master will return without notice and remove him from his position of trust and assign him to the place of the unfaithful. He will be severely punished, for though he knew his duty he refused to do it.

"But anyone who is not aware that he is doing wrong will be punished only lightly. Much is required from those to whom much is given, for their responsibility is greater." (LB)

What did Jesus teach about stewardship in Luke 12:42–48?

APPLY Can you think of examples of people you know who were *not* faithful stewards? What were their consequences?

_____

_____

_____

_____

_____

_____

Can you think of areas in your life in which you can be a better steward or manager? What can be done to improve on these areas? What can you begin to do differently this week?

_____

_____

_____

_____

_____

_____

In summary, stewardship is using and managing all of life's resources as God's faithful servants. It is the life-changing response to our calling as Christians. It is a way of life. In the next few days of this week's lesson, we will look at how we can be better stewards of our human resources. These will include our time, abilities, and work.

ARE YOU TRUSTWORTHY?

"Whoever can be trusted with very little can also be trusted with much, and whoever is dishonest with very little will also be dishonest with much. So if you have not been trustworthy in handling worldly wealth, who will trust you with true riches? And if you have not been trustworthy with someone else's property, who will give you property of your own?" (Luke 16:10–12)

STEWARDSHIP OF OUR TIME

We Are Stewards

DAY TWO

As Christians, we commit ourselves to responsible use of God's resources to us. An important resource God has given us is that of time. We may not think of this as a resource. Yet it is one of the most important resources we all have.

Have you ever heard someone exclaim, "I wish I had more hours in my day"? We may feel we do not have enough time to do what we want to do.

We may desire to have more time, but every one of us has only twenty-four hours in a day. What may seem as the problem of *lack of time*, actually has to do with *what we do with our time*. We *can* learn to manage our time more effectively as it passes, hour by hour, day by day.

Psalm 90:12 reminds us to be aware of the limited time we have in each of our days. *"Teach us to number our days and recognize how few they are; help us to spend them as we should"* (LB). The following account helps us visualize the time increments we have:

> If you had a bank that credited your account each morning with $86,000—that carried over no balance from day to day—and allowed you to keep no cash in your account. . . . and every evening cancelled whatever part of the amount you had failed to use during the day—what would you do? Draw out every cent, of course! Well, you do have such a bank—its name is 'time.' Every morning it credits you with 86,000 seconds. Every night it rules off as lost whatever of this you have failed to invest to good purposes. It carries over no balance, allows no overdrafts. Each day it opens a new account for you. If you fail to use the day's deposit, the loss is yours. There is no going back. There is no drawing against tomorrow. You must live in the present—on today's deposit. (Author unknown)

📖 Read the following Scripture verses on time and opportunities.

Ecclesiastes 3:1–2: what did Solomon say about time?

_____

_____

According to Ephesians 5:15–16, what directives are we given about time?

_____

_____

_____

Once we have a clear understanding of our priorities, we can apply our resources to the best opportunities given to us. We can make the most of every opportunity.

A Proper Balance of Our Time

How well do we manage the time given to us? Do we give enough time and importance to those areas we consider priorities? Sometimes we may feel life is a "balancing act" in a circus; we're trying to keep everything up in the air without dropping anything. We may be struggling to follow through with all of our responsibilities. Maybe it has been difficult keeping up with both work and home duties. Or perhaps we haven't set aside enough quiet time with our Father.

Let's look more closely at our daily routine. Do we include time for the following areas?

Our walk with God—our spiritual growth

Family—honoring them with our time and attention

Work

Play or relaxation

A problem many employers report is that of employees not making good

---

Paul strongly encourages readers of Ephesians 5:15–16 to be good stewards of time: "Be very careful, then, how you live—not as unwise but as wise, making the most of every opportunity, because the days are evil."

use of their paid time at work. Time that should be spent on the job is spent instead on long coffee or lunch breaks or frequent and long personal phone calls. In recent years, employers have been forced to implement stricter rules on personal use of computers on company time.

It is a sobering thought that we may stand before the Lord God and give an account of how we spent our time here on earth. It is so easy to get caught up with all of our daily activities and neglect our time seeking more of God and learning more of Him.

Think about how much time you set aside for the following activities every week:

> Bible study and quiet time
> prayer
> ministry—discipling or witnessing

John 15:1–11 reminds us of the importance of abiding in God. In John 15:4 we read: *"Abide in Me, and I in you. As the branch cannot bear fruit of itself, unless it abides in the vine, neither can you, unless you abide in Me"* (NKJV).

When we do not set aside quiet time with God, it is difficult to have a growing relationship with Him. When we spend time reading and studying God's Word, we move on in our maturity as believers. When we continue to be spiritually connected with Christ, we continue to bear fruit. As we stay and remain in Him, we learn more of how He wants us to live. Paul states: *"Clothe yourselves with the Lord Jesus Christ, and do not think about how to gratify the desires of the sinful nature"* (Romans 13:14).

APPLY Do you spend enough time on the priorities in your life?

_____

_____

_____

_____

As you think about how you spend your time, are there any ways you could improve on your use of time? What are they? As we learn to focus on our priorities, we will become more productive with our time.

Making the Most of Our Day
"This is the day the LORD has made; let us rejoice and be glad in it" (Psalm 118:24).

> This is the beginning of a new day. God has given me this day to use as I will. I can waste it or use it for good, but what I do today is important, because I am exchanging a day of my life for it. When tomorrow comes, this day will be gone forever, leaving in its place something that I have traded for it. I want it to be gain, and not loss; good, and not evil; success, and not failure. (Author unknown).

"Make the most of your chances to tell others the Good News. Be wise in all your contacts with them. Let your conversation be gracious as well as sensible, for then you will have the right answer for everyone."

Colossians 4:5–6 (LB)

STEWARDSHIP OF OUR ABILITIES AND WORK

Our stewardship can be lived out by wisely employing our God-given abilities. Each of us has been given abilities and gifts, which are especially assigned to us by our Creator. God wants us to use our talents wisely and to be productive for Him.

Some people may be aware of their innate abilities and capacities, yet they do not use these to their fullest because they are busy pursuing material success. There is nothing wrong with making a living. However, our talents can also be used in serving God in other ways, as well.

Can you think of some of the most talented people you knew in elementary school, high school, or in college? Did they continue to use their talents?

_____

_____

_____

_____

When we refer to someone as being talented in specific areas (such as music, academics, athletics, drama, etc.), we may not realize the use of the word "talent" is used in a parable in Matthew about a man who entrusted his property to three servants. Jesus used parables to reveal hidden truths of God's kingdom. In Matthew 13:13 He says, *"This is why I speak to them in parables: 'Though seeing, they do not see; though hearing, they do not hear or understand.'"*

When Jesus was on the Mount of Olives, His disciples came to Him and asked what the kingdom of heaven would be like. One of the parables Jesus told them that day was the parable of the talents. The parable begins with the master giving one servant five talents, another two talents, and the third servant one talent before leaving on a long trip. The Greek word *talanton* (translated *talents* in English Bibles) is derived from *tlao,* meaning, "to bear." Here it refers to "a balance" or supporting weight. It also refers to a sum of money. When Jesus told this parable, a talent was very valuable, worth about two years' wages.[2] The master divided his property and entrusted it to his servants to be managed wisely.

📖 Read the Parable of the Talents in Matthew 25:14–30.

What were Jesus' words to the two servants who doubled their investments (Matthew 25:21–23)?

_____

_____

Why did one servant hide his talent (Matthew 25:24–25)?

_____

_____

_____

> **"So whether you eat or drink or whatever you do, do it all for the glory of God."**
>
> **1 Corinthians 10:31**

What did the master say the servant should have done with his talent (Matthew 25:27)?

_____

_____

_____

What lesson can we learn from this parable?

_____

_____

_____

In Matthew 25:15 we read that the master gave the talents to his servants, *"according to his own ability."* This was not a decision that was made lightly. In his sovereignty the master distributed his talents with wisdom. He was well acquainted with his servants and knew what they could handle or manage. His desire was that they make proportionate improvement or increase.

In Matthew 25:14–30, we find characteristics of faithful servants and that of an unfaithful servant. The master distributed his goods to his three servants. Not one was forgotten. The faithful servants speedily got to business. They were prompt in getting to work (verses 16–17), knowing there was not a moment to lose. Even when their master took a long time to return, they persevered in their work, (verse 19). They looked forward to meeting their master and fearlessly awaited his return.

Contrary to the faithful servants, the third servant believed that his master was a harsh and unfeeling man (verse 24) and feared him. He approached his master with fear, knowing he wouldn't be rewarded for how he handled his talent. We are reminded that abiding love drives out fear. 1 John 4:18 states, *"There is no fear in love. But perfect love drives out fear, because fear has to do with punishment. The one who fears is not made perfect in love."* Fear involves harsh consequences. But God's love can be perfected in us.

The third servant had been given the same amount of time as the two other servants to improve and increase that which was bestowed upon him. Yet his talent remained buried in the ground, hidden, and useless. His master called him a *"wicked, lazy servant,"* (Matthew 25:26) and demanded, *"Take the talent from him and give it to the one who has the ten talents. For everyone who has will be given more"* (Matthew 25:28–29). The third servant was stripped of the small amount he possessed. Given a distinctive opportunity to serve his master, he ultimately proved himself unworthy of his master's trust and inevitably, his opportunity was taken away.

The master settled accounts with the third servant by saying, *"throw that worthless servant outside, into the darkness"* (Matthew 25:30). The outer darkness in this verse does not mean *Gehenna*, a place of suffering for unbelievers. The Greek word *skotos* ("obscurity" or "shadiness"), translated into the English phrase "into outer darkness," refers to a dark area just outside a lighted banquet hall. [3] Those people who managed to sneak into the banquet hall without suitable dress were removed to this area adjacent to the banquet hall where it was dark. This area wasn't as dense in darkness, however, as regions further away from the hall. Therefore, this verse must refer to a place for servants who were less diligent than those who used their talents to the fullest. We are reminded that our rewards in heaven will depend on how well we were faithful to Christ. When we who have a living faith remain faithful, we receive the crown of life.

"He said to me, 'My grace is sufficient for you, for my power is made perfect in weakness.'"

2 Corinthians 12:9

In Matthew 25:15 the word *"talents"* refers to endowments God has given to his people, or his disciples. God makes distinctions among his servants concerning their abilities. He distributes them diversely. This parable teaches us that each of us is given a certain number of gifts and opportunities, or talents, to use and to serve God. We can squander those abilities or faithfully use them as God intended. B. W. Johnson states: "The trust of the Lord to each servant is measured according to his mental ability, wealth, position, or influence. Everyone's opportunities as well as the character of his life and works will be considered."[4]

APPLY Do you think you are a five-talent, two-talent, or one-talent person? Why?

_____

_____

_____

_____

_____

_____

What are some of your talents?

_____

_____

_____

_____

Have you cultivated any of these? Are you useful to God according to your abilities?

_____

_____

_____

_____

What is your favorite excuse for not using some of your talents?

_____

_____

What will you do in the next month to begin using your talents wisely?

_____

_____

_____

_____

Paul wrote in 1 Corinthians 4:1–2: *"Men ought to regard us as servants of Christ and as those entrusted with the secret things of God. Now it is required that those who have been given a trust must prove faithful."* In this verse, the term *faithful* is derived from the Greek word *pistos,* meaning "trustworthy" or "trustful." It can also mean "believing," "sure," or "true."[5]

> **"Now it is required that those who have been given a trust must prove faithful."**
>
> **1 Corinthians 4:2**

Paul is an example of one who was found faithful to God. After his extraordinary conversion on the road to Damascus, God employed this talented man to further His kingdom in a great way. We know that Paul was highly educated in philosophy, history, and religion. Paul gave of his natural and learned abilities to reach the Jews and the Gentiles with the gospel. Once Paul was willing to surrender his life, desires, and will to God, the Lord mightily used him. The apostle Paul was able to say, *"I have fought the good fight, I have finished the race, I have kept the faith. Now there is in store for me the crown of righteousness, which the Lord, the righteous Judge, will award to me on that day—and not only to me, but also to all who have longed for his appearing"* (2 Timothy 4:7–8).

STEWARDSHIP OF OUR MATERIAL RESOURCES

G od has given us material blessings. We are accountable to Him to be good managers of the many resources He has given to us. We often use the term *"resources"* in reference to our possessions, money, or assets. As we acquire the "steward's mindset," we become more aware that we are the managers of what we have, not the owners. As we learn more biblical finance principles, we can manage what we own more wisely. When our focus turns from ourselves to what God wants for our lives, we can live far more satisfying lives.

King Solomon was known for his wisdom. When we read the book of Proverbs, we become aware of how he carefully questioned the thoughts and actions of people. His insights into practical life concepts are there for us to use, concepts, which we may not have pondered before. In Proverbs we find many verses and various views on money, how it helps and how it also brings worries and troubles to people. Solomon's book of wisdom provides us with understanding and discipline.

📖 Read these verses in Proverbs about poverty and wealth. Write them in your own words.

10:4

_____

_____

11:28

_____

_____

13:18

_____

_____

"Every good and perfect gift is from above, coming down from the Father of the heavenly lights, who does not change like shifting shadows."

James 1:17

15:16

_____

_____

19:17

_____

_____

> "He will always give you all you need from day to day if you will make the Kingdom of God your primary concern."
>
> **Luke 12:31 (LB)**

God looks at our attitude about wealth. We know that He never condemned wealth. In Luke 16:1–2 we read, *"There was a rich man whose manager was accused of wasting his possessions. So he called him in and asked him, 'What is this I hear about you? Give an account of your management, because you cannot be manager any longer.'"*

The manager was called in to give an account of his boss' inventory and possessions. How are we doing when it comes to managing our material resources? We may not be called into our bosses' office tomorrow morning, but some day we will be called for an accounting by our heavenly Father for how we lived our lives.

Luke 16:10–12 shows us that when we are good stewards of money, God can use us in greater things. It states:

> *"Whoever can be trusted with very little can also be trusted with much, and whoever is dishonest with very little will also be dishonest with much. So if you have not been trustworthy in handling worldly wealth, who will trust you with true riches? And if you have not been trustworthy with someone else's property, who will give you property of your own?"*

According to Luke 16:10, who can be trusted with much?

_____

_____

> "The man of integrity walks securely, but he who takes crooked paths will be found out."
>
> **Proverbs 10:9**

APPLY Do we portray a balanced lifestyle? Are we wasteful in any way? Name three ways you can be a better manager of your material possessions.

_____

_____

_____

_____

_____

_____

_____

_____

We Are Stewards of God's Word and His Grace

This week we have studied the importance of our stewardship of time, work, and abilities, and material resources. Stewardship can also include living and telling the good news of Jesus Christ. Empowered by the Holy Spirit, we play an important part in God's plan to be effective witnesses to others.

Our Role as Parents

We can first begin living and telling the good news as parents, as we are responsible to bring up our children with the knowledge of God's Word and His blessings. Proverbs 22:6 reminds us of the importance of training our children from an early age. It states: *"Train a child in the way he should go, and when he is old he will not turn from it."* How we raise our children plays a significant part in their character development. This puts the responsibility back onto us as to how we live as examples to our children. It takes time and dedication to teach our children God's principles and His ways.

Parents play a very important role in imparting knowledge to their children. Proverbs 1:7–9 exhorts children to listen to their parents' instruction. *"The fear of the Lord is the beginning of knowledge, but fools despise wisdom and discipline. Listen, my son, to your father's instruction and do not forsake your mother's teaching. They will be a garland to grace your head and a chain to adorn your neck."* This last verse paints a beautiful picture of how parents' teachings never leave their children.

📖 Read Proverbs 6:20–23.

What does Proverbs 6:20 tell us to do?

_____

_____

When will these instructions be a part of our lives (Proverbs 6:22)?

_____

_____

Write out Proverbs 6:23.

_____

_____

_____

_____

APPLY How are you teaching your children (or other children you influence) with the knowledge of God's Word? Can you do better in this area? How?

_____

_____

> **We must be responsible in using the abundance God has given us. Along with privileges come responsibility. Romans 14:10, 12 states, "For we will all stand before God's judgment seat. So then, each of us will give an account of himself to God."**

> **"That you may live a life worthy of the Lord and may please him in every way: bearing fruit in every good work, growing in the knowledge of God."**
>
> **Colossians 1:10**

Our Role as Christians

In the book of 1 Peter, Peter reminds Christians they are to be examples to believers. By the time he wrote this book, Peter had apparently mellowed, and was no longer filled with aggression and outrageous outbursts that he had once been known for. This is a man who had previously denied affiliation with Jesus three times shortly after Christ's arrest. Now we see a man who has earned his God-given name that means "rock." Peter has now become a disciple who has learned to hold steadfast in his faith and to not doubt God and His Word.

One of Jesus' last commands to Peter before He ascended up to heaven was *"Feed My sheep"* (John 21:17). Consequently, we see Peter giving similar advice to his readers:

> *"Be shepherds of God's flock that is under your care, serving as overseers— not because you must, but because you are willing, as God wants you to be; not greedy for money, but eager to serve; not lording it over those entrusted to you, but being examples to the flock. And when the Chief Shepherd appears, you will receive the crown of glory that will never fade away."* (1 Peter 5:2–4)

Note that God wants us to willingly serve in the building of His kingdom, in sharing God's Word, and in making disciples. He wants us to help other believers to grow in Christ.

Peter also earnestly urges fellow believers to live exemplary lives for the sake of the unbelievers around them. He tells them to *"abstain from sinful desires which war against the soul"* and warns them that their conduct should be honorable. The result is that when they (the Gentiles) observe their good works, they will *"glorify God"* (1 Peter 2:11–12). In these verses, he also encourages God's elect to remain faithful.

What does Peter encourage the believers to do in 1 Peter 4:10??

_____

_____

In Matthew 28:16–20, we read what is known as "The Great Commission." Shortly after Jesus had risen from the dead, He met with His eleven disciples at a mountain in Galilee, where He had instructed them to go. Jesus gave some final words to His followers who had been at His side during His last few years. Jesus was now resurrected, and many of the prophecies He talked about when He was with them had come true. This was their Messiah . . . alive . . . and with a few final instructions for them. What would His last words be?

Read Matthew 28:16–20.

What was the reaction of the disciples when they saw Jesus (verse 17)?

_____

_____

What is the promise we have from Jesus (verse 20)?

_____

_____

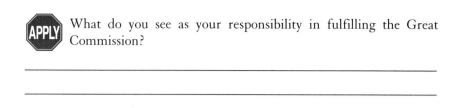 What do you see as your responsibility in fulfilling the Great Commission?

_____

_____

_____

_____

The word *responsibility* consists of two words, "response" and "ability." We may feel we don't have the ability to teach or be a part of the great commission. David Dawson, a Christian discipleship trainer, wrote: "Responsibility is responding not to our ability, but to God's ability to get the job done in and through us."[6] We can proceed without fear because Jesus said, *"All authority has been given to me in Heaven and on earth."* Once we have grasped the concept that Jesus has infinite power and resources at His disposal, it is easier for us to follow through with what Jesus has asked us to do. The objective of the Great Commission is to teach and make disciples of all nations.

Immediately after the Lord Jesus had spoken to His eleven disciples, He went up into heaven. His eleven disciples then *"went out and preached everywhere, and the Lord worked with them and confirmed His word by the signs that accompanied it"* (Mark 16:20). We can be reassured that the Lord will work with us. This is not something we need to do on our own. We can draw upon God's strength and power to help us.

 Lord, thank You for my many blessings that come from You. Help me to be a better steward of time. Thank You for my talents and abilities. I give them to You. Thank You for my material blessings. Show me where I can be a better steward in using the abundance You have given me. Lord, thank You for Your Holy Word, which is a light to my path. Help me to be an effective testimony for You. In Jesus' name. Amen.

Do we pray daily for God's guidance and strength in our lives? Are we steadfast in our faith? Revelation 2:10 gives us words of encouragement. "Be faithful, even to the point of death, and I will give you the crown of life."

NOTES

1. *The Student Bible, New International Version* (Grand Rapids, MI: The Zondervan Corporation, 1996), 1396.

2. Ibid., 1027.

3. *Strong's Hebrew and Greek Dictionaries*, In e-Sword Bible software database, 2005, Rick Meyers.

4. B. W. Johnson, *The People's New Testament*, "Matthew 25:15 Commentary." In e-Sword Bible software database, © 2005, Rick Meyers.

5. *Strong's Hebrew and Greek Dictionaries*, In e-Sword Bible software database, 2005, Rick Meyers.

6. David L. Dawson, *Equipping the Saints: Establishing the Vision*, "The Great Commission and Its Fulfilling" (Greenville: ETS Ministries, 1982), 7.

Notes

God's Commands Protect Us from Indebtedness

The Word of God teaches us to live in a manner pleasing to God. Knowing God's Word impacts our thinking on a daily basis. When we read from the pages of Scripture, we are made aware of what God expects from us in our relationship with Him and with others. The all-knowing God wants to reveal His heart and desires for us during our short lifetime here on earth. He wants to teach us about His nature and how we can obey and follow Him. He reveals His heart and teaches us through His Word, which operates much like a compass, giving direction to our lives. The Bible has profound truths for us to live by. The psalmist David wrote, *"Your word is a lamp to my feet and a light for my path"* (Psalms 119:105). This verse is also translated, *"Your words are a flashlight to light the path ahead of me, and keep me from stumbling"* (TLB). David also stated, *"Oh, how I love your law! I meditate on it all day long"* (Psalms 119:97).

God's laws are **precepts.** In Psalm 119 David states, *"I obey your precepts"* (verse 100) and *"I gain understanding from your precepts"* (verse 104). The word "precepts" is a translation of the Hebrew word *piqqud*, which means "commandment, mandate." God's commands are divine ones, serving as guidelines for righteous living. They are not human commands or laws, which can change and grow obsolete. They are always true and dependable.

In this lesson we will look at five of the commandments that relate to money, our possessions, and debt.

God revealed His nature to us when He gave us His laws. In Exodus 20 we have an account of the giving of the Ten Commandments to Moses on Mount Sinai. Earlier, God had led the Israelites out of the land of Egypt. As they camped in the Desert of Sinai, God made a tremendous appearance. When the people remained at a distance at the foot of the mountain, they saw that *"Mount Sinai was covered with smoke, because the LORD descended on it in fire"* (Exodus 19:18). The mountain where the Lord God descended was consecrated as a holy mountain.

Moses went up to the top of the mountain and approached Jehovah God to receive the laws and ordinances for His people. The Ten Commandments formed *"a central core of morality,"* serving to condense the many legal codes of the times. These laws are clear-cut commands that show us God's nature and character. They caution us to live a life pleasing to Him. God's laws warn us of harmful attitudes and actions. These wrong attitudes and actions are not only harmful to others, but to ourselves.

In this lesson we will look at five of the commandments that relate to money, our possessions, and debt. We'll examine how following these laws protects us from a life of indebtedness.

God's Commands

DAY ONE

THERE IS JUST ONE GOD

The first of the Ten Commandments states, *"You shall have no other gods before me"* (Exodus 20:3). All the other commands are based on this one. This first commandment concerns the object of worship, Jehovah, and Him only. Our worship includes obedience and allegiance focused on God. Adam Clarke, Bible scholar, has this to say concerning the first commandment:

> This commandment prohibits all inordinate attachment to earthly things. God is the fountain of happiness, and no intelligent creature can be happy but through Him. The very first commandment . . . is divinely calculated to prevent man's misery and promote his happiness by taking him off from false dependence, and leading him to God himself, the fountain of all good.[1]

"You shall have no other gods before me."

Exodus 20:3

When we show allegiance to God, we display steadfast devotion or loyalty to Him. Moses' words emphasize this first law: *"Acknowledge and take to heart this day that the LORD is God in heaven above and on the earth below. There is no other"* (Deuteronomy 4:39). The next verse offers a promise to those who acknowledge God's authority in their lives. It states, *"Keep his decrees and commands, which I am giving you today, so that it may go well with you and your children after you and that you may live long in the land the LORD your God gives you for all time"* (Deuteronomy 4:40).

📖 Psalm 19 clearly describes the Law of God and the benefits it offers us. Read each of the following verses. Fill in the blanks using the Scripture term used for the law and the description of the law.

19:7: *The _____ is _____, reviving the soul. The _____ are _____, making wise the simple.*

19:8: *The* _____ *are* _____, *giving joy to the heart. The* _____ *are* _____, *giving light to the eyes.*

19:9: *The* _____ *is* _____, *enduring forever. The* _____ *are* _____, *and altogether righteous.*

19:10: _____ *are* _____, *than much pure gold;* _____ *are* _____, *than honey from the comb.*

When the psalmist wrote Psalm 119, we observe that he had a thankful heart for God's laws. He didn't see them as restricting or dictatorial. David stated, *"Oh, how I love your law! I meditate on it all day long"* (verse 97). He delighted in God's laws, and this delight was shown by his frequent meditation on them.

📖 In Psalm 119:89–104, we are reminded how God's law frees us from the destructive consequences of sinful attitudes and actions. Read these verses.

Why did David say he will never forget God's precepts? (Psalms 119:93)

APPLY As we contemplate the words *"have no other gods before me,"* think of your personal relationship with God. Do you esteem Him highly? Do you regard Him as valuable in your life, deserving of your worship? Worship is the act of giving reverence and honor to God.

_____

_____

_____

_____

In your desire for spiritual health, do you make a daily commitment to have a right relationship with God and others? What personal application for your life do you see in the first of the Ten Commandments?

Don't Put Anything before God

Looking at our heart attitude, is our desire for wealth and possessions more important than seeking God and serving Him? Are we allowing any idols to lead us astray from God? What contemporary idols do we have today?

The second of the Ten Commandments states, *"You shall not make for yourself an idol in the form of anything in heaven above or on the earth beneath or in the water below,"* (Exodus 20:4). Just as in the first commandment, God wants our focus to be on Him.

The people of Israel had left Egypt, where idolatry was common among the people. The second commandment was made very clear to them:

ONE GOD

"There is no God but one. For even if there are so-called gods, whether in heaven or on earth (as indeed there are many "gods" and many "lords"), yet for us there is but one. . . ."God, the Father, from whom all things came and for whom we live; and there is but one Lord, Jesus Christ, through whom all things came and through whom we live." (1 Corinthians 8:4–6)

God's Commands

DAY TWO

Put Yourself in Their Shoes
WEALTH AN IDOL?

King Solomon stated, "For as he thinks in his heart, so is he" (Proverbs 23:7, NKJV). Although today we may not have idols made of wood or stone, greed may lead us astray from the adoration that belongs to God. Our money or wealth should not be a barrier to our spiritual growth or to our commitment to Christ.

"You shall not bow down to them or worship them; for I, the LORD your God, am a jealous God, punishing the children for the sin of the fathers to the third and fourth generation of those who hate me, but showing love to a thousand generations of those who love me and keep my commandments." (Exodus 20:5–6)

God had shown Himself to the Israelites by leading them out of Egypt and showing them many miraculous signs of His power. They had seen the Red Sea part so they could be freed from slavery in Egypt. As *"a jealous God"* he desired their allegiance and obedience. Yet they *"refused to obey him. Instead, they rejected him and in their hearts turned back to Egypt"* (Acts 7:39). They continued in their old ways, carving wooden images and making bronze statues. Idolatrous practices, pagan lifestyles, and revelry went unchecked while the people focused on themselves and their strong desires. It was not enough to have seen the great Jehovah perform miracles.

During the days of Jeremiah the prophet, idolatry was quite common. The people of Israel would not keep their devotion reserved for the true God of their fathers. They ignored the words of the prophets that the worship of God could not be shared with their devotion to idols. They mixed practices of idol-worshipping religions with their temple worship. We note what God's reaction is to this, *"This is what the Sovereign LORD says: My anger and my wrath will be poured out on this place . . . The people of Judah have done evil in my eyes . . . They have set up their detestable idols in the house that bears my Name and have defiled it"* (Jeremiah 7:20, 30). When they weren't sure that God was enough, they took a few idols with them to war for good luck with the assumption that nature and gods had power that would bring them success.

The Bible clearly shows us that idolatry is incompatible with the service of God.

Samuel told the people of Israel, *"If you are returning to the LORD with all your hearts, then rid yourselves of the foreign gods and Ashtoreths and commit yourselves to the LORD and serve him only, and he will deliver you out of the hand of the Philistines* (1 Samuel 7:3). God wants us to be totally committed to Him. In Paul's second letter to the Corinthian believers he asks, *"What does a believer have in common with an unbeliever? What agreement is there between the temple of God and idols? For we are the temple of the living God"* (2 Corinthians 6:15–16).

In the New Testament, Paul warns us that greed is a form of idolatry. He states, *"The kingdom of Christ and of God will never belong to anyone who is impure or greedy, for a greedy person is really an idol worshiper—he loves and worships the good things of this life more than God"* (Ephesians 5:5, TLB). Webster's Dictionary defines *greed* as *"selfish desire to acquire more than one needs or deserves."* Although today we may not have idols made of wood or stone, greed may lead us astray from the adoration that belongs to God. Our money or wealth should not be a barrier to our spiritual growth or to our commitment to Christ. Idolatry and selfish ambition are considered *"acts of the sinful nature"* (Galatians 5:19–20).

Greed is a harmful attitude that that leads to poor financial decisions and consequences. It motivates us to take on more debt for those things that we do not want to wait for. It deceives us into thinking that we will be satisfied if we have more things or bigger and better things. Greed can lead us astray from God's desire for us to depend totally on Him and give of our total devotion to Him.

LIVE BY THE SPIRIT

"So I say, live by the Spirit, and you will not gratify the desires of the sinful nature. For the sinful nature desires what is contrary to the Spirit, and the Spirit what is contrary to the sinful nature. They are in conflict with each other, so that you do not do what you want." (Galatians 5:16–17)

Greed is an attitude, which takes the focus off God and onto ourselves. It occurs when our focus is on the fulfillment of our desires and satisfaction, rather than a willingness to surrender to God's will and to His provisions for us. The *opposite of greed* is "self-denial, self-control, moderation, generosity."

Money itself isn't good or bad. It's how we use it that counts. It's our attitudes toward our money and possessions that are important. In Luke 16:13–15, Jesus reminds his disciples, the Pharisees, and us that God knows our hearts and He knows where our loyalties lie. As people were gathered around Jesus, eager to listen to Him speak, He presented them with two choices. Jesus said, *"No servant can serve two masters. Either he will hate the one and love the other, or he will be devoted to the one and despise the other. You cannot serve both God and Money* (Luke 16:13). (The word "money" in this verse is translated from the Chaldee *mammon,* meaning "wealth" or "riches.") When Jesus saw that the Pharisees took offense at Him after making this bold contrast of God and money, He responded to them by saying, *"You are the ones who justify yourselves in the eyes of men, but God knows your hearts. What is highly valued among men is detestable in God's sight"* (Luke 16:15).

📖 The Bible talks about greed and the love of money in the Old and New Testaments. Note what the following Scriptures say about it.

Luke 12:15—What did Jesus say we should be on guard against? Why?

_____

_____

Summarize these verses:

Ecclesiastes 5:10

_____

_____

Hebrews 13:5

_____

_____

1 Timothy 6:9

_____

_____

Dwight L. Moody was a great American evangelist who lived in the nineteenth century. He preached about the temporal and eternal views of life. He observed how "the church is full of people who want one eye for the world and the other for the kingdom of God. Therefore, everything is blurred."[2] The church today is no different. Moody stated, "When the Spirit of God is on us, the world looks very empty; the world has a very small hold on us, and we begin to let go our hold of it and lay hold of things eternal."[3]

Are your decisions and actions based on worldly standards or on your desire to please God? During today's lesson, have you been made aware of any contemporary idols getting in the way of your total commitment to Christ? Has the desire or love for particular possessions become idols in your life? You can ask God to help you turn away from any idol He has revealed to

"When the Spirit of God is on us, the world looks very empty; the world has a very small hold on us, and we begin to let go our hold of it and lay hold of things eternal."

—Dwight L. Moody

you. As believers we possess the keys to understanding life from God's perspective. We have God's Word to teach us and the Holy Spirit's power to work in our lives.

DON'T TAKE WHAT ISN'T YOURS

As we consider the Ten Commandments and how they relate to living with no indebtedness, we will examine the eighth commandment. God commands, *"You shall not steal"* (Exodus 20:15). This implies that a person's right of property is sanctioned and all theft is forbidden by law. The word *steal* in this commandment is translated from the Hebrew root *gawnab,* literally meaning to *"thieve"*; by implication it means to *"deceive."* It forbids us to hurt our neighbor in deed.

This law talks about more than the act of taking something that isn't ours. It expresses the importance of ownership. We are reminded of God's ownership and that everything belongs to Him. *"Yours, O LORD, is the greatness and the power and the glory and the majesty and the splendor, for everything in heaven and earth is yours"* (1 Chronicles 29:11). Not only are the heavens and the earth His, but we are His. *"The earth is the LORD's, and everything in it, the world, and all who live in it"* (Psalms 24:1).

This law also reminds us that God is our Provider. He is the One who gives us what we have. When we truly put our trust in our Creator and Heavenly Father for our needs, then stealing should not even be considered. As a loving Father, He already knows our needs and gives as He sees fit. When we put our confidence in Him and believe that He will provide for us, the thought of stealing should be far from us.

When we take from someone we are indebted to that person. The Lord God spoke to Moses in the book of Leviticus about stealing and dishonesty, saying:

> *If anyone sins and is unfaithful to the LORD by deceiving his neighbor about something entrusted to him or left in his care or stolen, or if he cheats him, or if he finds lost property and lies about it, or if he swears falsely, or if he commits any such sin that people may do—when he thus sins and becomes guilty, he must return what he has stolen or taken by extortion, or what was entrusted to him, or the lost property he found, or whatever it was he swore falsely about. (Leviticus 6:2–5)*

When we take what is not lawfully ours, we are obligated to return it or pay it back.

📖 Ezekiel 18:10–13 speaks about the unrighteous acts of a son. We read in verse 12 that the son did *"not return what he took in pledge."* By not returning what he promised to return, he does not restore that which is owed to the owner. In effect, he steals from him. He takes advantage of an act of kindness, and shows disrespect to the lender. In verse 13 we find that the son *"lends at usury and takes excessive interest."* This is another practice God considers sin. The son took financial advantage of a poor person, robbing him and oppressing him.

📖 Before Jesus began his ministry on earth, John the Baptist was sent as the messenger to prepare the way for His coming. John preached the

God is our Provider. He is the One who gives us what we have. When we put our confidence in Him and believe that He will provide for us, the thought of stealing should be far from us.

message of forgiveness of sins. Desiring to change their lives, tax collectors and soldiers asked him what they should do about their responsibilities. Read Luke 3:3–14 about John the Baptist's ministry.

What did John tell the tax collectors to do (verses 12–13)?

_____

_____

What did he tell the soldiers (verse 14)?

_____

_____

By telling the soldiers, *"Don't accuse people falsely,"* John said they should not defraud the citizens. Albert Barnes states it is probable that when the soldiers wanted property that wasn't theirs, and they couldn't take it by force, they would falsely accuse a person of a crime, thus obtaining what they wanted).[4] When John replied *"Be content with your pay,"* he emphasized that they should not unlawfully increase their wages.

The apostle Paul cautioned the church people at Ephesus about stealing. For in his letter to the Ephesians he wrote, *"He who has been stealing must steal no longer, but must work, doing something useful with his own hands, that he may have something to share with those in need"* (Ephesians 4:28). Paul wanted the new Christians to know that stealing was not acceptable. In their earlier days they may have been familiar with the pagan practice of taking property that was not guarded. They were no longer to continue in those ways; they were to live holy lives, work hard, make a living, and win the respect of others. They should look for honest employment. Just as during the times of Paul, people today are tempted to cheat and take what isn't rightfully theirs. The matters of personal responsibility and honesty are the same. We shouldn't have to be a burden on others.

📖 In Romans 13:8–10, Paul reminds us that love fulfills the law. When we steal, we do not show love.

What did Paul say about debt? (Romans 13:8)?

_____

_____

🛑 APPLY What personal application for your life do you see in the eighth of the Ten Commandments?

Reflect on the following areas of your life and how you are doing:

The Money I Make, Spend, and Give
Am I adequately providing for my family with my work?

_____

_____

Am I planning for my future by setting aside money?

_____

_____

> *"Yours, O LORD, is the greatness and the power and the glory and the majesty and the splendor, for everything in heaven and earth is yours."*
>
> **1 Chronicles 29:11**

Am I giving as the Lord directs me to give?

_____

_____

Have I been an honest steward or manager of my income?

_____

_____

Do I pay back what I owe, and take back what I borrow?

_____

_____

My Work
Do I put in the time I say I do? Am I using my time wisely?

_____

_____

Am I careful not to take from my employer what is not rightfully mine?

_____

_____

God's Commands

"Let no debt remain outstanding, except the continuing debt to love one another, for he who loves his fellowman has fulfilled the law."

Romans 13:8

DON'T DESIRE YOUR NEIGHBORS' THINGS.

As we continue to look at the Ten Commandments, we will now focus on the tenth commandment and how it can protect us from indebtedness to others. It tells us to guard against five different areas of coveting. Exodus 20:17 states, *"You shall not covet your neighbor's house. You shall not covet your neighbor's wife, or his manservant or maidservant, his ox or donkey, or anything that belongs to your neighbor."* God's covenant cautions against coveting in five different areas: **1)** a neighbor's house, **2)** the neighbor's wife or common-law spouse, **3)** his servants (today's servants may be maids, extra conveniences or services), **4)** his ox or donkey (the means one uses for transportation or to conduct business), or **5)** anything else he has.

What is meant by the word *covet*? It comes from the Hebrew term *chamad*, meaning *"to desire, to long for, to be desirable, costly, precious, to feel delight."* It is synonymous with jealousy, envy, and resentfulness. When we don't covet, we are better suited to be kind-hearted, charitable, helpful, and sympathetic. We have learned to be satisfied with what God has provided for us. We have learned to be thankful for what we have. We set our minds and hearts on kingdom values rather than earthly values.

The Hebrew word translated "covet," *chamad,* is first used in the Bible to describe the pleasant trees in the Garden of Eden. *"The LORD God made all kinds of trees grow out of the ground—trees that were pleasing* (chamad) *to the eye and good for food. In the middle of the garden were the tree of life and the tree of knowledge of good and evil"* (Genesis 2:9). God told Adam and Eve they could eat from the fruit of the trees in the garden, except for the tree in the middle of the garden. They were told not to eat the forbidden fruit from the tree or even touch it, or they would die (Genesis 3:3). They did not heed God's warning, and their beautiful existence in the garden ended. When Adam and Eve saw that the forbidden fruit was *"good for food"* and it became desirable (*chamad*), they ate it (Genesis 3:6).

The tenth commandment concerns our thoughts, which no human eye can see. Only God can see our personal thoughts. Coveting refers to an *"ungoverned and selfish desire."* This commandment forbids us to hurt our neighbor and is the *"root of all sins of word or deed against our neighbor"*[5] When one covets he is in a state of discontent that can lead to disobeying all of the other nine commandments. Our selfish thoughts and desires lead to an unrighteous lifestyle. The pursuit of possessions can dominate our lives. But we know that life is more than what we own.

Jesus told a parable at the beginning of His ministry about kingdom values. In the parable of the sower, He discussed the different ways people receive God's Word and either accept it, or don't apply it to their lives.

📖 Read Mark 4:1–20, and consider the different types of soil: the seed on the path, the rocky soil, the soil choked with thorns, and the good soil. Jesus reminds us that many people hear the message of redemption and forgiveness of sins, but not all of them yield their lives to Christ as their Lord.

According to Mark 4:19, what three things choke the Word, making it unfruitful?

1) _____

2) _____

3) _____

In the thorny soil, the seed has taken root and has begun to grow. This soil offers signs of fruitfulness and lots of promise. But kingdom values are crowded out and choked by the thorns of worries, riches, and the pleasures of this world. Just as in the days of Jesus, we can easily be swayed today to experience the thorns of this world.

APPLY Can you think of any thorns that are in your life now?

_____

_____

_____

_____

How have these thorns choked the word of God in your life or your faithfulness to Him?

_____

_____

_____

_____

"You shall not covet."

Exodus 20:17

MATTHEW 16:26–27

"What good will it be for a man if he gains the whole world, yet forfeits his soul? Or what can a man give in exchange for his soul? For the Son of Man is going to come in his Father's glory with his angels, and then he will reward each person according to what he has done."

What steps can you begin to take to allow the good soil to flourish?

_____

_____

_____

_____

Paul reminds Timothy, a young believer, that coveting and envy can cause those who know the Word to wander, leading to dire consequences. *"For the love of money is a root of all kinds of evil. Some people, eager for money, have wandered from the faith and pierced themselves with many griefs"* (1 Timothy 6:10). When Paul wrote this letter, he warned against selfish and profit-seeking motives, not money itself.

Jesus reprimands and condemns covetousness in a parable he tells about a rich man. Jesus warns against trusting completely in money and possessions. The wealthy man's desire for an indulgent lifestyle demonstrated where his heart was.

📖 Read Luke 12:13–21, and note the story of the parable in verses 16–21.

What was the person in the crowd concerned about (verse 13)?

_____

_____

What are we to be on our guard against (verse 15)?

_____

_____

What did the rich man decide to do with his surplus of crops (verses 17–18)

_____

_____

What were the man's plans after he stored his crops (verse 19)?

_____

_____

> *"For where your treasure is, there your heart will be also."*
>
> *Matthew 6:21*

What does it mean to be *"rich toward God"* (verse 21)?

_____

_____

What can we learn from this story?

_____

_____

_____

_____

As we conclude today's lesson, let's remember that although we are in this world, we are not to be of this world. Our thoughts and motives need to be continually examined and sifted through the screen of God's Word. His

Word judges our thoughts and discerns our intentions. Let us examine our motives and our hearts as we read the Psalmist David's prayer:

Search me, O God, and know my heart;
Test me and know my anxious thoughts.
See if there is any offensive way in me,
And lead me in the way everlasting. (Psalms 139:23–24)

FOLLOWING AND OBEYING GOD

God has given divine laws or commands that protect us against harmful and sinful tendencies that have been common to us throughout time. The hearts of people from the beginning of time to the present day have not changed. When God gave the Ten Commandments to the people whom He had freed from slavery in Egypt, the Israelites, His desire was that they would know Him as *Yahweh* their Redeemer. He desired their love, obedience, and allegiance. He told them *"I, the* LORD *your God, am a jealous God . . . showing love to a thousand generations of those who love me and keep my commandments"* (Exodus 20:5–6). God wanted them to *"live long in the land"* (Exodus 20:12).

Let's take a look at all of the Ten Commandments, the laws that God called His "covenant" to His people (Exodus 20:3–17):

You shall have no other gods before me.

You shall not make for yourself an idol in the form of anything in heaven above or on earth beneath or in the waters below.

You shall not misuse the name of the LORD *your God.*

Remember the Sabbath day by keeping it holy.

Honor your father and your mother.

You shall not murder.

You shall not commit adultery.

You shall not steal.

You shall not give false testimony against your neighbor.

You shall not covet.

Doctrine
GOD'S LAW AND GOD'S GRACE

God's laws serve as boundaries and guidelines for us. They also serve to evaluate where we are in our lives as we grow and mature as Christians. When we apply the Ten Commandments to our lives, we need to recognize that we do not work our way to heaven or attain righteousness by keeping these laws.

God's laws were given to us to show us the right way to live. Obeying God's laws should not be a burden to us; instead, they can be a source of liberation for us as believers. They serve as boundaries and guidelines for us. They also serve to evaluate where we are in our lives as we grow and mature as Christians. When we apply the Ten Commandments to our lives, we need to recognize that we do not work our way to heaven or attain righteousness by keeping these laws. To have eternal life we need to come to Christ with a repentant heart and ask Him to forgive us of our sins. We need to accept Him as the Savior of our sinful ways and unrighteousness. *"But God demonstrates His own love for us in this: While we were still sinners, Christ died for us"* (Romans 5:8). We can cross the bridge from eternal condemnation by putting our trust in Jesus Christ alone as the only hope of eternal life. Jesus Himself says, *"I am the way and the truth and the life. No one comes to the Father except through me* (John 14:6).

> **"He who conceals his sins does not prosper, but whoever confesses and renounces them finds mercy."**
>
> **Proverbs 28:13**

God's purpose for us is to honor and serve Him. We cannot do this of our own will. It is required that we turn from our own ways and trust Christ alone for our redemption and righteousness. It is through God's grace that we have passed from eternal death to life. It is through God's grace and power that we no longer need to be slaves to sin.

> *"For we know that our old self was crucified with him so that the body of sin might be done away with, that we should no longer be slaves to sin . . . In the same way, count yourselves dead to sin but alive to God in Christ Jesus. Therefore, do not let sin reign in your mortal body so that you obey its evil desires."* (Romans 6: 6, 11–12)

It is impossible for us to love and serve God when we are constantly sinning and breaking His law. We may say that we love God, but if we don't obey Him, how true is our claim? First John 2:5–6 says, *"But if anyone obeys his word, God's love is truly made complete in him. This is how we know we are in him: Whoever claims to live in him must walk as Jesus did."* How well does our walk go along with our talk? Do we claim to love God, yet still live with the "old nature" desires of coveting, envy, or pride?

📖 Read James 1:12–15. James emphasizes in his letter that as Christians, we need to stop sinning and submit to God.

According to verse 12, who is called *"blessed"*?

_____

_____

What will he receive *"when he has stood the test"* (verse 12)?

_____

_____

What should one not say, when he is tempted (verse 1:13)?

_____

_____

What does verse 14 say about temptation?

_____

_____

What does sin begin with (verse 15)?

_____

APPLY We act on our thoughts and beliefs about money and possessions. Our thoughts and attitudes play a very important part in why we make wise or poor financial choices. What reason might you have for overspending, living beyond your means, or remaining in debt? Could it be any one of these?

❑ feelings of insecurity

❑ searching for something to fill a void in your life

❑ the need to be respected for having nice things

❑ a sense of hopelessness of never being able to get out of debt

❑ the desire to be loved by people who notice the things you have

If not any of these reasons, write down your own.

_____

_____

_____

_____

_____

_____

Some of the following attitudes and beliefs have caused people to make unnecessary and foolish purchases. People's selfish or greedy desires show through with these attitudes:

- ■ "I may be broke, but I sure look good!"
- ■ "Showing high status is important to me."
- ■ "Eat, drink, and be merry. Live life today like there's no tomorrow."
- ■ "I just need to have the best there is. I deserve it."
- ■ Or fill in the blank . . . (I'll finally be somebody when I have _____.")

When it comes to material things, what areas have caused you to be greedy or to covet? Have any of the following areas caused your life to be off-balance financially and in your walk with God?

- ❑ Houses (bigger, with a lot more conveniences, in a nicer neighborhood, owning more than is necessary)
- ❑ more land and property
- ❑ cars (the latest, faster, classier, more expensive, bigger)
- ❑ furnishings
- ❑ clothing
- ❑ electronic gadgets for entertainment

A self-indulgent attitude is exposed in one's irresponsible spending for things that lead to temporary satisfaction and little benefit. If we are constantly desiring more stuff than what we presently own or the things we think everybody else has, we have not yet learned to be content with a moderate or balanced lifestyle.

Do we have proper attitudes toward material possessions and money? King Solomon said, *"A greedy man stirs up dissension, but he who trusts in the LORD will prosper"* (Proverbs 28:25). The antidote for wanting more things is seeking to have a heart of gratitude for what God has already given to us and for what He will give to us in the future. Although it may be difficult to understand everything now, we can trust God to provide our needs. We are to *"come before him with thanksgiving"* (Psalms 95:2), not complaining and grumbling as the Israelites did after they were delivered from slavery in Egypt.

For those who have felt a void in their lives and have tried to fill it with possessions or the appearance of wealth, God's love can fill that void. We can find real satisfaction in Him. The Holy Spirit will do God's work in us as we desire to do His will.

📖 As you read Ephesians 3:16–19, consider Paul's prayer for the Ephesians.

> **"Therefore, since we are receiving a kingdom that cannot be shaken, let us be thankful, and so worship God acceptably with reverence and awe, for our 'God is a consuming fire.'"**
>
> **Hebrews 12:28–29**

How are we strengthened with the Father's power (verse 16)?

_____

_____

According to verse 17, how does Christ dwell in our hearts?

_____

_____

In what are we to be _"rooted and established"_ (verse 17)?

_____

_____

 Most gracious, almighty God, full of lovingkindness and longsuffering:

We confess to Thee with our whole heart our neglect and forgetfulness of Thy commandments, our wrong doing, and speaking and thinking, and the hurts we have done to others, and the good we have left undone. O Lord, blot out the transgressions that are against us, for thy goodness and Thy glory, and for the sake of Thy Son, our Saviour, Jesus Christ Amen. (Anonymous)

NOTES

1. Adam Clarke, _Adam Clarke's Commentary on the Bible_, "Exodus 20:3 Commentary." In e-Sword Bible software database, © 2005, Rick Meyers.

2. Dwight L. Moody, _CloserWalk_ (August 2006), 17.

3. Ibid.

4. Albert Barnes, _Albert Barnes' Notes on the Bible,_ "Luke 3:14 Commentary." In e-Sword Bible software database, © 2005, Rick Meyers.

5. Ibid., "Exodus 20:17 Commentary."

Notes

Virtues That Help
Keep Debt at Bay

O ur attitudes about life in general play an important role in how we live and how we handle our money. Whether we are young or not-so-young we consistently display our beliefs about life through our actions. In this lesson we will look at five biblical virtues that can lead us to prosperous living. When we're abiding in God, we make conscious choices to live in a way that would please Him.

Industry, or Hard Work

Keep Debt at Bay
DAY ONE

H ere in Day One, we will examine the virtue of industry, or hard work. It is interesting to note that many wealthy people today consider their industriousness a determining factor leading to their fulfillment and well being, supporting biblical teachings on the importance of hard work. The Bible upholds good work characteristics while it repudiates the polar opposites of laziness, idleness, negligence, and sluggishness.

Genesis 2 tells us that after God made Adam He placed him in the Garden of Eden that He had planted specifically for him. This garden had *"all kinds of trees . . . trees that were pleasing to the eye and good for food"* (Genesis 2:9). A river naturally watered the garden, allowing the plants and trees to grow and bear fruit. Imagine what this beautiful garden may have looked like! It was a true paradise, full of lush greenery and flowers and fruit of many colors. One would think that Adam had it made. He had a beautiful place he could call home and all the nourishment he would ever need. Did God tell Adam that he could take it easy for the rest of his life and just enjoy the garden? Not exactly. He immediately directed Adam *"to work it and take care*

BENEFITS OF HARD WORK

"A man can do nothing better than to eat and drink and find satisfaction in his work. This too, I see, is from the hand of God, for without him, who can eat or find enjoyment? To the man who pleases him, God gives wisdom, knowledge and happiness."

(Ecclesiastes 2:24–26)

"Better to be a nobody and yet have a servant than to pretend to be somebody and have no food."

Proverbs 12:9

of it" (Genesis 2:15). Even before sin entered the world and Adam disobeyed God, God gave him specific instructions to work the Garden. We note that man was not to live a life of idleness. God specifically condemns the attitude of laziness and the one whose *"hands refuse to work"* (Proverbs 21:25).

Why did God place Adam in the Garden of Eden (Genesis 2:15)?

_____

_____

When we look at the Gospels, we note that when Jesus lived on this earth, He was not idle. Even as a child, He was devoted to His work. When Jesus was twelve years old, He and His parents went to Jerusalem for the Feast of the Passover. After the Feast, Mary and Joseph began their journey home. They returned to Jerusalem, however, when they realized that Jesus was not with their relatives and friends. After anxiously searching for Him, they found Him back in Jerusalem, spending time with the teachers of the law in the temple courts. When Mary and Joseph asked Jesus why He stayed behind, He answered, *"Why did you seek Me? Did you not know that I must be about My Father's business?"* (Luke 2:49, NKJV). Even as a child, Jesus was found faithful, doing what He knew His Father expected of Him. Luke records that Jesus then *"went down to Nazareth with them and was obedient to them . . . And Jesus grew in wisdom and stature, and in favor with God and men"* (Luke 2:51–52).

In the days of Jesus' ministry, He made it clear that He would never stop working, even if it meant healing the sick on the Sabbath. When Jesus was back in Jerusalem for a feast of the Jews, He went to the pool of Bethesda. Near the Sheep Gate, this pool often had many disabled people lying nearby. The blind, lame, and the paralyzed patiently waited for an angel of the Lord to come and stir the pool waters. The first person to get in the pool after the moving of the water was instantly made well. Jesus saw a man who had been lame for thirty-eight years, lying at the pool. Asking him if he wanted to get well, the man replied, *"Sir, I have no one to help me into the pool when the water is stirred. While I am trying to get in, someone else goes down ahead of me"* (John 5:7). Taking pity on him, Jesus instantly healed the man, telling him to pick up his mat and walk. Observing this man carrying his mat on the Sabbath, the Jews became upset and demanded to find out who made him well—for when they discovered it was Jesus, they were angry with Him and wanted to punish Him for "working" on the Sabbath. When confronted, Jesus replied, *"My Father is always at his work to this very day, and I, too, am working"* (John 5:17).

In both of his letters to the believers in Thessalonica, Paul strongly warns them against idleness. Paul was able to write to them of this concern of his, as he himself set a good example. He was a tentmaker by trade. Throughout his ministry he toiled and worked hard, not wanting to be a burden on others. In his second letter to the Thessalonians, Paul is critical of lazy church members. He said they should be contributing members of their society.

📖 Read 2 Thessalonians 3:6–13 and note what Paul tells the believers about idleness. Verse 10 mentions a rule about work. What is it?

_____

_____

According to verse 12, what does Paul command and urge?

_____

_____

In verse 13, what is Paul's final exhortation?

_____

Paul reminds the Thessalonians that when he and his workers had been with them, they were not idle and that they were careful to pay for the food they ate (verses 7–8). We note in verse 11 that Paul refers to citizens who meddle in other people's business. Apparently he heard of those who were not active enough with their own work and responsibilities. They were not engaged in minding their own business; instead, they were getting in the way of other peoples' business and work. Adam Clarke notes the usage of the term *busybodies* as meaning "prying into other people's circumstances and domestic affairs; magnifying or underrating everything."[1]

📖 The book of Proverbs gives ample treatment to the topic of being industrious. What do the following verses say about hard work versus laziness?

10:4

_____

_____

12:11

_____

_____

13:11

_____

_____

14:23

_____

_____

Let's look at two scenarios of fathers and note their work habits.

Example 1: Joe is 25 years old and is the father of a five-year old boy. The boy's mother has custody of the child and she has kept a steady job for several years. Joe has had a variety of jobs. Joe does not think it's important to keep a steady job. When Joe begins to make some "real" money, the boy's mother wants him to help out with expenses for raising their son. Joe is behind on many of his bills and often will spend his check on new video games, which he spends many hours playing. He switched jobs again to avoid money deduction for child support. Sometimes he'll get money from his mother or friends when he's spent his paycheck.

Example 2: Lee, a Christian, is a single father raising two boys. He makes sure they are involved in activities that keep them challenged academically and that encourage their spiritual growth as Christians. Planning his work around his sons' school day, Lee arrives at work before 6:00 AM so he can

"He who works his land will have abundant food."

Proverbs 12:11

"Laziness brings on deep sleep, and the shiftless man goes hungry."

Proverbs 19:15

be at home when his sons arrive from school. Providing stability for his boys, Lee is available to help them with their homework and have dinner with them. He's had the same job for five years, and his boss considers him a valuable asset to the company.

Consider how Joe and Lee lead their lives in terms of their work ethic. Which one of the two shows signs of negligence and laziness? Which father actively provides for his family's needs?

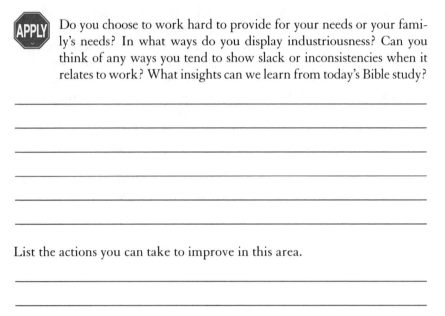 **APPLY** Do you choose to work hard to provide for your needs or your family's needs? In what ways do you display industriousness? Can you think of any ways you tend to show slack or inconsistencies when it relates to work? What insights can we learn from today's Bible study?

_____

_____

_____

_____

_____

_____

List the actions you can take to improve in this area.

_____

_____

The Bible encourages us to have good work characteristics. Industriousness leads to a richer sense of fulfillment in life. We can ask God for strength and wisdom to be useful and valuable family members and citizens.

Keep Debt at Bay

When we show responsibility, we recognize that we are accountable for our actions and are unafraid to carry out individual responsibilities.

RESPONSIBILITY, OR DEPENDABILITY

Have you ever heard someone ask a child in desperation, "Will you *ever* grow up?" Or perhaps you have heard that same disparaging question asked to an adult. Undoubtedly the questioner wasn't referring to the other person's physical growth, stature, or height. The person asking the question was likely more interested in seeing a higher maturity level or a semblance of responsibility.

What does *responsibility* mean? It means "being accountable; being answerable to a duty or trust; the ability to meet obligations or to act without superior authority or guidance."[2] When we show responsibility, we recognize that we are accountable for our actions and are unafraid to carry out individual responsibilities. On the other hand, when we show traits of irresponsibility, we appear uncontrolled and unrestrained. Irresponsible people prefer to be accountable to no one and can come up with a limitless number of excuses for wrong behavior. At times they may consider themselves immune to discipline or correction, and in some cases run afoul of the law or suffer dire financial consequences as a result of their neglectful tendencies (i.e., bankruptcy, foreclosure, garnishment, etc.).

From the fall of man onward, people have found it easier to blame others than to take responsibility for their actions. Paul, Apostle to the Gentiles, emphasizes in the first chapter of his letter to the Romans that when it comes to sin, all of us are without excuse. We all have racked up an insurmountable sin debt payable only through the death of God's Son, Jesus. Those who daily live their lives in humble recognition of this fact show a measure of responsibility that God truly honors.

At the very beginning of Jesus' ministry, He called a simple fisherman named Simon Peter to follow Him. Peter left his nets and followed, learning about the teachings of the Law, the prophets, and of the Master, namely, Jesus. One day when Jesus and His disciples were traveling together, Jesus and the disciples were discussing the various opinions and rumors flying around as to who Christ was. Jesus then pointedly asked the disciples, *"But what about you? . . . Who do you say I am?"* Peter immediately responded saying, *"You are the Christ"* (Mark 8:29).

Yet learning how he should live did not instantly change Peter to willingly follow the Master's teachings. He had several run-ins with the government authority, and he knew what it was like to not submit to it. As a "babe" in his faith, he stumbled often. At the time of Christ's crucifixion, he adamantly denied knowing Christ. Years later, however, as a responsible and mature disciple, he wrote the letter of 1 Peter to the believers. In this letter, the apostle teaches the importance of self-control, honoring authority, and serving God willingly.

📖 Read 1 Peter 4:10–11 regarding service to others.

What does Peter tell us to do (verse 10a)?

_____

_____

How should we serve (10b)?

_____

_____

With what should we serve (11)?

_____

_____

Who is to be honored through our work (11)?

_____

_____

Some of us may wonder what our special abilities may be. Peter encourages us to *"use whatever gift"* we have received to help others (verse 10), which leads us to believe that each of us has at least one special ability we can use. Peter offers the challenge to do our work wholeheartedly with the desire to please God. He encourages his readers to live responsibly as examples to others.

The author of Hebrews (of whom no one is certain) wrote his letter to challenge Jewish believers to remain faithful to the teachings they had received. In this letter he warns them against falling away from the "elementary

CLEAR CONSCIENCE

"Dearly loved friends, if our consciences are clear, we can come to the Lord with perfect assurance and trust, and get whatever we ask for because we are obeying him and doing the things that please him."

(1 John 3:21, 22 [LB])

truths" of God's Word, and he encourages them to enjoy the triumphs of being faithful in their walk with God. He also encourages them to live by faith as their forefathers had done before them: Abel, Enoch, Noah, and Abraham (see Hebrews 11:4–11).

📖 Look at Hebrews 13:17–18 and consider our responsibilities as believers.

_____

_____

According to verse 17, what two things are we to do?

_____

_____

Whom do you consider to be the "leaders," or those who have authority in your life?

_____

_____

What is the author's request in verse 18?

_____

_____

According to Hebrews 13:18, what does the author desire to do?

_____

_____

Parents play an important role in teaching their children about obedience. They are the first teachers of responsibility to their children. Parents who want the best for their children encourage them and instruct them in ways that mold and shape them to grow to be responsible and mature adults. Good parents set general rules in the household to teach respect for each other, to keep order, and to keep their children from harm. Parents give their children different jobs or assignments, showing how to do them correctly. When their children can be found faithful with the smaller chores or jobs, they are given larger ones. Children are taught to carry out their work or instructions carefully. They are encouraged to be mindful of their actions.

Whenever necessary, parents correct their children and discipline them, teaching them the importance of being accountable to leaders and people in charge. We see how people who have not learned the value of responsibility get in trouble at home, school, at work, or even on the roads and highways. They look for excuses to do their own thing; it doesn't matter to them what the consequences may be. Solomon talked about the importance and the rewards of teaching responsibility in Proverbs. He states,

> "The rod of correction imparts wisdom, but a child left to himself disgraces his mother. When the wicked thrive, so does sin, but the righteous will see their downfall. Discipline your son, and he will give you peace; he will bring delight to your soul." (Proverbs 29:15–17)

When we live responsibly, we deliberately and carefully carry out our indi-

"Train a child in the way he should go, and when he is old he will not turn from it."

Proverbs 22:6

vidual assignments or duties. We pursue excellence. Paul was one who was found faithful in this regard. In his first letter to Timothy, Paul writes, *"I thank Christ Jesus our Lord, who has given me strength, that he considered me faithful, appointing me to his service"* (1:12). As Christians, after we have followed through with our duties, we should be able to look over what we have done and not be dissatisfied with our work. In 2 Timothy 2:15, Paul reminds us how we must work: *"Do your best to present yourself to God as one approved, a workman who does not need to be ashamed and who correctly handles the word of truth."* Paul also states, *"Now it is required that those who have been given a trust must prove faithful"* (1 Corinthians 4:2).

 How are you doing in the area of responsibility? How well do you carry out your individual duties in the settings of your home, church, or business? Do you give of your best to the duties to which you are assigned? Having too many responsibilities can be overwhelming. Do you need to consider saying "no" to taking on any new responsibilities and requests, so you can be more attentive to what is important at this time in your life? Write down any changes that need to be made and then pray for God to give you wisdom in these areas.

_____

_____

_____

_____

_____

_____

_____

 Now let's look at responsibility as it relates to personal finances. Examine how you rate in the following areas: 1) paying your bills on time, 2) keeping up-to-date balances in your checkbook and other accounts from which you pay your bills, 3) keeping accurate records for taxes and paying what is due in a reasonable amount of time, 4) evaluating your purchases before buying, 5) providing for your family's needs, 6) saving money regularly. What are some steps you can begin to take now to improve in the area of personal finances? List these action steps below.

_____

_____

_____

_____

_____

We enjoy life to the fullest when we have a more disciplined lifestyle. The key is to have balance, which comes from heeding God's directives for our lives. When we have stumbled in our walk and we need to get back on track, we can go to the One who is always faithful to us. We have the promise of 1 John 1:9, *"If we confess our sins, he is faithful and just and will forgive*

"Work hard so God can say to you, 'Well done.' Be a good workman, one who does not need to be ashamed when God examines your work. Know what his Word says and means."

2 Timothy 2:15 (LB)

us our sins and purify us from all unrighteousness." When we desire to "listen" with our hearts to what God is saying to us, we move on in our spiritual walk to become imitators of Christ. We become more willing to be accountable to other believers, taking heed to their words of advice and encouragement. As we ask God to help us live more responsibly, He'll reveal these ways to us.

> **"Whatever your hand finds to do, do it with all your might."**
>
> **Ecclesiastes 9:10**

DILIGENCE, OR PERSEVERANCE

Another virtue written about in the Bible that can keep debt at bay is diligence, or perseverance. One does not find this quality of moral excellence in a lazy person or a person who is content to meet the bare minimum standards asked of him. This virtuous characteristic reveals a strength that one possesses to *not* give up but to "keep on keeping on." People who exhibit the traits of diligence and perseverance are the ones who persistently carry on with their work or duties. They do not give up easily, but display a persevering effort, often in spite of difficulties. Having good intentions is not enough. We can ask God to help us carry out our work with diligence and to continue persevering.

Having an idea or a noble plan is not enough. How often have we started a project with enthusiasm, then after some time elapsed, found our enthusiasm waning? As our eagerness dwindled, so did our effort. The longer we procrastinated, the harder it became to continue the project. The apostle Paul knew the importance of completing one's work. He encouraged the Corinthians when he learned of a noble plan they had. Paul knew of their zeal for the extraordinary project and told them: *"Now finish the work, so that your eager willingness to do it may be matched by your completion of it, according to your means"* (2 Corinthians 8:11). Another translation records the verse this way: *"But now finish doing it also; that just as there was the readiness to desire it, so there may be also the completion of it by your ability"* (NASB).

Solomon, author of thousands of proverbs, often contrasts the righteous and the wicked in his writings. He emphasizes in his wise sayings that *"diligent hands will rule"* (Proverbs 12:24). Note what he says about the diligent person in this proverb:

> *Poor is he who works with a negligent hand,*
> *But the hand of the diligent makes rich.*
> *He who gathers in summer is a son who acts wisely,*
> *But he who sleeps in harvest is a son who acts shamefully.*

📖 Look up other proverbs about the diligent person and write the verses below:

Proverbs 12:27

_____

_____

Proverbs 13:4

_____

_____

_____

_____

_____

_____

APPLY Solomon gives us the charge, *"watch over your heart with all diligence, for from it flow the springs of life"* (Proverbs 4:23 NASB). What do you think this means? Are you daily watching over your heart?

_____

_____

_____

_____

_____

📖 Paul exhorts us in Romans 12 to be dedicated in our service as servants of Christ. Read Romans 12:4–11, and summarize how we can we be faithful in our duties.

_____

_____

According to Romans 12:11, what should we never lack?

_____

The author of Hebrews encourages believers to continue in their faith. He tells us that God will not forget our work and the commitment we have shown Him through our diligence:

> *God is not unjust; he will not forget your work and the love you have shown him as you have helped his people and continue to help them. We want each of you to show this same diligence to the very end, in order to make your hope sure. We do not want you to become lazy, but to imitate those who through faith and patience inherit what has been promised.* (Hebrews 6:10–12)

The believers *"who obey God's commandments and remain faithful to Jesus"* will be greatly rewarded in Heaven. The saints who have remained steadfast in their faith will be called *"Blessed,"* and *"they will rest from their labor, for their deeds will follow them"* (Revelation 14:12–13).

APPLY In what ways do we display diligence and perseverance in our life? Are there times we could have done better?

_____

_____

_____

When we are discouraged or tempted to give up, we can ask God for His strength and help. We can continually depend on God and the Holy Spirit's power to change us into the people God desires us to be. And as we see growth and transformation in our life, we can thank God for working in us.

"Patience and diligence, like faith, remove mountains."

—William Penn

"Be devoted to one another in brotherly love; give preference to one another in honor; not lagging behind in diligence, fervent in spirit, serving the Lord."

Romans 12:10–11 (NASB)

PATIENCE

We have probably at one time or another heard someone say, "Patience is a virtue." When we are patient we "possess or demonstrate quiet, uncomplaining endurance under distress or annoyance."[3] It is an admirable trait of inner strength. When we are patient we tend to be composed and calm about the issues at hand. When we're not patient we tend to be hasty, high-strung, restless, or easily flustered. We would rather not deal with the long delays. As impatient people, we find it difficult to wait for whatever we look forward to, such as a reward.

A true example of one who displays patience is our Father God. God reminds us of His longsuffering and patient endurance with sinners so that they will repent of their sinful ways. Romans 2:4 states, *"Do you show contempt for the riches of his kindness, tolerance and patience, not realizing that God's kindness leads you toward repentance?"*

Second Peter 3:9 also reminds us of His loving patience: *"The Lord is not slow in keeping his promise, as some understand slowness. He is patient with you, not wanting anyone to perish, but everyone to come to repentance."* God is forbearing, giving us enough time to accept His plan of salvation to obtain eternal life. His patience toward sinners shows His desire for them to be saved.

The apostle Paul continually reminds believers through his letters to act worthy of their calling. In several of his letters, he extols the virtue of patience, or endurance. He is a good example of one who exercised patience. His writings stressed the importance of this quality as a "fruit of the Spirit." It is listed as the fourth fruit of the Spirit in the following passage:

> *But the fruit of the Spirit is love, joy, peace, patience, kindness, goodness, faithfulness, gentleness and self-control. Against such things there is no law. Those who belong to Christ Jesus have crucified the sinful nature with its passions and desires. Since we live by the Spirit, let us keep in step with the Spirit.* (Galatians 5:22–25)

The fruit of the Spirit has its beginning when we respond to God's love and His grace. This fruit is a result of the Spirit-filled life, rather than taking the approach of doing things in our own strength.

📖 Look at Ephesians 4:1–3.

What qualities should we have as Christians (Ephesians 4:2)?

_____

_____

How are we to live with one another (Ephesians 4:3)?

_____

_____

Paul emphasizes the importance of the unity of the Church. The death and resurrection of Jesus broke down the wall separating the Gentiles and Jews. They are now one in Christ; they are now on equal footing. Christ is the

A true example of one who displays patience is our Father God. God reminds us of His longsuffering and patient endurance with sinners so that they will repent of their sinful ways.

head of the Church. Ephesians 4:4–6 states, *"There is one body and one Spirit—just as you were called to one hope when you were called—one Lord, one faith, one baptism; one God and Father of all."* Paul encourages the believers to continue living out their faith, to which they were called.

📖 Read the beginning of Paul's letter to the Thessalonians in 1 Thessalonians 1:1–3.

According to verses 1 and 2, who does Paul mention in his prayers?

_____

_____

_____

Paul and his companions planted a church in Thessalonica. Paul's preaching led to a large following of believers here. This new church was comprised of some of the Jews and many God-fearing Greek men and women. Even from the beginning of Paul's ministry there, the church had experienced strong opposition. The faith of the Thessalonians became known throughout Macedonia, Achaia, and throughout the region (1 Thessalonians 1:8).

Fill in the blanks to complete verse 3.

"We _____ remember before our God and Father your _____ produced by _____, your _____ prompted by _____, and your _____ inspired by _____ in our Lord Jesus Christ."

Paul commended them for their endurance, or patience, as they endured persecution for their faith. Paul's gratitude for their steadfastness of faith is evident.

We learn patience as we go through hard times. In the New Testament, James emphasizes the importance of being Christ-like even when situations may be difficult for us. His writings emphasize that our works make our faith visible to others. A leader of the church in Jerusalem, James' practical writings show how Christians are to live day-to-day. (Some call the letter of James the "Proverbs of the New Testament.") He points out that our trials could be productive for us in the end; we can discover joy as a result of our troubling times. Read what James has to say about patience:

> *"Consider it all joy, my brethren, when you encounter various trials, knowing that the testing of your faith produces endurance. And let endurance have its perfect result, that you may be perfect and complete, lacking in nothing. But if any of you lacks wisdom, let him ask of God, who gives to all men generously and without reproach, and it will be given to him."* (James 1:2–5, NASB)

In these verses, *endurance* is a translation of the Greek word *"hupomone,"* which "is associated with hope and refers to the quality that does not surrender to circumstances or succumb under trial."[4] As patience is exercised, the outcome or goal is completed and attained, as it ought to be. Our strong hope in God can help us endure the situations that come our way.

God helps us, as His children, accept the difficult circumstances that come our way. We can be assured that we will be rewarded for our patience: *"Blessed is the man who perseveres under trial, because when he has stood the test,*

PAUL'S CHARGE TO TIMOTHY

"But you, man of God, . . . pursue righteousness, godliness, faith, love, endurance and gentleness. Fight the good fight of the faith." (1 Timothy 6:11–12)

he will receive the crown of life that God has promised to those who love him" (James 1:12). James reminds us that our future rewards in heaven depend on how we faithfully live here on earth.

📖 Referring to these verses in James 1:2–5 and verse 12, answer the following questions:

What is the result of perseverance (James 1:4)?

_____

_____

According to James 1:12, what has God promised to those who love him?

_____

_____

APPLY In Romans 12:12, Paul writes the believers and encourages them to action by exercising three different qualities: *"Be joyful in hope, patient in affliction, faithful in prayer."* Consider how you are doing in these areas (at home, work, church, and your community) and make a brief note of it.

"Be joyful in hope."

_____

_____

"Patient in affliction."

_____

_____

_____

"Faithful in prayer."

_____

_____

"Be joyful in hope, patient in affliction, faithful in prayer."

Romans 12:12

How patient are you in the area of personal finances? Do you exercise patience and caution in your financial decisions, whether large or small? Are you willing to wait for the items you want and to purchase them with cash, instead of charging them to your credit cards? Can you patiently wait for your money to earn interest, or are you tempted to jump into hasty "investment" decisions? Do you have long-range plans for your savings? Spend some time in prayerful consideration as you ponder these questions. Write any observations or areas for improvement below. Praise God for the materials and resources He has entrusted to you and ask Him to help you in areas where you have not been the best stewards.

_____

_____

_____

_____

_____

_____

Courage to Do the Right Thing

When we think of a courageous person, we may think of a daring soldier who is eager to fight in a war. Or a person who may be dealing stoically with a difficult illness or a tragic situation. Or perhaps it may be someone who fearlessly follows through with a dangerous task or job.

As people who believe in the all-powerful God, we can approach God and ask Him for courage to face whatever may come our way, whether known or unknown. There's a story of an Old Testament king who was confronted unexpectedly with war. King Jehoshaphat took over as king of Judah after his father, King Asa. Jehoshaphat brought order to a country that abounded in crime. He organized a national court system; taught his citizens about the laws of God; and had a large army based in Jerusalem.

One day King Jehoshaphat heard there was a vast army from Syria coming and declaring war against him and the people of Judah. Shaken from the news, feeling helpless and fearful, he announced to the people of Judah to intercede before God for their safety and deliverance. He joined the citizens who came from all across the nation to the new court of the temple in Jerusalem.

📖 Read the king's prayer for guidance in 2 Chronicles 20:6–12.

The king began his prayer with adoration to God. According to verse 6, what are in God's hands?

_____

_____

What will God do when we *"cry out to* [Him] *in our distress"* (verse 9)?

_____

_____

Fill in the blanks for 2 Chronicles 20:12: *"For we have no _____ to face this vast army that is attacking us. We do not know what to _____, but our eyes are upon _____."*

The citizens from Judah came together to seek the Lord for help. Then God told King Jehoshaphat and people of Judah and Jerusalem through a messenger: *"Do not be afraid or discouraged because of this vast army. For the battle is not yours, but God's"* (2 Chronicles 20:15). Encouraged by God's promise, early the next morning, the army of Judah went out to the desert of Tekoa. When the king met with the people, he assigned those who would lead the march by singing to the Lord and acknowledging God's holiness as they went out to meet the army. They sang *"Give thanks to the LORD, for his love endures forever."* At that moment, when they began to praise and sing, the Lord God caused the other armies to fight among themselves, and Judah's enemies were killed (2 Chronicles 20:20–22). King Jehoshaphat passed the test of courage, and his faith inspired others.

Many times we fail to realize or acknowledge that the Lord our God, the all-powerful God, is here to help us and to fight our battles. There's a saying,

> **As people who believe in the all-powerful God, we can approach God and ask Him for courage to face whatever may come our way, whether known or unknown.**

"Do not be afraid or discouraged because of this vast army. For the battle is not yours, but God's."

2 Chronicles 20:15

"The greatness of our fears shows us the littleness of our faith." Fear can paralyze, hold us back in life, and accentuate the obstacles. Can you recall when fear caused you to be ineffective and powerless? We don't like to dwell on these times for very long, do we?

God wants us to face our problems with courage. As His children whom He loves dearly, we can ask Him for courage so we can think and act calmly as we deal with the important decisions we face every day in our lives. As we are open to God's leading in our lives, He will show us what we need to do to follow Him more closely. But we mustn't just think about making the necessary changes sometime later. We need to get past the stage of deciding to make important changes in our lives, and get to the action part, doing what we sense God telling us to do. Our heavenly Father will give us the courage we need to follow His directives for our lives.

Forty years after crossing the Red Sea, Joshua took over as leader of the Israelites. Before leading Joshua and the people to the Promised Land, God summoned him three times in His speech with these words: *"Be strong and courageous"* (Joshua 1). In this chapter, *strong* is derived from the Hebrew word *chazaq,* meaning to be "bound fast, to hold firm, to conquer."[5] *Chazaq* is often used to describe battle scenes.

📖 Read what Joshua 1:8–9 says about how we can live a prosperous life:

"Do not let this Book of the Law depart from your mouth; meditate on it day and night, so that you may be careful to do everything written in it. Then you will be prosperous and successful. Have I not commanded you? Be strong and courageous. Do not be terrified; do not be discouraged, for the LORD your God will be with you wherever you go."

Why are we to be strong and courageous (Joshua 1:9)?

_____

_____

When we have the resources of God's Word and His presence, we are equipped to be courageous. Our faith enables us to be strong and of good courage.

📖 Courage wipes out fear and worry. Look up the following passages on worry and write them below:

Psalms 50:15

_____

_____

_____

Proverbs 12:25

_____

_____

_____

Philippians 4:6

_____

_____

_____

1 Peter 5:6–7

_____

_____

_____

We can ask God for courage when we're dealing with difficult problems in our lives. He can help us act calmly and bravely in our actions, helping us to make sound judgments. If we are faced with moral dilemmas, we can have the courage to stand firm and do what is morally right. We can have this courage because we know that God is in control of everything and He is with us. For He has promised us, _"Never will I leave you; never will I forsake you"_ (Hebrews 13:5). We can say to God "I will trust in you," and we can count on His faithfulness. Then, God will honor our courage.

When times come that trouble and test us, we can remember to take the long view of things. God's timing is always right. With the strength God gives us, we can be encouraged as we go through the valleys before us. We can hold firm to the blessings that will be ours.

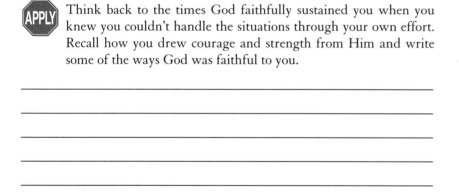 Think back to the times God faithfully sustained you when you knew you couldn't handle the situations through your own effort. Recall how you drew courage and strength from Him and write some of the ways God was faithful to you.

_____

_____

_____

_____

_____

As we think about our money management, it takes courage to make important changes that will affect our future for the better. It takes courage to follow though with our financially smart decisions, when we have taken the easy route in the past. With this new courage we will see God work in new and great ways in our lives. We can work through our financial challenges with God's presence and principles to guide us. Just as we did not lose hope in the past, we can have that same hope every day for whatever may come our way.

 Lord, most Holy God, I thank You that Your love endures forever. I am thankful that I can put my trust in You. Give me the strength and courage that I need each day to do the right and wise thing in every situation. Show me the areas in my life that I need to change to become more like You. May I receive your Word with a receptive heart and a willing attitude. In Jesus' name, Amen.

> "Never will I leave you; never will I forsake you."
>
> Hebrews 13:5

Write your own prayer or a journal here.

_____

_____

_____

_____

_____

_____

_____

_____

_____

_____

_____

NOTES

1. Adam Clarke, *Adam Clarke's Commentary on the Bible,* "2 Thessalonians 3:11 Commentary." In e-Sword Bible software database, 2005, Rick Meyers.

2. *Funk & Wagnalls Standard Desk Dictionary,* Vol. 2, (USA: Harper & Row Publishers, Inc. 1984), 568.

3. Ibid., 480.

4. Spiros Zodhiates, *Hebrew-Greek Key Word Study Bible,* (Chattanooga: AMG Publishers, 1990), 1883.

5. Ibid., 1724.

PRINCIPLES FOR LEARNING GOD'S WILL IN OUR LIVES

*H*ow can I find out God's will for my life? How can I know if I'm making the right decisions? Do I just follow the crowd or do what "feels" like the right thing to do? How can I know what's important for me now at this point in my life? Am I doing the right thing when it comes to my relationships, career, or even where I live? Which direction should I be going when it comes to making important financial decisions? These questions can be answered as we desire to grow closer to God and we are open to His leading.

Many people struggle to discover their purpose in life. This week we will look at five principles that help us find God's will for our lives. Whether we are new in the Christian faith or not, these principles can serve as signposts in following God. They will indicate to us that we are either going in the right direction or the wrong direction. These principles will guide us in our primary objective of living for God. God wants us to live our lives with significance and real purpose.

Which direction should you be going when it comes to making important financial decisions?

FEED ON GOD'S WORD

Today we will see how God reveals His purpose for us in His book. By feeding on God's Word, we are taught how to live obedient and holy lives. The Bible says, *"All Scripture is God-breathed and is useful for teaching, rebuking, correcting and training in righteousness, so that the man of God may be thoroughly equipped for every good work"* (2 Timothy 3:16–17). This verse makes it unmistakable that God is the source of the Scriptures. God inspired the writers to communicate His truths to us.

Our purpose is discovered as we learn to please God in our lives. It's not about us, but about Him. In the Old and New Testaments, we are told to be a holy people, for which we were created. In Leviticus 11:44 God stated, *"I am the LORD your God; consecrate yourselves and be holy; because I am holy."* The apostle Peter quoted from this verse when writing to the believers: *"But just as he who called you is holy, so be holy in all you do; for it is written: 'Be holy, because I am holy' "* (1 Peter 1:15–16). Peter wrote letters to encourage the believers, emphasizing the importance of living a pure life, set apart from the world. At the beginning of his first letter, he reminds them of their *"living hope"* (verse 3) through Christ's resurrection. Because death has been conquered, those who receive Jesus Christ can have salvation and life eternal. Peter states,

> *"Though you have not seen him, you love him; and even though you do not see him now, you believe in him and are filled with an inexpressible and glorious joy, for you are receiving the goal of your faith, the salvation of your souls."* (1 Peter 1:8–9)

📖 Peter wrote about practical issues for daily living. Read 1 Peter 1:13–17, looking for the five commands he gives us.

What five commands does Peter give (verses 13–16)?

_____

_____

_____

_____

_____

Which command sums up the other four (verses 15–16)?

_____

_____

How does living a holy life make us strangers here?

_____

_____

_____

_____

"Continually restate to yourself what the purpose of your life is. The destined end of an individual is not happiness, not health, but holiness."

—Oswald Chambers

APPLY Are you like a stranger in this world, or do you feel right at home? Why?

_____

_____

_____

_____

_____

_____

Has your life been more holy or less holy in the last year? How?

_____

_____

_____

_____

_____

_____

What part of your life do you have the most difficulty keeping holy? What will you do this week to let God take control of this area?

_____

_____

_____

_____

When we read the Bible, we learn the direction God wants us to take in our lives. _"Your Word is a lamp to my feet and a light for my path"_ (Psalms 119:105). When James wrote to the believers, he was concerned with their ethical behavior and their outward behavior. In his letter, he stresses the importance of not only being _listeners_ of the Word but _doers_ of the Word. He wrote about how to _live_ like a Christian.

📖 Read James 1:21–25 and consider his instruction.

According to verse 21, what are we to get rid of?

_____

How are we to accept the Word of God (verse 21)?

_____

_____

What can the Word planted in us do (verse 21)?

_____

In verse 22, James tells us that listening to the Word isn't enough. What else must happen?

_____

> **"I will instruct you and teach you in the way you should go; I will counsel you and watch over you."**
>
> **Psalms 32:8**

Who will be blessed in whatever they do (verse 25)?

_____

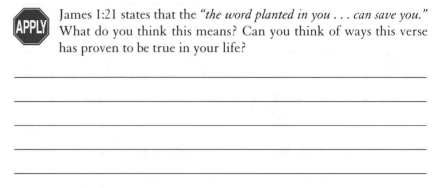

James 1:21 states that the *"the word planted in you . . . can save you."* What do you think this means? Can you think of ways this verse has proven to be true in your life?

_____

_____

_____

_____

_____

Secondly, by feeding on God's Word, we come to *"know the mystery of God, namely, Christ, in whom are hidden all the treasures of wisdom and knowledge* (Colossians 2:2–3). As Christians we can have access to these bountiful nuggets of wisdom, as we abide in Christ. Paul and Timothy wrote regarding this previously hidden "mystery":

> *"this mystery among the Gentiles, which is Christ in you, the hope of glory. And we proclaim Him, admonishing every man and teaching every man with all wisdom, that we may present every man complete in Christ."* (Colossians 1:27–28, NASB)

Christ is our hope. He is sufficient. Warren Wiersbe notes,

> Why follow empty philosophy when we have all fullness in Christ? The fundamental test of any religious teaching is, "Where does it put Jesus Christ—His Person and His Work? Does it rob Him of His fullness? Does it deny either His deity or His humanity?" If so, that teaching is wrong and dangerous.[1]

The Word tells us:

> *"See to it that no one takes you captive through hollow and deceptive philosophy, which depends on human tradition and the basic principles of this world rather than on Christ. For in Christ all the fullness of the Deity lives in bodily form, and you have been given fullness in Christ, who is the head over every power and authority."* (Colossians 2:8–10)

Are we "Christians" by name only, or are we truly drawn to God and to His Word? Are we "along for the ride," perhaps following family traditions and warming a church pew, or do we desire to seek all that Christ has to offer us? Paul warned Titus about people that *"claim to know God, but by their actions they deny him. They are detestable, disobedient and unfit for doing anything good"* (Titus 1:16). These people profess to know God, but in their daily lives they do not walk their talk. There is a vast difference between *knowing about* God and knowing Him *personally*.

After the Lord's Supper, and after washing his disciples' feet, Jesus told his disciples about things to come. He told them, *"Whoever has my commands and obeys them, he is the one who loves me. He who loves me will be loved by my Father, and I too will love him and show myself to him"* (John 14:21). Here we see the correlation between knowing the Word, obeying it, and Jesus revealing Himself to us. Jesus then spoke to his disciples saying, *"I am the vine; you are the branches. If a man remains in me and I in him, he will bear much fruit; apart from me you can do nothing"* (John 15:5). Jesus emphasized that we need to draw upon Him as *"the vine"* of our spiritual life so that we can be fruitful. Without an ongoing relationship with the Lord Jesus, our lives are unsatisfying and oftentimes disappointing. Jesus told His disciples that they were His dear friends. He told them, *"I have called you friends, for everything that I learned from my Father I have made known to you"* (John 15:15).

 Read the following verses as a prayer to God.

You have laid down precepts that are to be fully obeyed.
Oh, that my ways were steadfast in obeying your decrees!
I seek you with all my heart; do not let me stray from your commands.
I have hidden your word in my heart that I might not sin against you.
I rejoice in following your statutes as one rejoices in great riches.
I meditate on your precepts and consider your ways.
Do good to your servant, and I will live; I will obey your word.
Open my eyes that I may see wonderful things in your law.

Psalm 119:4–5, 10–11, 14–15, 17–18.

COMMIT TO DO GOD'S WILL FIRST

A second principle in finding our purpose in life is to make a commitment to do God's will *first*. When we make a commitment, we are promising to do something and to carry it out faithfully. We make a resolute decision to be faithful to someone or to a cause. King Solomon taught these words of wisdom: *"So you will find favor and good repute in the sight of God and man, Trust in the LORD with all your heart, and do not lean on your own understanding. In all your ways acknowledge Him, and He will make your paths straight"* (Proverbs 3:4–6, NASB). When we "acknowledge" God, we are familiar with His ways, and we understand His ways. Note that the root word in *acknowledge* is *"know."* The term *acknowledge* in verse 6 is translated from the Hebrew word *Yada,* meaning, "to perceive, to understand, to acquire knowledge, to know, to discern, to be acquainted with." It is used to describe knowledge that is gained through the senses. Knowing this, how can we know our purpose in life if we don't have a genuine and growing relationship with the One who can show us the way? Without an awareness of God in our lives, we cannot be certain of our future.

A paraphrase of Proverbs 3:4–6 says,

> *"If you want favor with both God and man, and a reputation for good judgment and common sense, then trust the Lord completely; don't ever trust yourself. In everything you do, put God first, and he will direct you and crown your efforts with success."* (LB)

Solomon also stated, *"Commit your works to the LORD, and your plans will be established"* (Proverbs 16:3, NASB). In this verse the word *"plans"* relates to "thought, imaginations, intentions, purpose" and *"established"* means "to stand firm, steadfast, sure, certain."[2] Spiros Zodhiates states, "The deep satisfaction and sense of well-being comes from the certainty that our hearts are fixed upon God. We can be confident that He will direct our paths"[3]

"If the Lord delights in a man's way, He makes his steps firm; Though he stumble, he will not fall, for the Lord upholds him with his hand."

Psalms 37:23

When Jesus is the Lord of my life, I will put Him on the throne of my life. I will yield myself to Him. My interests and desires will be in accord and in agreement with His directives. He will be honored in my life, and I will be loyal to Him. I will be inclined to follow His ways consistently, every day and be assured that I can and will enjoy God's blessings when He is first in my life.

📖 What were King Solomon's words of wisdom concerning God's leading in our lives (Proverbs 3:5–6)?

_____

_____

📖 David had a heart for God, and his psalms exalt and honor God and God's eternal faithfulness. Psalm 37 is a psalm of trust. David declared that he could confide in God completely because of who God is; he learned to trust God. Read Psalm 37:1–6 concerning the heritage of the righteous, then fill in the blanks to complete verses 3–6.

"_____ in the LORD and do _____; dwell in the land and enjoy safe pasture. _____ yourself in the LORD and he will give you the desires of your _____. _____ your way to the LORD; _____ in him and he will do this: He will make your _____ shine like the dawn, the _____ of your cause like the noonday sun."

APPLY Have you ever worn a blindfold and allowed someone to lead you around a room or another area? How did you feel about the experience? If you knew and trusted that person leading you, most likely you were not hesitant to allow him or her to guide you.

_____

_____

_____

_____

What areas of your life are hard to trust God with? Ask God to help you entrust these areas to Him.

📖 We read the story in Mark of a young ruler who held back from making an important commitment because of his riches. Read Mark 10:17–27 to learn more about this man.

How did the young man approach Jesus (verse 17)?

_____

_____

What did the young man ask Jesus (verse 17)?

_____

What did the rich young ruler say he had done since he was a boy (verses 19–20)?

_____

_____

"So we say with confidence, 'The Lord is my helper; I will not be afraid.'"

Hebrews 13:6

According to verse 21, what did Jesus lovingly tell him he needed to do?

_____

_____

How did the young man go away (verse 22)?

_____

What did Jesus tell His disciples afterward (verse 23)?

_____

_____

Note the contrast of how the young man approached the *"Good Teacher"* and then how he left. He undoubtedly heard of this great teacher making his way throughout the land of Judea. He was able to run and to catch up with Jesus soon after Jesus had picked up the children in His arms and blessed them.

He must have desired to obey God, for he said he followed the laws from the time he was a young boy. He wanted to know for sure how he could have eternal life. The rich young ruler left with a heavy heart after hearing the counsel of Jesus. For there was still another commandment he needed to take into account. He needed to give up the idol of riches and to love God instead. At the end of the story Jesus reminded the disciples that salvation is from God. There is nothing too hard for Him (Mark 10:26–27). The rich young ruler was not ready to commit his life to God by faith. He was not ready to make this commitment concerning his money.

The apostle Paul's charge to Timothy was, *"Command those who are rich in this present world not to be arrogant nor to put their hope in wealth, which is so uncertain, but to put their hope in God, who richly provides us with everything for our enjoyment"* (1 Timothy 6:17). The term *"hope"* in this verse refers to "the hope of future good fortune."

When we make a commitment to doing God's will first, it is important to be obedient to His priorities. God has promised that He will be with us. The degree to which we can experience His presence depends on us. How we relate to God in our Christian walk, our love, obedience, and faith, plays a vital role in the vastness of experiencing his presence.

APPLY Have we submitted our lives to Him? Is it apparent to others that we want Christ to have first place in our lives? Is there evidence that God is using us for His purposes?

_____

_____

_____

_____

 "Set before our minds and hearts, O heavenly Father, the example of our Lord Jesus Christ, who when He was upon earth, found His refinement in doing the will of Him who sent Him, and in finishing His work. Give us grace to remember Him who knew neither impatience of spirit nor confusion of work, but in the midst

> **"Command those who are rich in this present world not to be arrogant nor to put their hope in wealth, which is so uncertain, but to put their hope in God, who richly provides us with everything for our enjoyment."**
>
> **1 Timothy 6:17**

of all His labors held communion with Thee, and even upon earth was still in heaven; where now He reigneth with Thee and the Holy Spirit, world without end."—Dean C. J. Vaughan

Learning God's Will

DAY THREE

DAILY ASK FOR GOD'S GUIDANCE

How can we learn God's will for our lives? We can feed on God's Word. Oswald Sanders comments, "Let us recognize that all matters of moral and spiritual principle are clearly dealt with in the Scriptures. It is our responsibility to search out what is revealed. Where the Scriptures speak clearly, we need seek no further guidance."[4] Secondly, we can make a commitment to *first* do His will. We can confidently trust Him to do what is in our best interest. We make a resolute decision to trust and obey Him.

Thirdly, we must *daily* ask for God's guidance in our lives. We can seek God's will through prayer and supplication without expecting to know *today* what we will be doing five or ten years from now. Learning God's will is a lifelong process, so we shouldn't worry about tomorrow. It is unreasonable to expect to have all the answers *today* for our lives. But we can live in the present and know we are doing *today* what we should be doing; that we are doing God's will. It is reassuring to know that we can go to someone who loves us and knows us. When we pray, we can seek the Holy Spirit to show us and guide us in His direction for our lives.

An author on the subject of prayer, Oswald Sanders reminds us "true prayer is not asking God for what *we* want, but for what *He* wants." His words are well spoken:

> Prayer is not a convenient method of getting one's own way or of bending God to one's desires. Prayer is the means by which our desires can be redirected and aligned with the will of God. As we expectantly pray for light concerning the will of God on any matter, if our desires are not in line with His will, He will make it clear. If we are willing, He will change and redirect our desires, as Paul assures us: *"It is God who is at work in you, both to will and to work for His good pleasure"* (Philippians 2:13). . . . The supreme example of the redirection of the will in prayer is that of our Lord in Gethsemane's garden. As Son of Man, Jesus was utterly submissive to His Father's will. Yet in His humanity He shrank from the unutterable sufferings involved in His work as Mediator. In His distress He prayed, *"Father if Thou art willing, remove this cup from Me; yet not My will, but Thine be done"* (Luke 22:42).[5]

Pray with a Clean Heart
When we pray, we must pray with a clean heart. We need to confess our sins for our prayers to be heard. When Job was pleading and praying for relief from his suffering he prayed, *"My prayer is pure"* (Job 16:17). The term *"pure"* alludes to purity, innocence, and clarity, as in the clarity of olive oil. In the book of Job it is "used figuratively of the soul and morality." In the book of Psalm, David said, *"If I had cherished sin in my heart, the Lord would not have listened"* (Psalms 66:18).

"For God is at work within you, helping you want to obey him, and then helping you do what he wants."

Philippians 2:13 (LB)

68   FOLLOWING GOD – LIVING A BALANCED FINANCIAL LIFE

James reminds us that, for our prayers to be effective, we must have clean hearts before God. James 5:16 states, *"Therefore confess your sins to each other and pray for each other so that you may be healed. The prayer of a righteous man is powerful and effective."* Another translation tells us *"The effective prayer of a righteous man can accomplish much"* (NASB). In this verse, the term *"effective"* is translated from the Greek *energeo*, meaning "to be active and energetic, prove oneself strong."[6] Spiros Zodhiates points out that "in James 5:16 it [*energeo*] seems to denote the inspired prayer or the prayer of a righteous man wrought by the operation or energy of the Holy Spirit."[7] When we come with clean hearts before God with our needs, we can have confidence that He will hear us.

Pray with Adoration and Thanksgiving

When we pray, we can acknowledge that God is sovereign and holy. He made us and He deserves our adoration and worship. *"Come, let us bow down in worship, let us kneel before the LORD our Maker; for he is our God and we are the people of his pasture, the flock under his care"* (Psalms 95:6–7). We tell God of our love for Him. Jude concluded his letter with beautiful words of adoration:

> *"To him who is able to keep you from falling and to present you before his glorious presence without fault and with great joy—to the only God our Savior be glory, majesty, power and authority, through Jesus Christ our Lord, before all ages, now and forevermore! Amen."* (Jude 1:24–25)

It is also important to pray with thanksgiving. We are grateful for God's many blessings. We acknowledge His kindness and His love bestowed on us. When we pray with thankful hearts, we can experience God's peace in our lives.

> *"Do not be anxious about anything, but in everything, by prayer and petition, with thanksgiving, present your requests to God. And the peace of God, which transcends all understanding, will guard your hearts and your minds in Christ Jesus."* (Philippians 4:6–7)

Pray Without Doubting

When we pray, we should not doubt that we will receive help. When we are searching for God's will in our lives, we must have a deep sense of conviction that He will answer our prayers. James states,

> *"But when he asks, he must believe and not doubt, because he who doubts is like a wave of the sea, blown and tossed by the wind. That man should not think he will receive anything from the Lord; he is a double-minded man, unstable in all he does."* (James 1:6–7)

We must not waver in our thinking; instead we must have faith. In Hebrews 11, the chapter naming several legends of the faith, we are reminded, *"And without faith it is impossible to please God, because anyone who comes to him must believe that he exists and that he rewards those who earnestly seek him"* (verse 6). We can pray with confidence.

Pray Continually

When we pray, we can have the assurance that God hears us. We can pray at any time and wherever we are, for God is omnipresent. Prayer should be natural for us. We are encouraged to *"pray continually"* (1 Thessalonians 5:17) and to pray persistently about our concerns.

📖 In Luke 11, Jesus taught about prayer. Read Luke 11:5–10 about persistence in asking.

"Because of the LORD's great love we are not consumed, for his compassions never fail. They are new every morning; great is your faithfulness."

Lamentations 3:22–23

What does Jesus tell us to do about our needs (Luke 11:9)?

_____

📖 Jesus told a parable of the persistent widow as a lesson that we should never give up when we pray. Read Jesus' parable in Luke 18:1–8.

Is there a relationship between faith and answered prayer?

_____

Is there a relationship between persistence and answered prayer?

_____

Put Yourself in Their Shoes
WATCH AND PRAY

Jesus told His disciples to watch and pray. Do we watch and pray as we make important decisions that not only affect us but our family and those around us? Are we "on guard" as we make financial decisions, whether large or small?

Watch and Pray

After the Passover feast, (also known as the Lord's Supper), Jesus and His disciples Peter, James, and John went to Gethsemane, at the Mount of Olives. Knowing what was ahead of Him, Jesus told His disciples to *"watch and pray so that you will not fall into temptation. The spirit is willing, but the body is weak"* (Matthew 26:41). They were instructed to watch (be on guard) and pray. Jesus was extremely distressed, dreading what may come before Him. We note how, as the Son of Man, Jesus was dealing with His own humanity at this time.

📖 Find out how the will of God became clear to Jesus by reading about His experience in the Garden of Gethsemane. Read Matthew 26:36–45.

While in the garden Jesus prayed to His Father three different times. According to Matthew 26:39, what were the words of His first prayer? (The term "cup" in this verse refers to the bitter suffering Jesus would endure.)

How did Jesus pray the second and third times (verses 42, 44)?

_____

_____

Jesus was ready to accept His death when He told the disciples, *"Rise, let us go! Here comes my betrayer!"* (Matthew 26:46). The answer to the Son of Man's prayers had become clear. He had committed His future with its sufferings into His Father's hands. It was His Father's will that He would endure the trials ahead.

APPLY In what areas have you gone to God in distress and sorrow? Where has your Gethsemane been? Reflect on how you handled the results of your prayers. Are you facing a Gethsemane experience now, or will you be facing it in the near future? Trust God to help you as you go through the challenging times.

_____

_____

_____

_____

_____

Jesus told His disciples to watch and pray. Do we watch and pray as we make important decisions that not only affect us but our family and those around us? Are we "on guard" as we make financial decisions, whether large or small? We can bring these matters to God for *"the spirit is willing, but the body is weak"* (Matthew 26:41).

 "Blessed Jesus, it is Thyself in whom our faith must be rooted if it is to grow strong. Thy work has freed us from the power of sin, and opened the way to the Father; Thy Spirit is always drawing us upward into a life of perfect faith and confidence; we are assured that in Thy teaching we shall learn to pray the prayer of faith. Thou will train us to pray so that we believe that we receive, to believe that we really have what we ask. Lord, teach me so to love and trust Thee that my soul may have in Thee assurance that I am heard." (Anonymous)

BE AWARE OF THE QUIET CONVICTION

In this lesson we have looked at three ways we can learn God's will for our lives. They are: 1) feed on God's Word, 2) commit to do God's will first, and 3) daily ask for God's guidance. Today we will examine the principle of listening to quiet conviction as another way to learn what He would have us do.

God's Word gives us written truths and morals to live by. Passed down for generations, God speaks to us through the words of Scripture. While teaching in the synagogue in Capernaum, Jesus told the disciples, *"The words I have spoken to you are spirit and they are life"* (John 6:63). God speaks to us through His Word and through our prayers with Him. We can learn to be aware of the quiet conviction of God speaking to us. He speaks to us as our hearts and ears are attuned to His still, small voice.

The young boy Samuel was attentive to the voice of God, even though *"in those days the word of the LORD was rare; there were not many visions"* (1 Samuel 3:1). His mother Hannah had prayed incessantly for a son, and she was granted her desire. When the time came to take him as a young child to the temple, she joyfully dedicated him for the Lord's service. From the time he was a young boy, Samuel obeyed and worshiped God.

While resting in the temple, Samuel heard his name called on three different occasions and went to Eli, the temple priest. After the third time, Eli told Samuel that if he was called again, to say, *"Speak, LORD, for your servant is listening"* (1 Samuel 3:9). Samuel followed Eli's instructions, and then the LORD told him that God would judge Eli's family *"because of the sin he* [Eli] *knew about; his sons made themselves contemptible, and he failed to restrain them"* (1 Samuel 3:13). The next morning Samuel told Eli the vision; he was a faithful messenger. Samuel was known as a great prophet of the Lord and was used mightily throughout his life.

God spoke to a young boy who desired to obey God in spite of the corruption going on around him, even in the Temple. The young boy Samuel heard God's voice when he was resting, in the still of the night. Are we crowding out God's voice with all the noise and activity around us? We are told, *"Be still, and know that I am God"* (Psalms 46:10). Have we learned to recognize His voice?

> "Speak, LORD, for your servant is listening."
>
> I Samuel 3:9

The parable of the Good Shepherd and his flock reminds us that the sheep know their shepherd's voice. In John 10:3–4 Jesus states, *"To him the doorkeeper opens, and the sheep hear his voice; and he calls his own sheep by name and leads them out. And when he brings out his own sheep, he goes before them; and the sheep follow him, for they know his voice* (NKJV)." Each shepherd cares for his own flock and protects his sheep from danger. The sheep enjoy safety and peace in the presence of their shepherd. Throughout the day, when it is time for the sheep to move on, the shepherd calls them, and they follow their shepherd's voice.

Jesus is our Good Shepherd and He knows us. On a winter day, Jesus stood in the porch of Solomon's temple in Jerusalem and told the Jews, *"My sheep hear My voice, and I know them, and they follow Me; and I give eternal life to them, and they shall never perish; and no one shall snatch them out of My hand"* (John 10:27–28, NKJV). We can decide to be more attentive to the voice of the Good Shepherd and daily learn to be more aware of His presence.

God is everywhere. He is with us wherever we are. The psalmist wrote, *"Where can I go from your Spirit? Where can I flee from your presence?"* (Psalms 139:7). We can make time for stillness in our hearts once we decide to be receptive to His presence.

The prophet Isaiah lived in turbulent political times. Yet he wrote about having peace in God's presence. Read Isaiah 26:3–4; 32:17.

Who will have perfect peace (26:3)?

_____

What is the fruit of righteousness (32:17)?

_____

What is the effect of righteousness? (32:17)?

_____

_____

God uses our conscience to show us whether we are doing the right things or not. The apostle Paul talked about keeping a clear conscience and doing what is right *"for conscience' sake"* (Romans 13:5, NASB). We keep our conscience clear by paying attention to it and steering away from sin. In a letter to Timothy, Paul wrote about two men who had "shipwrecked their faith" by not following their conscience. He exhorted, *". . . fight the good fight, holding on to faith and a good conscience. Some have rejected these and so have shipwrecked their faith. Among them are Hymenaeus and Alexander"* (1 Timothy 1:18–20). These men ignored the voice of their consciences and lost the good fight. Our conscience can be an excellent guide when God's Word produces conviction.

In this same letter to Timothy, Paul again mentions the idea of conscience. He states, *"The Spirit clearly says that in later times some will abandon the faith and follow deceiving spirits . . . . Such teachings come through hypocritical liars, whose consciences have been seared as with a hot iron"* (1 Timothy 4:1–2). May we be this sensitive and receptive to our conscience and to the voice of the Holy Spirit within us.

At times God uses godly friends to give us the biblical advice and counsel that we need to hear. Sometimes the Holy Spirit prompts the hearts of our acquaintances or friends and they sense the need to talk with us about how we need to live as believers. They are undoubtedly sensitive to the Spirit's voice about important matters. Sometimes they encourage us to continue on the path we've begun. Or they may counsel us to go in another direction. God uses Christian people to help confirm which direction we should go in our Christian walk. He also uses them to lead strays back to the truth.

📖 Read James 5:16–20, concerning Christian fellowship.

Whose prayers ended and started the rain (verses 17–18)?

_____

To whom did James direct this exhortation (verses 19–20)?

_____

📖 Look up the following verses and note what each says regarding the idea of counsel.

Psalm 1:1

_____

_____

Proverbs 11:14

_____

_____

Proverbs 19:20

_____

_____

APPLY Do you live your life in such a way that you can easily listen to the voice of God speaking to you? If not, what lifestyle changes need to be made?

_____

_____

_____

_____

 "Lord, teach me to listen. The times are noisy and my ears are weary with the thousand raucous sounds, which continuously assault them. Give me the spirit of the boy Samuel when he said to Thee, 'Speak, for thy servant heareth.' Let me hear Thee speaking in my heart. Let me get used to the sound of Thy voice, that its tones may be familiar when the sounds of earth die away and the only sound will be the music of Thy speaking voice. Amen.' "[8] (A. W. Tozer)

> **"I have been cruci-fied with Christ; it is no longer I who live, but Christ lives in me; and the life which I now live in the flesh I live by faith in the Son of God, who loved me and gave Himself for me."**
>
> **Galatians 2:20 (NKJV)**

> **"But whoever drinks the water I give him will never thirst. Indeed, the water I give him will become in him a spring of water welling up to eter-nal life."**
>
> **John 4:14**

FOR ME TO FOLLOW GOD

Many people today are content to focus on the message of God's love, mercy, and goodness. They don't want to believe that there will be an accounting for their "bad choices." After all, God loves all people, so how could a loving God punish them? They see God mainly as a giver, expecting Him to bring great prosperity and blessings to them, no matter how they live. This is an unbalanced view of God's loving nature, for He does not overlook sin.

I once knew a man who professed to be a Christian. This man went to church with his family and participated in church activities, and on the surface it seemed he had it all together spiritually speaking. Yet he complained to his wife that God was not blessing their home. Soon, the truth came out that this man had been cheating on his wife and had been hiding this adulterous relationship for some time. This story brings me to this probing question: how can individuals profess to be Christians, live like sinners, and still expect God to work in them and through them?

When people choose to continue living with the old sin nature, they are content to hold on to their own natural thoughts, emotions, and desires. They miss out on the wonderful and full life available for them through the work of the Holy Spirit.

Paul wrote to the Corinthians about the evils of immorality and reminded them that their bodies were temples of the Holy Spirit. The word picture of a temple shows us the importance of living holy lives. The temple is a structure for worship. *"Do you not know that your body is a temple of the Holy Spirit, who is in you, whom you have received from God? You are not your own; you were bought at a price. Therefore honor God with your body"* (1 Corinthians 6:19–20). Jesus called His own body a temple (Mark 14:58). When Solomon's great temple was built in Jerusalem, the inside was overlaid with pure gold (see 2 Chronicles 3:4). Gold symbolizes purity. The psalmist David wrote, *"The LORD is in His holy temple; and the LORD's throne is in heaven"* (Psalms 11:4, NASB).

As the song "I Have Decided to Follow Jesus" suggests, we no longer want to turn back to our old way of life. When the Samaritan woman met Jesus at the well and asked Him about the "living water," He answered, *"But whoever drinks the water I give him will never thirst. Indeed, the water I give him will become in him a spring of water welling up to eternal life"* (John 4:14). Jesus' grace and His Spirit will fill and satisfy those who truly embrace Him and follow Him.

📖 Read the story of the woman of Samaria in John 4:1–26.

What kind of worshipers does the Father seek (John 4:23)?

_____

According to verse 24, who did Jesus say God is (verse 24)?

_____

The Samaritan woman turned her life around. Her testimony led others to believe in Christ. We can have a constant supply of His Spirit, as a fountain bubbling up. Our lives are open vessels ready to be filled with this living water. Jesus' grace and His Spirit will fill and satisfy us when we truly embrace and follow Him.

It is difficult to have an "intimate knowledge of God" when we have sin in our lives. We must first confess and repent of all the Holy Spirit has shown us. Paul exhorts us, *"You have taken off your old self with its practices and have put on the new self, which is being renewed in knowledge in the image of its Creator"* (Colossians 3:9–10). Galatians 5:16 states, *"Walk by the Spirit, and you will not carry out the desire of the flesh"* (NASB).

Jesus promised his disciples that the Holy Spirit would be sent in His place as our Counselor (John 14:16). The Bible tells us when we are "born again" we receive a new heart and a new spirit. We desire to be aware of the Holy Spirit's prompting in our lives.

 Are we living the life that counts now and in eternity? Jesus is our example for purposeful living. Before being taken to the cross, Jesus looked up to heaven and prayed to His Father saying, *"I have brought you glory on earth by completing the work you gave me to do"* (John 17:4). Jesus completed the assignment His Father gave Him. May we be faithful to continue abiding in Christ's love.

 "O Holy Spirit, Giver of light and life, impart to us thoughts higher than our own thoughts, and prayers better than our own prayers, and powers beyond our own powers; that we may spend and be spent in the ways of love and goodness, after the perfect image of our Lord and Savior, Jesus Christ." (Anonymous)

JUSTIFIED THROUGH FAITH

"Therefore, since we have been justified through faith, we have peace with God through our Lord Jesus Christ, through whom we have gained access by faith into this grace in which we now stand. And we rejoice in the hope of the glory of God." (Romans 5:1–2)

NOTES

1. Warren Wiersbe, *A Time to Be Renewed* (Wheaton, IL: Scripture Press Publications, 1986), 264.

2. *Hebrew-Greek Key Word Study Bible* (Chattanooga, TN: AMG Publishers, 1990), 1734, 1740.

3. Ibid., 1735.

4. J. Oswald Sanders, *Prayer Power Unlimited* (Chicago, IL: Moody Bible Institute, 1977), 45.

5. Ibid., 42–43.

6. *Hebrew-Greek Key Word Study Bible*, 1832.

7. Ibid., 1832.

8. A. W. Tozer, *The Pursuit of God* (Camp Hill, PA: Christian Publications, 1993), 78.

Notes

EVALUATING OUR LIFE-GOALS: DESIRING TO PLEASE GOD

In the previous lesson, we studied the importance of being open to following God's will for our lives. To do this, we feed on His Word, commit to do His will first, daily ask for His guidance, and remain aware of the quiet conviction. We can be aware of what God is saying to us through His Word, our prayers, through our worship, and from what our godly leaders and friends tell us. We can learn to be attuned to what the Holy Spirit is showing us as we go about our daily activities.

It is also important to have clear and definite goals. Goals that have been thoughtfully made can help guide us in purposeful living. What do we aim or strive for? What are we committed to doing and accomplishing? In this lesson we will look at and evaluate our goals in four main areas of our life: our faith, family, career and work, and finances. How we choose to live today affects our family and others. How we live today affects how we spend our resources and money and whether we can save for the future. We will examine our priorities and how they fit with a biblical perspective.

> **"Do not conform any longer to the pattern of this world, but be transformed by the renewing of your mind. Then you will be able to test and approve what God's will is—his good, pleasing and perfect will."**
>
> **Romans 12:2**

OUR FAITH GOALS

Today we will look at our faith goals, or our spiritual goals. If we say we want to commit to do God's will first, we need to make this a priority. When we get to heaven, God may ask us these words: "What *on earth* were you doing?" Recognizing that our desire is to please Him, hopefully we will be able to answer our Savior with certainty and confidence. For we will need to be accountable for how we lived here on earth:

> *So our aim is to please him always in everything we do, whether we are here in this body or away from this body and with him in heaven. For we must all stand before Christ to be judged and have our lives laid bare—before him. Each of us will receive whatever he deserves for the good or bad things he has done in his earthly body.* (2 Corinthians 5:9–10, LB)

Paul and Timothy reminded the believers in the book of Colossians that since they are alive in Christ, they must be more like Christ. Read Colossians 3:1–4.

According to verse 1, where should we set our hearts?

_____

_____

Where is Christ seated (verse 1)?

_____

On what should we set our minds (verse 2)?

_____

According to verse 4, who is our life?

_____

Paul says, *"Set your minds on things above, not on earthly things"* (verse 2). Here, the term *"set your minds"* means "be intent on." This same term also appears in Matthew. Jesus was talking to His disciples and foretelling His suffering and death, when Peter quickly took Him aside. He exclaimed, *"Never, Lord! This shall never happen to you!"* (Matthew 16:22). Jesus responded with these words, *". . . You are a stumbling block to Me; for you are not setting your mind on God's interests, but man's"* (Matthew 16:23, NASB). Soon after His response to Peter, Jesus continued talking with His disciples on the costs of discipleship.

Paul and Timothy warned the believers in Philippi about the *"enemies of the cross of Christ, whose end is destruction . . . who set their minds on earthly things"* (Philippians 3:18–19, NASB). They wrote:

> *"Dear brothers, pattern your lives after mine and notice who else lives up to my example. For I have told you often before, and I say it again now with tears in my eyes, there are many who walk along the Christian road who are really enemies of the cross of Christ. Their future is eternal loss, for their god is their appetite: they are proud of what they should be ashamed of; and all they think about is this life here on earth."* (Philippians 3:17–19, LB)

We are encouraged to be attracted to heavenly things, not earthly things, for our *"citizenship is in heaven"* (Philippians 3:20). Heaven is our final homeland.

Paul writes in Romans to be transformed *"by the renewing of your mind."* He declared, *"Do not conform any longer to the pattern of this world, but be transformed by the renewing of your mind. Then you will be able to test and approve what God's will is—his good, pleasing and perfect will"* (Romans 12:2). Here, the term *"renewing"* refers to "a renovation which makes a person different than in the past; to renew qualitatively."[1] The flesh controls the "old mind" and leads to death while the Holy Spirit should control the new mind. When our minds are clear and pure, we can focus on God more easily and have effective communication with Him. We will take the time to open our Bibles to read and learn what God would teach us for that day. Our desires become more of what God would desire for us. The world offers many distractions and temptations leading Christians away from a full relationship with Christ. We need to make a real commitment to having our minds controlled by the Holy Spirit.

📖 Read about the mind controlled by the flesh and the mind controlled by the Spirit in Romans 8:5–11.

Looking at verse 5, who lives according to the sinful nature?

_____

In verse 5, who lives in accordance with the Spirit?

_____

📖 Read Romans 8:6–8, and fill in the blanks.

"The mind of sinful man is _____, but the mind controlled by the Spirit is _____ and _____; the sinful mind is _____. It does not submit to _____, nor can it do so. Those controlled by the sinful nature cannot _____."

What controls us if the Spirit of God lives in us (Romans 8:9)?

_____

It may only take a moment for us to decide to follow Jesus. But we grow and mature in the faith for a lifetime. Individuals who *"live a life worthy of the calling"* can grow to be *"mature, attaining to the whole measure of the fullness of Christ"* (Ephesians 4:1, 13). So, in which direction are we headed? Is our relationship with Christ barely alive or is it thriving? Ephesians 2:4–5 tells us, *"But because of his great love for us, God, who is rich in mercy, made us alive with Christ even when we were dead in transgressions—it is by grace you have been saved."* God has made us alive together with Christ. What an awesome promise. Consequently, we should have a growing relationship with Christ. What are we doing to nurture it?

When we abide in Christ, our life continues to grow in our relationship with Him. Philippians 3:10 says, *"I want to know Christ and the power of his resurrection."* The Greek word translated *"know"* in this verse means "to know experientially."[2] The church today, just as in the days of the early apostles after Christ's resurrection, can know the living power of His resurrection. He is still transforming lives.

We may have habits we need to let go of, and God can give us the strength to do that.

We may need to seriously consider what it means to be "followers of Jesus." Our spiritual growth doesn't just happen. It comes from yielding to the Holy Spirit's leading. It comes from turning the reigns of our lives over to One who knows what is best for us. We may have habits we need to let go of, and God can give us the strength and ability to do that. Obedient Christians consider the value of a consistent walk with God and act upon it. They can walk freely knowing that they are right with Him. Obedient Christians desire that their character becomes more like Christ's. How consistent are we in studying the Bible, praying, being in fellowship with other Christians, and witnessing? What has hindered our progress in these areas in the past?

If we look at the life of Jesus Christ, we note that in His days of ministry, He had a frantic schedule and noisy surroundings. There were crowds of people following Him and wanting His attention. Yet, Jesus made time to pray and commune with His Heavenly Father. He went away by boat to be alone (Matthew 14:13). He went to the mountainside by Himself to pray (Matthew 14:23). He prayed late at night when troubled (Matthew 26:36), and spent the whole night in prayer (Luke 6:12) before choosing His disciples. While He lived on earth, Jesus knew how critical it was to spend time with His Father.

 What have we been focused on lately? Concerns of this world can take our minds off of the better things for us. Where do we find our attention and energy directed to: fulfilling our natural desires, accumulating more stuff, the upkeep of our possessions, our own entertainment? Distractions from our fellowship with Christ can come so easily. He longs for our time with Him. He is desirous of our faithfulness to Him.

What faith goals do we have? What do we want to accomplish? How can we become more useful as Christians? Our usefulness depends on our commitment. Fill in the following chart with goals that will help you grow and mature as a Christian. Beside each goal, write down a plan of action. An example is provided.

Faith Goals I will be consistent in reading my Bible.	Plan of Action Get up fifteen minutes earlier in the morning to have my devotions.
1. _____	_____
2. _____	_____
3. _____	_____
4. _____	_____
5. _____	_____
6. _____	_____
7. _____	

OUR FAMILY GOALS

It takes a lot of teamwork and cooperation to keep our families happy and healthy. Parenting is not easy. We want to balance our schedules so that everyone can get needed attention. We want to appropriately balance our time between work and family, encouraging our family members continually as they go through their week. It takes a lot of love to keep our families healthy emotionally. Sometimes it takes sacrificial love.

First Corinthians 13 reminds us what real love is:

> *"Love is patient, love is kind. It does not envy, it does not boast, it is not proud. It is not rude, it is not self-seeking, it is not easily angered, it keeps no record of wrongs. Love does not delight in evil but rejoices with the truth. It always protects, always trusts, always hopes, always perseveres."* (1 Corinthians 13:4–7)

Bible scholar and teacher Warren Wiersbe states, "The home is the first place where Christian love should be practiced. A Christian home begins with a Christian marriage in the will of God. This means loyalty and purity."[3] In Ephesians 5 and 6, Paul reminds family members to live peaceably. He writes, *"Each one of you [husbands] also must love his wife as he loves himself, and the wife must respect her husband."* To the children he writes, *"Obey your parents in the Lord, for this is right."* (Ephesians 5:33; 6:1). Paul wrote specifically to the fathers saying, *"Do not exasperate your children; instead, bring them up in the training and instruction of the Lord"* (Ephesians 6:4).

As parents, we play a very important role in our children's spiritual and moral education. From the time our children are young, we should teach them important kingdom values. The Bible teaches responsibility and trust, truthfulness and integrity, and the importance of respect for authority. Although the task of bringing up our children may seem enormous at times, we can ask God for wisdom. We can pray for our children, acknowledging God's ownership of and love for them. We are given a great promise in Psalm 55:22, *"Cast your cares on the LORD and he will sustain you; he will never let the righteous fall."*

📖 Read Deuteronomy 6:5–7 about the diligence parents and families should have in teaching God's Word to their children.

With what should we love the LORD our God (verse 5)?

_____

_____

Where should we keep these commandments (verse 6)?

_____

What instructions concerning God's commandments are given to parents in Deuteronomy 6:7?

_____

_____

Psalm 55:22 states: "Cast your cares on the LORD and he will sustain you; he will never let the righteous fall."

> ## "Reverence for God gives a man deep strength; his children have a place of refuge and security."
>
> ## Proverbs 14:26 (LB)

The Bible tells us that if we don't teach the Word of God to our children, the teachings will not continue on to future generations. Moses instructed the people of Israel, *"Be careful, and watch yourselves closely so that you do not forget the things your eyes have seen or let them slip from your heart as long as you live. Teach them to your children and to their children after them"* (Deuteronomy 4:9). Moses warned that future generations would be in peril if God's people did not teach their children about Him.

It is evident from the actions and words of Jesus that children are important in God's kingdom. One day, Jesus' disciples saw that little children had been brought to Jesus so He could bless them and pray for them. The disciples scolded the ones who brought them, for they didn't believe the children were important enough to take up their Master's time (Matthew 19:13). With compassion for the children, Jesus said, *"Let the little children come to me, and do not hinder them, for the kingdom of heaven belongs to such as these"* (19:14).

Jesus warned against anyone causing *"one of these little ones who believe in me to sin"* (Matthew 18:6). He had strong words when he stated,

> *"And whoever receives one such child in My name receives Me; but whoever causes one of these little ones who believe in Me to stumble, it is better for him that a heavy millstone be hung around his neck, and that he be drowned in the depth of the sea."* (Matthew 18:5–6, NASB)

As parents and trusted friends, we should not cause children to stumble or "entice them to sin." Children are vulnerable and trust us to guide them with wisdom.

An example of godly upbringing is seen in the life of Timothy. In his second letter to Timothy, Paul remembers his family heritage. Looking forward to seeing him again, Paul writes, *"I have been reminded of your sincere faith, which first lived in your grandmother Lois and in your mother Eunice and, I am persuaded, now lives in you also. . . . For God did not give us a spirit of timidity, but a spirit of power, of love and of self-discipline* (2 Timothy 1:5, 7). Timothy was one of the youngest missionaries Paul sent out to share the gospel. Yet, Paul had confidence that he could depend on Timothy to stand firm in his faith, continuing to teach the message of salvation. Paul recognized Timothy's sure foundation in his upbringing, and Timothy proved to be a reliable and trustworthy person for the ministry.

When we build our lives on the Word of God, we have a sure foundation that will last a lifetime. Are we giving our children this foundation? It is important to make time to learn God's Word and worship together. For the readers who have grandchildren, are we helping them to have a firm foundation?

📖 Jesus told a parable about wise and foolish builders and their foundations. Read Luke 6:46–49 on the importance of putting the Word of God into practice. Summarize this parable in your own words.

_____

_____

_____

_____

 Many families today, including Christian families, are unstable for lack of a firm foundation. How are you doing when it comes to building a strong foundation for your children? Do you feel God's presence in your family? Consider the time and attention you are giving each member of the family. Do you focus more on giving your family material things than on teaching them biblical values they will keep for a lifetime?

Do you exhibit the values of self-discipline and perseverance when it comes to material things, or are you choosing to live beyond your means? Children often pick up our values from how we live rather than what we say.

Fill in the following chart with goals that will help meet your family members' needs. Beside each goal, write a plan of action. An example is completed for you.

Family Goals Our family will attend church every Sunday.	Plan of Action Go to bed earlier on Saturday night, so we can get up on time Sunday morning.
1. _____	
2. _____	
3. _____	
4. _____	
5. _____	

OUR CAREER AND WORK GOALS

God knows our physical needs and our needs as a family. He wants to give us what is good for us (Psalms 85:12). We have been given the wonderful promise that He will supply all of our needs (Philippians 4:19). Our jobs and work duties help provide for our needs. God wants to bless our work (Deuteronomy 28:12), and He wants our work to prosper (Deuteronomy 30:9).

The psalmist David comments that work is a reality of life: *"Then man goes out to his work, to his labor until evening"* (Psalms 104:23). Although the author of Ecclesiastes wrote about how despairing life can be, he also added some nuggets of wisdom in his writings. Consider his words:

"Enjoy life with your wife, whom you love, all the days of this . . . life that God has given you under the sun . . . For this is your lot in life and in your toilsome labor under the sun. Whatever your hand finds to do, do it with all your might, for in the grave, where you are going, there is neither working nor planning nor knowledge nor wisdom." (Ecclesiastes 9:9–10)

In his letter to the believers in Thessalonica, Paul stresses the importance of not being a burden on others and living at the expense of others. He had received news that some of them were not working at all. Paul reminded them of a familiar rule: *"If a man will not work, he shall not eat"* (2 Thessalonians 3:10). He emphasized their responsibility to provide for their own needs.

"I will show you what he is like who comes to me and hears my words and puts them into practice. He is like a man building a house, who dug down deep and laid the foundation on rock."

Luke 6:47–48

Life Goals
DAY THREE

"The LORD will fulfill his purpose for me; Your love, O LORD, endures forever—Do not abandon the works of your hands."

Psalm 138:8

In 1 Corinthians 3:9, Paul reminds the new believers in Corinth that they are "God's fellow workers". The idea here is that they were "God's employees." They were "fellow laborers with one another in God's employment."[4]

Paul, Silas, and Timothy wrote that they "continually remember" the Thessalonian believers' *"labor prompted by love"* (1 Thessalonians 1:3). They were pleased the Thessalonians' work was done eagerly and readily because of their love. The second letter encouraged them to continue their good work: *"Now may our Lord Jesus Christ Himself and God our Father, who has loved us and given us eternal comfort and good hope by grace, comfort and strengthen your hearts in every good work and word"* (2 Thessalonians 2:16–17 NASB). Whatever our jobs require of us, and whatever we do, we should be worthy workers, working as unto the Lord. The quality of our work matters.

Read Colossians 3:22–24 for directives on employee responsibility.

According to verse 22, what two characteristics should Christian employees have when obeying their employers?

_____

_____

How should we work (Colossians 3:23)?

_____

_____

What is the worker's promised reward (verse 24)?

_____

Who are we serving (verse 24)?

_____

_____

> "Our callings are not simply secular means of making money or a living, but are God's means of utilizing our gifts and interests to His glory."
>
> Martin Luther (paraphrased)

In Deuteronomy 24:14–15, employers are told, *"Do not take advantage of a hired man"* but *"pay him his wages."* The employers' authority over others is a responsibility that should not be held lightly. The employers' authority does not give him or her the right to overlook the welfare of others. Employers and employees are responsible to do their work with excellence. Whatever our jobs may demand of us, we should pray that God will give us the strength and wisdom to carry out our responsibilities. God will provide the necessary strength and stamina, as Scripture teaches that we are *"strengthened with all power according to his glorious might."* (Colossians 1:11)

When it comes to our vocation and work, have we been seeking God's will in our lives? David reminds us, *"The steps of a good man are ordered by the LORD"* (Psalms 37:23, NKJV). Those who search for and discern God's will for their lives put Him first. They realize that life is a series of decisions, and they are open to the direction where God leads them.

George Müller, 19th century English evangelist, was known to have said, "The *stops* of a good man, as well as his *steps*, are ordered by the Lord."[5] Lettie Burd (better known as L. B. or Mrs. Charles E.) Cowman, a 20th century missionary to Asia and author, wrote about how God directs us. She states,

We often make a great mistake thinking that God is not guiding us at all, because we cannot see far ahead. But He only undertakes that the steps of a good man should be ordered by the Lord; not next year, but tomorrow; not for the next mile, but the next yard. . . . I shall never be able to go too fast, if the Lord is in front of me; and I can never go too slowly, if I follow Him always, everywhere.[6] *As we are open to God's leading in our lives, He will show us His will for us. We can trust God to guide us with an opened door as well as a closed door ahead of us.*

Individuals who contemplate a vocation examine their interests, talents, and unique abilities. They observe how these can fit in with God's plan for their vocation or career. They consider the counsel and advice their perceptive teachers and professors give them. As they seek God for His direction in their lives, they can receive the Counselor's help. *"But when he, the Spirit of truth, comes, he will guide you into all truth"* (John 16:13). These individuals may already use their gifts and abilities in a small way—within their families, in their local church, or in their community. They are rewarded for being open to God's leading. *"Humility and the fear of the LORD bring wealth and honor and life"* (Proverbs 22:4).

What is the basis for a person's decision in choosing a career and job? Does the job meet the individual's inner needs and self-fulfillment? Is the person serving God, using God-given gifts and abilities? Is he or she able to be of help to others? Or is the person working only for the money? As the author of Ecclesiastes explains, money is a temporary satisfier: *"Whoever loves money never has money enough; whoever loves wealth is never satisfied with his income. This too is meaningless"* (Ecclesiastes 5:10).

 When it comes to a career, have you focused on the jobs that will bring you the most money and the most possessions? The quest for things and possessions can get in the way of the better things God may have planned for our lives. Sometimes the things we think *we* own actually own and possess us. Not that there is anything inherently wrong with making a lot of money, as money is one of many resources that God entrusts to us. As is the case with all resources God entrusts with us, we need to see that we are faithful with money and learn to be excellent managers of it.

Fill in the following chart with goals that you have for your work and career. Beside each goal, write a plan of action. An example is completed for you.

Career and Work Goals	Plan of Action
Acquire an advanced degree.	Do research on colleges and universities and the programs they offer.
1. _____	_____
2. _____	_____
3. _____	_____
4. _____	_____
5. _____	_____

ADVICE FOR DAILY LIVING

"Make it your ambition to lead a quiet life, to mind your own business and to work with your hands, just as we told you, so that your daily life may win the respect of outsiders and so that you will not be dependent on anybody."

I Thessalonians 4:11–12

OUR FINANCIAL GOALS

In Day Four we'll look at financial goals in general. A few lessons down the road, we'll look in more detail at ordering our finances and using a spending plan.

It is essential to establish financial goals. Many people are in trouble financially today because they have not set any goals. They have drifted along year after year, barely able to get by on their income. They have a vague hope that in the future things will work out for them. Yet they haven't taken the effort or time to plan ahead and set any goals. They say things like, "I'll *never* be able to pay off my credit cards!" or "I guess I'll always be stuck with debt." Some families don't think it's even *possible* to live a debt-free lifestyle.

Families with above-average wealth may have few financial worries. The more affluent seem to have it relatively easy. Yet by not setting financial goals for the future, they may be unable to maintain the same level of living as they grow older. Maybe they haven't taken into account that as times change, so does the economy along with our financial needs and priorities. As life expectancy increases, we must learn to stretch our resources further. The ever-increasing cost of health care as we grow older will put greater demands on our budgets. Many who are healthy today do not take into account that prescription drugs will one day be a much larger percentage of their annual budget.

Without the focus of financial goals, we tend to be more careless with our money and not the best stewards that we can be. We are tempted to spend our income on whatever seems appropriate at the moment, not planning ahead for the anticipated bills coming later or leaner times. We don't save for the things that we should consider as more essential and significant for our family's well being. Without thinking twice about it, we'll quickly spend all of our cash and purchase what we desire with credit.

With God's help, it becomes easier to develop discipline and to have a singleness of purpose. It's easier to let go of the things that get in the way of helping us achieve the goals we're striving for. By establishing financial goals, we can look ahead with hope and more confidence. As we work toward them, we will be sure to reap positive results.

As we set our financial goals, we want to consider whether we are setting them with wisdom and with the right motives. Our goals reflect who we are. They identify our values. Our Bible study in this lesson has led us to take a look at what is important to us as Christians: our spiritual growth including service to others, our desire for a happy and healthy family, and fulfillment in life (careers and personal achievement). How will our financial goals fit with the other goals we looked at earlier in this lesson?

Solomon has a lot to say about the importance of making plans and planning wisely. He prayed for wisdom and demonstrated wisdom as king. His father David left him with the huge task of building the great temple in Jerusalem. Solomon emphasizes, *"We should make plans—counting on God to direct us"* (Proverbs 16:9, LB).

📖 Look at two more verses on planning found in Proverbs 21.

> Without the focus of financial goals, we tend to be more careless with our money and not the best stewards that we can be.

According to Proverbs 21:5, what leads to profit and what leads to poverty?

_____

_____

Read Proverbs 21:30, and record your perception of this verse.

_____

_____

_____

Is our tendency to spend impulsively, whittling away at our goals or dreams? Whether our work brings in a fat paycheck or a small one, if we're having difficulty living on our income, we need to consider why. If we want to get our lives together financially, the change begins in our daily choices. We can begin each day as a new opportunity to work on making better choices by deciding to be in control of what we spend. New habits will need to be made.

APPLY What are some of our financial goals? Consider the following areas:

paying off credit cards

_____

_____

_____

saving for an emergency fund

_____

_____

_____

buying a house

_____

_____

_____

funding for children's education

_____

_____

_____

retirement savings

_____

_____

_____

helping others

_____

_____

Think of three financial goals that are most important to you at this time, and list them in the chart below. Write a plan of action for each goal that you can act on within the next week or two.

Financial Goals	Plan of Action
1. _____	_____
2. _____	_____
3. _____	_____

Now that we have listed three financial goals that are a top priority for us, let's consider our attitudes or motives behind them. If a person desires to "make millions and live in a luxury house" what are his motives? If she desires to buy a new car every two years, what are her motives? If he desires to send his children to a private school, what are his motives? God looks at our hearts. He's interested in our motives and our attitudes. He wants our motives to be right and just.

As we take a quick look back at the history of Israel, we remember a young boy named David who was delivered from a lion and a bear as he cared for his father's sheep. David told King Saul that the Lord could also deliver them from the Philistine giant (see 1 Samuel 17:34, 37). David saw God's protection and deliverance throughout his life. This boy who would be king was known to be a man "after God's heart. He worshiped God with zeal and passion. This is evidenced by his statement, *"Righteousness goes before him and prepares the way for his steps"* (Psalms 85:13). In other words, righteousness, or a clean heart, produces blessings.

Some people are driven to wealth and prosperity out of envy. We are warned against envying the wealthy in Psalms 73:2–3: *"But as for me, my feet came close to stumbling; my steps had almost slipped. For I was envious of the arrogant, as I saw the prosperity of the wicked"* (NASB). Solomon states, *"Do not let your heart envy sinners, but always be zealous for the fear of the LORD"* (Proverbs 23:17). He also says, *"A sound heart is life to the body, but envy is rottenness to the bones"* (Proverbs 14:30, NKJV). Albert Barnes notes that *sound heart* literally means a "heart of health, that in which all emotions and appetites are in a healthy equilibrium. . . . The contrast with this is the envy which eats, like a consuming disease, into the very bones of a man's moral life."[7] Adam Clarke notes, "A healthy state . . . is the grand cause, in the hand of God, of health and longevity. If the heart be diseased, life cannot be continued for long."[8] A righteous and contented person tends to be healthy and and is one who enjoys life. Someone who envies the happiness and prosperity of other people will have it eat away at him. A paraphrase of this verse says, *"A relaxed attitude lengthens a man's life; jealousy rots it away"* (Proverbs 14:30, LB).

The Bible warns us against the attitudes of conceit and pride. *"Pride goes before destruction, a haughty spirit before a fall"* (Proverbs 16:18). *"A man's pride brings him low, but a man of lowly spirit gains honor"* (Proverbs 29:23). God is the giver of all things, including our possessions. We are privileged to enjoy what is ours for the time it is ours. David warns about not depending too heavily on our riches in Psalm 62:10: *"Though your riches increase, do not set your heart on them."*

> "All a man's ways seem right to him, but the LORD weighs the heart. To do what is right and just is more acceptable to the LORD than sacrifice."
>
> **Proverbs 21:2–3**

> "Money never made a man happy yet, nor will it. There is nothing in its nature to produce happiness. The more a man has, the more he wants. Instead of filling a vacuum, it makes one."
>
> **Benjamin Franklin**

People may be tempted to boast and brag about their wisdom, accomplishments, and possessions. But Jeremiah reminds us that we must acknowledge the source of all of our blessings. We can give God the glory for the knowledge we have and for the spiritual and physical strength enabling us to work. We shouldn't be prideful of what we own and what we have, since it ultimately comes from God.

📖 Read Jeremiah 9:23–24 to learn what the Lord says about bragging. Fill in the blanks:

"Let not the _____ boast of his _____ or the _____ boast of his _____ or the _____ boast of his _____, but let him who boasts boast about this: that he _____ and _____ me, that I am the LORD, *who exercises _____, _____, and _____ on earth, for in these I delight."*

When we understand our calling and purpose in life, we can set objectives for a fulfilled life. We can ask God to direct our steps as we seek Him. He desires our faithfulness.

 Lord, I am grateful for all the ways You provide for me. Thank You for Your Word and the truths in Your Word. Thank You for my family, those whom You have entrusted to me to love and care for. Thank You for my work, and the strength You give me so I can earn a living. Keep me from getting caught up in the trappings of the world. I pray the words that King David prayed, *"Create in me a new, clean heart, O God, filled with clean thoughts and right desires."[9]* May Your will be done in my life. Amen.

FOR ME TO FOLLOW GOD

This week we have been examining our priorities and how they fit in with a biblical perspective. We have learned the importance of growing and maturing for a lifetime in our faith, not just for a short season. We have asked God to renew our minds so that we can focus on Him more clearly. Now it is time to have closer communion with Him, ever mindful of how our usefulness as Christians depends on our level of surrender to His leading. As we have considered our priorities and goals, we have asked God to help us make goals that would best fit with His will and our lives as we seek harmony and balance in our lifestyles. Let's reflect on some of the verses we read this week as they relate to our goals.

On Faith Goals
We will need to be accountable for how we lived our lives here on earth:

So our aim is to please him always in everything we do, whether we are here in this body or away from this body and with him in heaven. For we must all stand before Christ to be judged and have our lives laid bare—before him. Each of us will receive whatever he deserves for the good or bad things he has done in his earthly body. (2 Corinthians 5:9–10, LB)

Life Goals

DAY FIVE

PRESS ON!

"But one thing I do: Forgetting what is behind and straining toward what is ahead, I press on toward the goal to win the prize for which God has called me heavenward in Christ Jesus." (Philippians 3:13–14)

When we abide in Christ, our life continues to grow in our relationship with Him. Philippians 3:10 says, *"I want to know Christ and the power of his resurrection."* The word *know* in this verse is translated from the Greek *ginosko*, which means "to know experientially." The church today, just as in the days of the early apostles after Christ's resurrection, can know the living power of His resurrection.

On Family Goals:

After Moses summoned all Israel, he told them about the diligence parents and families should have in teaching God's Word to their children.

> *"Love the LORD your God with all your heart and with all your soul and with all your strength. These commandments that I give you today are to be upon your hearts. Impress them on your children. Talk about them when you sit at home and when you walk along the road, when you lie down and when you get up."* (Deuteronomy 6:5–7)

In Ephesians 5:33, Paul reminds family members to live peaceably. He states, *"Each one of you [husbands] also must love his wife as he loves himself, and the wife must respect her husband."* Later in this same epistle, he encourages children to *"obey your parents in the Lord, for this is right."* (6:1). Fathers are told, *"Bring [your children] up with the loving discipline the Lord himself approves, with suggestions and godly advice "* (Ephesians 6:4, LB).

On Career and Work Goals:

Those who are contemplating a vocation examine their interests, talents, and unique abilities and observe how these can fit in with God's plan for their vocation or career. As they seek God for His direction in their lives, they can have the Counselor's help. *"But when he, the Spirit of truth, comes, he will guide you into all truth"* (John 16:13).

Whatever our jobs may demand of us, we pray that we will have the strength and wisdom to carry out our responsibilities well. We can receive the needed strength and stamina from God. *"That you may live a life worthy of the Lord and may please him in every way: bearing fruit in every good work, growing in the knowledge of God, being strengthened with all power according to his glorious might"* (Colossians 1:10–11).

On Financial Goals:

It is important to make plans and have a course of action for our finances. *"We should make plans—counting on God to direct us"* (Proverbs 16:9, LB). When we establish financial goals, we can look ahead with hope and more confidence. As we work toward our financial goals, we will be sure to reap positive results. We can plan for a better future.

We've had a great deal to think about and reflect on this week. Perhaps we've thought about how short our lives really are here on earth, compared to eternity. Perhaps we have been reminded of some great ideas or goals that we've had in the past; this is an opportune time to follow through with them. As we seek God's will for our lives, He will reveal His direction for us.

📖 Paul wrote about pressing on toward the goal and not giving up. Read Philippians 3:12–14.

What did Paul do with singleness of purpose (Philippians 3:13)?

_____

_____

Fill in the blanks to complete Philippians 3:14.

"I _____ toward _____ to win the _____ for which God has called me _____ in _____."

In his book *Turning Vision into Action*, George Barna writes how we can be vision-directed Christians. What is vision? He defines it as "a clear and precise mental portrait of a preferable future."[10] "Vision is not a solution to a current problem. . . . Vision is not a quick fix. It is a long-term solution to long-term opportunities."[11] He explains that as Christians, we hunger to invest our time on earth in activities that have spiritual significance. Such meaning comes by understanding how He created us and how we can employ every resource at our disposal—time, energy, money, relationships, materials, knowledge—to unfold God's ultimate plan for humankind.[12]

George Barna emphasizes that vision-directed Christians maintain the most optimistic and hopeful perspectives about the future. They are, after all, involved in the spiritual redemption and interpersonal redevelopment of the world, employed by the Lord Jesus Christ.[13] Imagine the impact that believers in Jesus Christ can make as they obey Him.

Write a prayer or a journal entry.

_____

_____

_____

_____

_____

_____

_____

_____

_____

"We should make plans—counting on God to direct us."

Proverbs 16:9, LB

NOTES

1. Spiros Zodhiates, *Hebrew-Greek Key Word Study Bible*, (Chattanooga: AMG Publishers, 1990), 1804–1805.

2. Ibid., 1817.

3. Warren Wiersbe, *A Time To Be Renewed* (Wheaton: Victor Books), 1986), 271.

4. Albert Barnes, *Albert Barnes' Notes on the Bible*, "1 Corinthians 3:9 Commentary." In e-Sword Bible software database, 2005, Rick Meyers.

5. Mrs. Charles E. Cowman, *Springs in the Valley* (Grand Rapids, MI: Zondervan Publishing House, 1977), 248.

6. Ibid.

7. Albert Barnes, *Albert Barnes' Notes on the Bible*, "Proverbs 14:30 Commentary." In e-Sword Bible software database, 2005, Rick Meyers.

8. Adam Clarke, *Adam Clarke's Commentary on the Bible,* "Proverbs 14:30 Commentary." In e-Sword Bible software database, 2005, Rick Meyers.

9. Psalm 51:10 (The Living Bible).

10. George Barna, *Turning Vision into Action,* (Ventura: Regal, 1996), 36.

11. Ibid., 14.

12. Ibid., 50

13 Ibid., 117.

FAITHFULNESS
IN HANDLING OUR MONEY

In Week 6, we evaluated our life goals and the importance of asking God for His direction in our lives. We made goals for our faith, family, career, and finances, along with a beginning plan of action. We were reminded to have a singleness of purpose as we go about our daily lives. Be encouraged this week as you get started right away on the steps you need to take to attain your goals.

In this lesson, we will look at the importance of handling our money as faithful stewards, or money managers, with a special emphasis concerning the areas of honesty, self-control, and resourcefulness. We will consider what it means to be salt and light as Christians as we examine how responsible we are in handling our own money.

In Day One we're going to take a look at a parable that Jesus told of the prodigal son. Most of us have heard a sermon or two on this story. I have heard sermons delivered from the perspective of the older son, which were quite intriguing. It is quite interesting to look at this parable from the viewpoint of the older son, who was the obedient and dependable one.

Jesus told three parables to his audience of "tax collectors and sinners." These parables are recorded in Luke 15 in the following order: the parables of the lost sheep, the lost coin, and the lost son. In each of these parables, the owners did not give up their

In this lesson, we will look at the importance of handling our money as faithful stewards, or money managers, with a special emphasis concerning the areas of honesty, self-control, and resourcefulness.

right of ownership for what was lost. They rejoiced when what had been lost was found. With happy hearts, they asked their friends to rejoice with them. Eminent New Testament Greek scholar, Spiros Zodhiates, emphasizes that in these three parables, "God is presented as still claiming His right of ownership even of those who are lost. When they are reclaimed, it is not He who becomes their Father or their rightful owner, but they become His again."[1]

> **"A man's heart is closer to his wallet than almost anything else."**
>
> **—Billy Graham**

ENTRUSTED WITH MONEY

We're going to read and observe the story of the lost son in today's lesson. In this parable Jesus describes a man who was a poor money manager, even though he came from a wealthy family. We don't use the term *prodigal* very often these days. It means "addicted to wasteful expenditure; extravagant." This prodigal son spent money lavishly and was known as one who had *"sinned against heaven"* (verse 18) and was *"dead"* (verse 32). He is a biblical example to us of how *not* to live.

Luke 15:12 tells us that the younger of two sons asked for his share of the inheritance. So the father divided his wealth between his two sons. Within a few days, the younger son left with his portion of the estate. According to *Barnes's Notes on the Bible,* "It seems the younger son received only money or movable property, and the older chose to remain with his father and dwell on the paternal estate. The lands and fixed property remained in their possession."[2] It was customary for the sons to receive the part that would be theirs before their father died. The younger son's downfall was *how* he chose to use the money.

📖 Read the parable of the lost son in Luke 15:11–32. As you read, consider two things: 1) the younger son's philosophy of life after he received his inheritance, and 2) what he did that shows poor choices in money management.

According to Luke 15:13, what did the younger son take with him when he went to a country far away?

_____

_____

What did he do with his wealth (verse 13)?

_____

_____

What amount of his inheritance did he spend (verse 14)?

_____

_____

What was he hired to do (verse 15)?

_____

_____

When did he begin thinking about his father's home (verse 17)?

_____

_____

Luke 15:14 says, *"After he had spent everything, there was a severe famine in that whole country, and he began to be in need."* Barnes comments that famines were not uncommon in Eastern nations, since they often were caused by crop failure. He adds, "In this case it is very naturally connected with the luxury, indolence, wastefulness, and lavishness of the people in that land."[3]

When the prodigal son traveled to another country, he not only left his family behind. He also left a valuable system of accountability. Living on his own, his new friends and way of life were vastly different from his moral upbringing. The prodigal son made foolish choices when it came to choosing his friends and managing his money. When he was hungry, his new friends were not there for him. *"No one gave him anything"* (verse 16). Yet he knew that back home, even his *"father's hired men have food to spare"* (verse 17).

After considering the prodigal son's poor choices with money, what lessons on money does this parable offer? Briefly list them.

_____

_____

_____

_____

_____

_____

APPLY How have you been like the prodigal son in your money management? Consider the areas of planning, saving, and spending.

_____

_____

_____

_____

_____

_____

_____

The prodigal son is an example of someone who loved the world. Selfishly spending all he had, there was little concern for his future—his spiritual or monetary future.

📖 Read 1 John 2:15–17.

What should we *not* love (verse 15)?

_____

_____

According to verse 16, what three specific things come from the world?

_____

_____

What will pass away (verse 17)?

_____

Who lives forever (verse 17)?

_____

We'll conclude our Day One study by briefly going back to the story of the prodigal son. The repentant son returns to his father, who has been anxiously looking forward to his return. Luke 15:20 tells us that when the wayward son *"was still a long way off, his father saw him and was filled with compassion for him. He ran to his son, threw his arms around him and kissed him."* Through compassionate grace, the prodigal son is welcomed back home. What a grand picture of a loving, heavenly Father! It is grace that brings us all to the throne of God.

The returning son is obviously remorseful for his actions. He is ready to accept personal responsibility for his choices. Now that he has lost all of his possessions and self-respect, he doesn't reciprocate with excuses. The younger son doesn't approach his father with weak defenses as to why things didn't turn out the way he thought they would. He doesn't blame anyone or anything. When he approaches his father, he simply and humbly admits, *"Father, I have sinned against heaven and against you. I am no longer worthy to be called your son"* (Luke 15:21).

His actions show that he has experienced a change of heart and attitude. He is ready and willing to be one of his father's hired hands, just another of the many servants his father oversees on his estate. The younger son is ready to give up his rights as a son and become a servant who obeys and follows his father's orders willingly. When we humbly approach our heavenly Father and come to Him with our faults and our sins, He lovingly receives us with open arms. He will not turn us away. God's love is unmerited and unconditional. We are His, and He is ours. We are no longer dead in our sins. We are alive again.

Through compassionate grace, the prodigal son is welcomed back home. What a grand picture of a loving, heavenly Father! It is grace that brings us all to the throne of God.

Handling Money

DAY TWO

LIVING HONESTLY

This week we are focusing on our faithfulness in handling money. An important aspect of being faithful is how honest we are as we deal with money. Today we'll look at handling our money honestly. Living *honestly* means living "in a manner that is not given to lying, cheating, stealing, etc.; not characterized by falsehood or intent to mislead; giving or having full worth or value; performed or earned in a conscientious manner."[4] As we want our Christian walk to be pleasing to the Lord, we need to reflect on honesty.

In Ezekiel 22, God reveals His strong displeasure with Jerusalem and the city's unrighteous ways. God had not approved of their dishonest ways of making a profit. The people were idolaters, and their consciences had been hardened. God says, *"I will surely strike my hands together at the unjust gain you have made"* (verse 13). He tells the prophet Ezekiel: *"The people of the land practice extortion and commit robbery; they oppress the poor and needy and mistreat the alien, denying them justice"* (verse 29). Evidently even Jerusalem's priests had not been preaching or exemplifying honest living. *"Her priests do violence to my law and profane my holy things; they do not distinguish between the holy and the common; they teach that there is no difference between the unclean and the clean"* (verse 26). In this passage God shows He is angry with them for their unjust actions (verse 31).

In 1 Kings 3 we find that King Solomon desired to reign justly and have his people conduct business matters honestly. His instructions include plans for a commerce system where items were weighed and measured accurately. Under such plans, neither the vendor nor the buyer was to be wronged. They were to carry out their transactions with honest units of measurement. The merchants were not to be deceitful and cunningly outwit the poor or common people.

📖 Read Proverbs 11:1; 16:11; 20:10, dealing with weights and measures. Then summarize all three verses.

_____

_____

_____

_____

_____

_____

> **"The Lord demands fairness in every business deal. He established this principle."**
>
> **Proverbs 16:11 (LB)**

In Psalm 15, King David describes a citizen who lives an honest life:

"Lord, who may dwell in your sanctuary? Who may live on your holy hill? He whose walk is blameless and who does what is righteous, who speaks the truth from his heart and has no slander on his tongue, who does his neighbor no wrong and casts no slur on his fellowman, who despises a vile man but honors those who fear the Lord, who keeps his oath even when it hurts, who lends his money without usury and does not accept a bribe against the innocent. He who does these things will never be shaken."

King David desired to please God and live a blameless life and said, *"You, O Lord, are loving. Surely you will reward each person according to what he has done"* (Psalms 62:12).

📖 Fill in the following chart with the results of the honest or dishonest life.

Verse	How People Live	The Result or Outcome
Psalm 37:37	blameless, upright	
Proverbs 11:18	wicked	
	he who sows righteousness	
Proverbs 15:27	greedy man	
	he who hates bribes	
Proverbs 17:20	man of perverse heart	
	he whose tongue is deceitful	
Proverbs 20:7	righteous man	

> ## "Dishonest gain will never last, so why take the risk?"
>
> ### Proverbs 21:6 (LB)

A dishonest or greedy man can cause trouble for his family (Proverbs 15:27). There are many examples in the Bible showing evidence of how the whole family was punished for the sins of the father. (For extra reading, see the story of Achan in Joshua 7.) Achan disobeyed God's battle commands, and his greed led to his death and the deaths of his family members. Lamentations 5:7 states, *"Our fathers sinned and are no more, and we bear their punishment."* The sins and deceitfulness of one person affect the whole family. Dishonest living today can lead to jail time, unemployment, repossession and foreclosure on automobiles and homes, and garnishment of wages. It can also lead to the loss of family relationships that were once strong and whole. Relationships between parents and children become strained and broken. Fathers and mothers may never really know the grief and hurt they have caused their families by their deceitful and dishonest living.

On the other hand, when people seek to live upright lives, God blesses the whole family. *"A righteous man who walks in his integrity—how blessed are his sons after him"* (Proverbs 20:7, NASB). Often when a family member comes to Christ, the whole household follows that member in saving faith. We know this is true based upon what Paul and Silas told their jailer: *"Believe in the Lord Jesus, and you will be saved—you and your household"* (Acts 16:31).

When we read the parable of the sower, we note that the people who bear fruit are the ones that have heard the Word of God with *"a noble and good heart"* (Luke 8:15). It is evident that such people have made a life-changing decision, for their actions show it. When a person has been known to live dishonestly and then makes a sudden change, desiring to live with integrity, people take notice.

In Luke 19:1–10, read the story of a rich man who made his money dishonestly. His life changed instantly the day he met Jesus. All it took was one visit and he was convicted of his deceitfulness.

Zacchaeus was a tax collector who decided to change his business practices and collect revenues honestly. We know that Jesus did not object to paying taxes. When He is asked whether it was right to pay taxes to Caesar, Jesus answers, *"Give to Caesar what is Caesar's"* (Mark 12:14, 17). Paul comments, *"Give everyone what you owe him: If you owe taxes, pay taxes; if revenue, then revenue; if respect, then respect; if honor, then honor"* (Romans 13:7). Just as in the day of Jesus, taxes need to be paid in our culture. We are to be honest and accountable with our record keeping.

> ## "A good man is guided by his honesty; the evil man is destroyed by his dishonesty."
>
> ### Proverbs 11:3 (LB)

APPLY How trustworthy are we when it comes to handling our money and other people's money? Do we desire to live with honor and a clear conscience? Do we need to begin repairing what we have done dishonestly in the past?

_____

_____

_____

_____

_____

_____

Read Proverbs 10:9 to conclude our lesson today. According to Proverbs 10:9, who walks securely? Who will be found out?

_____

_____

 Loving Father, I want to live honestly and walk securely in Your ways.. As I live in Your presence, help me to please You each day with my words and my actions. Help me to live an upright and honest life in everything that I do. In Jesus' name, Amen.

HAVING SELF-CONTROL

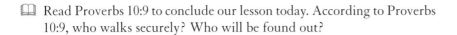

Handling Money

DAY THREE

Faithfulness in handling our money requires self-control. Self-control is one part of the fruit of the Spirit.

Faithfulness in handling our money requires self-control. Self-control is one part of the fruit of the Spirit. *"But the fruit of the Spirit is love, joy, peace, patience, kindness, goodness, faithfulness, gentleness and self-control"* (Galatians 5:22–23). Self-control is defined as "the act, power, or habit of having one's faculties or energies under control of the will."[5] When we have self-control, we have a rewarding life.

Self-control is necessary in a Christian's life. We can make important choices and decisions and carry them out well, because we have self-control. The apostle Paul wrote, *"Live by the Spirit, and you will not gratify the desires of the sinful nature."* Another translation states, *"But I say, walk by the Spirit, and you will not carry out the desire of the flesh"* (Galatians 5:16, NASB). The word *desire* here is derived from the Greek *epithumia,* meaning "the active and individual desire resulting from *pathos,* the diseased condition of the soul."[6] When we *"walk by the Spirit"* we will not perform or execute the natural impulses of the sinful nature. Galatians 5:25 states, *"Since we live by the Spirit, let us keep in step with the Spirit."* The word *live* comes from the Greek *zao,* and it relates to being warm, having life, or being alive."[7] Dr. Zodhiates notes, "To live in the Spirit (Galatians 5:25) is to live under His constant guidance and influence." When we live in the Spirit, we follow the Holy Spirit's leading, rather than our natural inclinations and impulses. When we live holy and godly lives, we display the fruit of the Spirit.

In his instructions to Timothy, Paul urges him to develop a godly way of life. He says, *"Train yourself to be godly"* (1 Timothy 4:7). Another translation says, *"Discipline yourself for the purpose of godliness"* (NASB). Paul uses the analogy of an athlete training for competition. Athletes discipline themselves during training. They carry out their training instructions faithfully to improve their skills, constantly pushing themselves as far as they can go. Paul continues his charge to Timothy: *"For physical training is of some value, but godliness has value for all things, holding promise for both the present life and the life to come"* (1 Timothy 4:8).

Paul is a model of self-control and discipline for us. He talks confidently about training himself to do what he should do. He knew the recipients of his letters would be familiar with the Greek Olympian Games and its emphasis on running the race to obtain the prize. Athletics had been important to people of Paul's day. He writes to the Corinthians using the analogy of an athlete:

In a race, everyone runs but only one person gets first prize. So run your race to win. To win the contest you must deny yourselves many things that would keep you from doing your best. An athlete goes to all this trouble just to win a blue ribbon or a silver cup, but we do it for a heavenly reward that never disappears. So I run straight to the goal with purpose in every step. I fight to win. I'm not just shadow-boxing or playing around. Like an athlete I punish my body, treating it roughly, training it to do what it should, not what it wants to. Otherwise I fear that after enlisting others for the race, I myself might be declared unfit and ordered to stand aside. (1 Corinthians 9:24–27, LB)

In his second letter to Timothy, Paul compares the believer's life to one of a good soldier. He encouraged him saying, *"As Christ's soldier do not let yourself become tied up in worldly affairs, for then you cannot satisfy the one who has enlisted you in his army"* (2 Timothy 2:4, LB). Are we effective "soldiers" for Christ? If we are, we should be willing to work at the discipline of self-control. A believer can have self-control through the power of the Holy Spirit.

 How well do you show self-control in your personal finances? If you exhibit self-control in your money management, then you are likely reaping positive rewards. If you don't show it, you may already have found yourself in some kind of trouble. Consider your self-control in the following areas:

Making purchases—Do you often make quick purchases for unnecessary items that look good and are pleasing at the moment?

_____

_____

_____

_____

_____

_____

Decision-making—Do you tend to make financial decisions quickly before thinking through the ramifications of your decisions?

_____

_____

Planning your spending—Do you spend all of your income quickly without planning ahead for expenses?

_____

_____

Paying your bills—Have you been late in paying your bills and making monthly payments?

_____

_____

Saving for expenses—Do you consistently make credit card purchases without paying the balance every month?

_____

_____

If you answer *yes* to any of these questions, you may need to work more on self-control. *"A wise man keeps himself under control"* (Proverbs 29:11). What are some ways that we can keep ourselves "under control" in these areas of money matters? Let's look at some solutions:

Making Purchases—Plan ahead or make a list beforehand for necessary purchases.

Decision-Making—When we are forced to make decisions hastily, we don't have all of the facts in front of us to make the best decision. Take the time necessary to think about the options and to talk with your spouse or financial advisor before making a decision. Refuse to make quick decisions.

Planning Our Spending—There needs to be a written spending plan or budget. Follow it carefully for successful results.

Paying our Bills—It's always best to pay bills on time every time. Find an effective system for getting organized, so there won't be any late payments.

Saving for Expenses—Save regularly for future needs. If you "can't afford to save" then you can't afford to buy things on credit.

James reminds us that, *"each one is tempted when, by his own evil desire, he is dragged away and enticed"* (James 1:14). We may not reap the consequences of indulging in our selfish desires immediately. Just as the prodigal son enjoyed frolicking in his wealth for a time, the "high life" eventually came to an end. He came to his senses when his money ran out. Suddenly, his world of free spending and reckless abandon had come to an end for him.

📖 Read 2 Peter 1:3–8 for evidence of fruitful growth in the Christian faith. According to 2 Peter 1:3, what has God's divine power given us?

_____

_____

According to verse 4, why has He given us His great promises?

_____

_____

What seven character traits should we make every effort to add to our faith (verses 5–7)?

_____

_____

_____

_____

_____

_____

_____

Why should we possess these qualities in increasing measure (verse 8)?

_____

_____

> *"It is for freedom that Christ has set us free. Stand firm, then, and do not let yourselves be burdened again by a yoke of slavery."*
>
> *Galatians 5:1*

When we enjoy self-controlled and disciplined lives, we ultimately experience many more freedoms in life. *"It is for freedom that Christ has set us free. Stand firm, then, and do not let yourselves be burdened again by a yoke of slavery"* (Galatians 5:1). We carry out necessary tasks with discipline, giving up something now for greater and better rewards in the future.

When Christ walked on earth, He often talked about the principle of sowing and reaping. When we sow the seeds of financial responsibility, understanding that all we have belongs to God, we will reap the blessings of surrendering to God greater control over our lives. God will then guide us in our daily choices, and our families and others will reap the rewards of our God-ordained self-control.

BEING RESOURCEFUL

Have you ever heard people comment, "It seems that I can never get ahead"? They may have been given great opportunities to earn and save money. Yet they spent or lost almost everything they earned. Maybe they were handed an inheritance or substantial monetary gift from a benefactor. Perhaps they made poor investment decisions and now have nothing to show for years of hard work. Another possibility: they were able to work with great leaders and mentors in a particular field of expertise but failed to use the privilege and position in a way that would be beneficial to others. Maybe the expert advice and knowledge given to them wasn't passed on to others. It could be that at one time these individuals had a clear idea of how they could use their talents and gifts to serve others, but they did not proceed to use and develop these talents.

Today we're looking at examples of women who were resourceful with what they had and with what was available to them. They learned to handle their money and resources to better benefit themselves and others. God rewards those who faithfully and resourcefully manage what they have.

Proverbs 31 describes a woman who knew what her talents were and developed them. This ideal woman is business-savvy and works from her home, carefully selecting wool and flax and spinning the thread to make beautiful fabric and fine linen garments that she can sell for extra household income. She uses her sewing skills to take care of her own family, by designing and making beautiful purple linen clothing items for them and bed coverings for their home. Her children are clothed well for the winter (Proverbs 31:13, 19, 21, 22, 24).

"She watches over the affairs of her household and does not eat the bread of idleness."

Proverbs 31:27

This entrepreneur also invests wisely. She "considers a field and buys it" (verse 16, NASB). The word "considers" derives from the Greek *zamam*, meaning "to meditate, to think, to resolve"[8] and shows us that the woman cleverly plans out her best options for purchasing property. Once she takes possession of property, she plants a vineyard with her earnings.

This businesswoman manages her time well, rising when it is still dark (Proverbs 31:15). Although she has servants, she gets up early and provides food for her household. She sees to it that the household activities are running smoothly (verse 27). She doesn't forget the needs of the poor and needy, but finds ways to help them (verse 20). She shares of her blessings and acquires even more. A person *"gives freely, yet gains even more; another withholds unduly, but comes to poverty"* (Prov. 11:24).

We've gained insight into the daily activities of this nobleman's wife. Let's learn more about her character traits. *"Her husband has full confidence in her"* (31:11). She is responsible with what she has, earning the trust of her husband. *"She brings him good, not harm, all the days of her life"* (verse 12). The term *good* is derived from the word *towb,* meaning "moral goodness, virtue, pleasantness."[9] Proverbs 31:25–26 states, *"She is clothed with strength and dignity; she can laugh at the days to come. She speaks with wisdom, and faithful instruction is on her tongue."* Strength and dignity are a part of her. No doubt she derives her strength from God for she *"fears the LORD"* (verse 30). She can confidently look forward to her future. This godly woman is honored by her family, friends, and those in her community as someone of great value (verses 28, 31).

In the book of Acts we learn of two other women who feared God and were known for using their resources well.

📖 Look at Acts 9:36–42.

What was Dorcas, a disciple, known for doing (verse 36)?

_____

_____

How did Dorcas help the poor (verse 39)?

_____

_____

What miracle took place (verses 40–41)?

_____

_____

What was a result of this miracle (verse 42)?

_____

_____

Dorcas used her skills to make clothing for others. She was loved and well respected by the people in her seaside community of Joppa.

📖 Read Acts 16:12–15, 40.

Where did Paul and his companions stay for several days (verse 12)?

_____

_____

What did Lydia do for a living (verse 14)?

_____

_____

After Lydia and her household were baptized, what invitation did she make (verse 15)?

_____

_____

When did Paul and Silas see her again (verse 40)?

_____

_____

Lydia was a seller of expensive purple cloth. It was mainly worn by the "princes and the rich," most likely making it a very profitable business. Lydia's invitation of hospitality to Paul and Silas led to their visit at her home. Not only did it provide a safe haven for them, but they were able to meet with other believers at Lydia's home and greatly encourage them there.

We've learned of examples of three women who were productive with their resources. They made the most of God-given abilities and developed them. Their faith in God helped them to be confident in their achievements.

What leads to wisdom in handling our resources? Note what these proverbs say:

"Listen to advice and accept instruction, and in the end you will be wise" (Proverbs 19:20).

"The way of a fool seems right to him, but a wise man listens to advice" (Proverbs 12:15).

"A simple man believes anything, but a prudent man gives thought to his steps" (Proverbs 14:15).

_____

_____

📖 Look at Proverbs 16:20.

Who prospers in their endeavors and receives blessings?

_____

_____

Giving people money is not going to solve their money problems. Paying off someone's financial debts may help temporarily, but unless they've learned to manage their own money, they'll go back to the same faulty habits. Until they've learned to be self-sufficient with their own resources, they will live troubled lives financially. No doubt you've seen examples of this truth. It takes more than a one-time sum of money to run a household or business successfully and to keep it running successfully. Proverbs 17:16 states, *"Of what use is money in the hand of a fool, since he has no desire to get wisdom?"* It takes proactive living to make the most of all of our resources. We need to be willing to learn from our past mistakes and take the necessary steps to handle our money wisely.

 List the resources that are available to you now. Consider the following: people (at home, in your neighborhood and community, at work, at your church, financial advisors, experts in their field of work)

> ## "Listen to advice and accept instruction, and in the end you will be wise."
>
> ### Proverbs 19:20

FAITHFUL STEWARD

"It is not what you'd do with a million
If riches should ever be your lot.
But what you are doing at present
With the dollar and a quarter you've got."

R. G. LETOURNEAU

your natural skills or abilities, talents, and spiritual gifts; your possessions (your home, other property or land, vehicles, transportation, businesses) products from your businesses or land; your income and jobs; your savings and investments.

Are you making the most of what you have? List new ways you can begin making the most of your resources. Tell someone about them and ask him or her to hold you accountable to them from time to time.

_____

_____

_____

_____

_____

_____

FOR ME TO FOLLOW GOD

Handling Money

DAY FIVE

God's instructions were written to give us more freedom in our lives and more enjoyment throughout our lifetimes. When we decide to apply biblical principles to our lives, we can experience God's blessings. When we ignore His warnings, many times the end result is financial troubles. Many families find themselves struggling to meet their financial obligations, including Christian families.

What are ways people can avoid financial troubles and handle their money faithfully? Consider what this verse says: *"The plans of the diligent lead to profit as surely as haste leads to poverty"* (Proverbs 21:5).

The first part of this verse says, *"The plans of the diligent lead to profit."* We need a plan (or perhaps multiple plans) to be profitable. Here, the Hebrew word translated as *"plans"* refers to "thought, imaginations, intentions, purpose."[10] We also need to carefully follow the plans. And we can have success by being steadfast and patient while following through with plans. The word *"diligence"* implies a level of "carefulness, attention, alertness, perseverance, industry." The opposite of *diligence* is "carelessness, indifference, unconcern, laziness."[11]

The second part of the verse says, *"haste leads to poverty."* What changes need to be made so we can get out of money troubles? We can stop making *quick* financial decisions. Maybe we haven't taken the time to do "homework." Some consumers make purchasing decisions based on the monthly payments. They don't take into account the total cost of the item over the years. They don't consider the added cost such as upkeep or interest in the long run.

We also can learn to be cautious about making a fast "profit" on a deal. Quick decisions are often made with a quick "profit" in mind. Without weighing the consequences, some people are taken in by get-rich-quick schemes. Hoping to not miss out on the deal of a lifetime, they are unable to resist the pull of the smooth sales pitch. Greed gets in the way of what would otherwise be recognized as an obvious bad choice or proposition.

The company we keep often plays a part in how we choose to live and spend our money. If our friends are preoccupied with wearing the latest fashions, spending frivolously on entertainment, or driving the newest vehicles, we may be swayed to imitate their ways. We can easily imitate those we enjoy being with. Those we spend time with often determine our character and reputation.

📖 Read Proverbs 13:20.

How does a person grow wise?

_____

_____

When we spend time with people who are knowledgeable and have good judgment, we will likewise grow in knowledge and discernment. A way we can grow in our relationship with God is to choose friends whose words and actions show Christian maturity. Getting involved in a church that teaches the Bible and in Bible study groups can lead to a deeper knowledge of God. Those who make poor choices in friends reap the consequences. People who associate with bad company often get into trouble themselves.

📖 Look at Proverbs 15:22.

What causes plans to fail?

_____

_____

We can avoid financial problems by getting advice on important matters. Consider the friendships and relationships we have as possible resources for advice. Plans succeed *"with many advisors"* (Proverbs 15:22). We benefit when we consult others and learn from them. How often do we share our ideas or plans with those we trust or get advice from them? We can avoid disappointment and be more successful by taking the time to confer with others.

When Jesus was teaching His disciples, He discussed the importance of being trustworthy with one's present resources, however small. Jesus told the parable of the clever manager who planned ahead for his inevitable time of unemployment (Luke 16:1–9). This shrewd manager made use of the resources available to him at the time.

📖 Read what Jesus said about being trustworthy in Luke 16:10–12.

According to Luke 16:10, who can be trusted with much?

_____

Who will be dishonest with much (Luke 16:10)?

_____

_____

HONESTY IN SMALL MATTERS

"For unless you are honest in small matters, you won't be in large ones. If you cheat even a little, you won't be honest with greater responsibilities. And if you are untrustworthy about worldly wealth, who will trust you with the true riches of heaven? And if you are not faithful with other people's money, why should you be entrusted with money of your own?" (Luke 16:10–12 [LB])

APPLY When it comes to managing your money and resources, do you think you have become *more* trustworthy or *less* trustworthy over time? In what ways?

_____

_____

_____

_____

_____

_____

 Heavenly Father, thank You for entrusting me with these earthly goods. I pray for Your wisdom that every day I may faithfully manage what You have entrusted to me. If I haven't been trustworthy with my money and possessions, show me ways I can improve and become trustworthy. Help me to be resourceful with all that You have given me. In Jesus' name, Amen.

NOTES

1. Spiros Zodhiates, *Hebrew-Greek Key Word Study Bible* (Chattanooga: AMG Publishers, 1990), 1375.

2. Albert Barnes, *Albert Barnes' Notes on the Bible,* "Luke 15:12 Commentary." In e-Sword Bible software database, 2005, Rick Meyers.

3. Ibid., "Luke 5:14 Commentary."

4. *Funk & Wagnalls Standard Desk Dictionary*, Vol. 1 (USA: Harper & Row Publishers, Inc. 1984), 308.

5. Ibid., Vol. 2, 607.

6. Spiros Zodhiates, *Hebrew-Greek Key Word Study Bible* (Chattanooga: AMG Publishers, 1990), 1834.

7. Ibid., 1838.

8. Ibid., 1722.

9. Ibid., 1729.

10. Ibid., 1740.

11. Joseph Devlin, *A Dictionary of Synonyms and Antonyms* (New York: Warner Books, 1982), 71.

Notes

Getting Our Finances in Order With a Spending Plan

This week we are focusing on ordering our finances with a spending plan. One reason people have trouble with their finances is that they don't have a spending plan. They don't plan ahead, yet they wonder why they struggle to pay their bills each month. They somehow manage to just get by month after month. Perhaps their credit card helps them make up for the difference. Still, they do not set funds aside for any extra costs that may come their way. Proverbs 22:3 states, *"A prudent man sees danger and takes refuge, but the simple keep going and suffer for it."*

In the Old Testament we read of King Hezekiah who was told to set his affairs in order. When the king became gravely ill, the prophet Isaiah came to him. Isaiah approached the King Hezekiah with these words, *"This is what the LORD says: 'Set your house in order, because you are going to die; you will not recover"* (2 Kings 20:1–2). The king was instructed to arrange and manage his affairs in an orderly system. He was to get his household ready for the day he would no longer be with them.

The Christian family should be characterized as having good money management skills. It should not be known as a family with disorganized records, consistently late payments, or financial chaos. The family that seeks to honor God desires to have orderliness in money management.

The Christian family should be characterized as having good money management skills. The family that seeks to honor God desires to have orderliness in money management.

GET ORGANIZED

Today we'll look at having a plan for organizing and storing our bills, receipts, and financial records. What system do you use to organize and pay your bills? Does it work well for you? If you occasionally get "past due" notices in the mail, it may not be because you are strapped for cash. It may be a matter of not being financially organized.

In order to pay your bills on time every time you need an efficient system. Developing an efficient system for bill paying helps you save time, money, and frustration. Some customers may have the money to cover the bills. When they get "past due" notices or the bank calls them about a late car payment, they feel they have no control of their finances. Taking a small amount of time to set up a system for paying monthly bills would save many hours of time and frustration in the future.

First of all, you need to make sure you have a place to keep all unpaid bills. As soon as the bill comes in the mail, check for the due date and write it on the front of the envelope. Organize the bills due with earliest due dates in the front. Decide when and where you are comfortable making the payments. You may choose to pay bills within a day of when they come in the mail. This way the chore of making the payment isn't delayed, and you may feel you have more control of your finances with such a rapid response in payment.

Some choose to pay bills by setting up electronic bill paying with a bank or credit union. This option allows people to use their computers to pay bills either manually or automatically (same day each month). If you choose electronic bill paying, money is deducted from your checking account each time a bill is paid. For the bills that you would rather pay by hand, have all the bill-paying items you will need in one easy location. This includes checkbook, calculator, stamps, mailing labels, and envelopes.

Keep a record of the date of payment and check number or form of payment for the bills. When using a spending plan or budget sheet, enter the date and payment amount on the budget sheet. Organize and save the tax-related bills and paid invoices by category in folders.

Using a debit card for purchases or ATM withdrawals can be convenient. But it's important to have a system for keeping the receipts and entering the purchase or withdrawal amounts in your checkbook. It's best to enter the purchase amount the same day as the purchase. You should also keep an up-to-date record of "floating" items when you balance your checkbook. Again, it's important to keep all the transaction receipts in one location.

Taking advantage of home banking has made it so much easier to be in control of our finances. We can see our transaction history and note the current balances in our accounts. We can transfer money from other accounts to our checking account when necessary. We can balance our checkbook any time we want within minutes—especially when we keep up with it regularly.

It is essential to learn how to balance a checkbook. I read of a finance counselor who discovered that fewer than two of ten couples knew how to keep their checkbooks balanced. Don't invite overdraft charges on checks written with insufficient funds. Some couples prefer to use a joint checkbook, while others like to have separate checkbooks. Whichever way is more convenient, it is important that bills are paid on time and accurate records are kept.

When we don't take charge of our financial obligations, late payments harm us in several ways. They can cost us money with additional charges and late fees. They harm our credit score. Lower credit scores make us riskier consumers to lenders. Late payments on our credit record lead to steep credit card interest rate hikes. Slow or late payments can also compromise our ability to get better interest rates for auto insurance or other forms of insurance.

Some consumers are not aware of their spending patterns, and they find it difficult to plan ahead. They take on financial obligations without looking at their total financial picture. When unexpected bills come their way, it becomes even harder for them to make the payments.

If someone were to ask you what your total income and expenditures were last month, would you be able to give an answer right away? Today we will take the time to estimate monthly income and expenses. (If you already have a budget system set up, it will be advantageous for you to refer to the expense totals). Estimating our income and expenses is a first step to becoming aware of where hard-earned money goes. It helps us be more observant of how much money we have access to.

As you estimate the expenses, remember to factor in variable expenses when estimating your average monthly expenses. These variable expenses take into account irregular expenses such as home repairs, car repairs, health costs, and utilities (gas, electric, water, phone, etc.). Quickly jot down what you pay during an average month for each category. You will need a calculator at the end of this exercise.

"A prudent man sees danger and takes refuge, but the simple keep going and suffer for it."

Proverbs 22:3

Monthly Income and Expenses Estimate
Total Family Monthly Income: $_____

Expenses:
1. Charitable Giving $_____
2. Housing (mortgage/rent,
    homeowner's insurance, property taxes,
    gas, electricity, water, sanitation,
    phones, internet service, repairs) $_____
3. Transportation (auto loans, insurance, gas,
    maintenance, plates, repairs) $_____
4. Food (groceries, school lunches) $_____
5. Insurance (medical, dental, life, other) $_____
6. Health (doctor, dentist, prescriptions) $_____
7. Entertainment (eating out, movies,
    babysitting, club fees, newspapers,
    magazines, books, computer games and software) $_____
8. Clothing, shoes, and accessories $_____
9. School tuition, daycare $_____
10. Miscellaneous (household and pet products,
    hair care, stamps, allowances, gifts, etc.) $_____
11. Debt obligations (credit cards, loans) $_____
12. Vacation and travel $_____
13. Savings (emergency fund, 401k, IRA, college) $_____

Total Estimated Living Expenses $_____
Cash Flow Margin (net spendable income
minus living expenses) $_____

Now that you have subtracted the monthly expenses from your income, do you have a positive or negative cash flow margin? If it shows a negative cash flow, the time is now to begin making lifestyle changes. If it shows a positive cash flow, you have already developed some great money habits! That's great!

If you find it difficult to estimate your monthly expenses, it is indicative that either you don't handle all of your financial affairs or your finances may not be in order. The wise King Solomon wrote about watching our business interests very carefully. In his time one way a man's wealth was measured was by how many flocks and herds of animals he had.

📖 Read Proverbs 27:23–24.

What two directives did King Solomon give in Proverbs 27:23?

_____

_____

What does not endure forever (verse 24)?

_____

_____

APPLY Write Proverbs 27:23 in your own words, making it applicable to you and your situation.

_____

_____

Write Proverbs 27:24 in your own words.

_____

_____

_____

We can break the cycle of disorganization and endless bills and obligations. We can bring order to our life and learn to enjoy a simpler and less stressful way of life. In Day Two we will begin a system of tracking our spending. This will help us take a step in the right direction of being better money managers.

Spending Plan

DAY TWO

DECIDE ON A SPENDING PLAN

In Day One, we estimated our average total income and expenditures. During Week Six of our *Following God* Bible study we evaluated life goals for faith, families, careers, and finances. How closely does our spending correlate with our goals? If we set a goal to eat out less in order to save more, our spending needs to reflect that. If we made it a goal to begin saving money for an emergency fund, our records should show that. When we set attainable goals, we will follow through with them one day at a time. We can ask God daily to help us do what will be impossible for us to do in our own power.

If we struggle to pay monthly bills, it is probably time to make changes. We don't need to continue living in survival mode when it comes to money. We have been learning God's promises and principles for how He wants us to live. As we read and learn more of God's Word, we will gain more of His wisdom. As we put God in the center of our life, He will show more of Himself to us. We can trust Him to help us with our everyday decisions, including our spending decisions.

📖 God is our source of wisdom. Read Proverbs 2:6–11 to read how the pursuit of wisdom brings security.

What comes from the Lord's mouth (Proverbs 2:6)?

_____

_____

According to Proverbs 2:7, what does the Lord store up for the upright?

_____

_____

The Lord is a shield for whom (Proverbs 2:7)?

_____

_____

📖 Fill in the blanks for verses 8–11.

"For he _____ the course of the just and _____ the way of his faithful ones. Then you will _____ what is right and just and fair—every good path. For wisdom will enter your _____, and knowledge will be pleasant to your _____. Discretion will _____ you, and understanding will _____ you."

Until we know exactly what our financial situations are, it is difficult to put our houses in order. When we take the time to observe the inflow and outgo of our money, we can develop more effective financial plans. On the flip side, when there are no financial plans or budgets in place, financial difficulties eventually overtake us. Thorough financial planning is key to staying in control of our money.

It is difficult to recognize spending patterns when we don't take the time to track spending. Monitoring personal and home expenditures on a regular basis through carefully recording the expenditure amounts enables us to fine-tune our future expenditures.

I hope your Day Two study is encouraging you to decide on a spending plan to help bring your income and expenses more into balance so that you can save more of your hard-earned income. In just a few moments, you will complete an exercise in which you will begin to record all of your spending for one month. Refer back to the expense estimates you made yesterday for the different categories. Look for particular areas where you will need to lower spending this coming month. For example, if your goal is to balance the monthly budget, can you lower your food or miscellaneous expense amounts? By how much? If you plan to spend one hundred dollars less on groceries this month, write "–$100" next to the food category. If you decide

We have been learning God's promises and principles for how He wants us to live. As we read and learn more of God's Word, we will gain more of His wisdom.

"For the LORD gives wisdom, and from his mouth come knowledge and understanding."

Proverbs 2:6

to cut your miscellaneous spending by fifty dollars, write "–$50" next to the miscellaneous category. Consider the ways you can cut costs in as many areas as possible. Decide how much you are willing to cut back on monthly expenses. Look for all the possible ways that will enable you to have a positive cash flow at the end of the month.

Husbands and wives need to be accountable to each other when it comes to how their money is spent. If you are married, it is important for you to establish spending goals with your spouse. If you establish them together, it will be easier for both of you to follow them. You'll be working as a team. Come to an agreement on what could work best for your family. Keep your family's interest in mind.

Go to the Monthly Expenses Worksheet located in the Appendix of this book. Find the areas on the Monthly Expenses Worksheet where you intend to make changes in spending. Above the columns, write down dollar amounts you plan to spend this month. Consider the highest dollar amounts you plan to pay in each category. These will serve as your spending limits. Keep all of your receipts for credit and debit transactions, and, when possible, your cash purchases in order to get an accurate dollar amount for recording purchases on the Monthly Expenses Worksheet. Remember to enter debit card purchases in your checkbook ledger as soon as possible.

 How would your friends describe your spending habits? In the past, have you recorded expenses in an effort to analyze your spending habits? What are some spending patterns you have been aware of for some time that need to changed?

Any new spending plan you formulate can be viewed as a road map that will boost confidence as you head in the right direction. Your goals should include goals for wise and balanced money management. Remember to record your expenses regularly. In four weeks you'll be able to see how well you followed your spending objectives.

Spending Plan

DAY THREE

MAINTAIN YOUR SPENDING PLAN

Many families have racked up burdensome credit card debt because they are using their credit cards to make up the difference for their desired standard of living. In other words, they use credit cards to "make ends meet." When families make an effort to follow through with spending plans or budgets, they shouldn't have to rely on credit cards for essential purchases. They will see an increase in cash flow when they begin to eliminate unnecessary purchases and lower standard of living expectations.

The advertising industry capitalizes on selling us bigger and better things. Advertisements entice us to always want more. Businesses often advertise their products for no money down or no interest for one year. Department stores lure us with an instant discount on our purchase if we sign up for their credit card. Such tactics sometimes lure us into making purchases for items that we haven't planned for. We may be convinced to buy unplanned items by listening to any of these sales pitches: "You deserve it," "Everybody else owns one," and "You can't live without it." Many people have developed a sense of entitlement, to their financial detriment. A false sense of entitlement can lead to higher interest rates or monthly payments than what we can handle. If we aren't careful, this feeling of entitlement will lead to unmanageable debt.

We need to take ownership of the spending plans we create with our own unique situations in mind. Using a spending plan, or budget, is a powerful way to manage money. It serves as a reality check and shows where our spending is excessive. It helps us control discretionary spending. We should already have a clear understanding of what causes us to make poor spending choices. Our spending plan helps us stay disciplined in money management.

The author of the book of Hebrews talked about discipline and its rewards. He said, *"No discipline seems pleasant at the time, but painful. Later on, however, it produces a harvest of righteousness and peace for those who have been trained by it"* (Hebrews 12:11). Adam Clarke comments:

> Neither correction, wholesome restraint, domestic regulations, nor gymnastic discipline, are pleasant to them that are thus exercised; but it is by these means that obedient children, scholars, and great men are made. And it is by God's discipline that Christians are made.

Concerning *"a harvest of righteousness and peace"* he writes: "The joyous, prosperous fruits; those fruits by which we gain much, and through which we are happy."[1]

📖 Look at Proverbs 13:18 on discipline.

What happens to the person who ignores discipline (Proverbs 13:18)?

_____

_____

What is the result for the person who heeds correction?

_____

_____

Matthew Henry explains this verse in more depth. He describes the person *"who ignores discipline"* as "he that is so proud that he scorns to be taught; he that refuses the good instruction offered him." He describes the *"honored"* person as "humble, avoiding that which would be a disgrace to him."[2] Compare this description with the picture of an undisciplined person who is full of pride.

📖 Read Proverbs 15:32, then fill in the blanks.

"He who ignores _____ despises himself, but whoever heeds correction gains _____."

In this verse, the word *despises* is translated from a word that literally means "to melt, to feel undone, to dissolve." The term "has the sense of flowing or running out"—similar to the concept of feeling "drained."[3]

Individuals who choose to ignore a semblance of order and discipline in financial choices will find that such choices eventually lead to harm and trouble. Their schemes and plans do not remain "held together" and eventually unravel and fall apart. To ignore discipline is to reject what is in one's best interest. Practice and training help us control our behavior and develop character.

We need to take ownership of the spending plans we create with our own unique situation in mind. Using a spending plan, or budget, is a powerful way to manage our money.

"No discipline seems pleasant at the time, but painful. Later on, however, it produces a harvest of righteousness and peace for those who have been trained by it."

Hebrews 12:11

Our faith in Christ and good discipline go hand in hand. When apostle Paul wrote to the Colossians, he was happy to hear about their level of discipline. He comments, *"For even though I am absent in body, nevertheless I am with you in spirit, rejoicing to see your good discipline and the stability of your faith in Christ"* (Colossians 2:5, NASB). He continued to encourage them saying, *"As you therefore have received Christ Jesus the Lord, so walk in Him, having been firmly rooted and now being built up in Him and established in your faith, just as you were instructed"* (Colossians 2:6–7, NASB).

The author of Hebrews emphasized in chapter twelve that God disciplines His children. *"My son, do not make light of the Lord's discipline, and do not lose heart when he rebukes you, because the Lord disciplines those He loves* (Hebrews 12:5–6). As parents we know how important it is that our children learn the skills of discipline. The process may not be enjoyable or easy, yet we know that our children will benefit from it in the end. We love them, and we desire to teach our children important kingdom values and life skills that they can keep for a lifetime. The author of Hebrews continued with these words of encouragement, *"Our fathers disciplined us for a little while as they thought best; but God disciplines us for our good, that we may share in his holiness"* (Hebrews 12:10). With discipline comes growth in grace and in character.

Many people assume their money problems come from not earning enough. Often the issue isn't that they *can't* live on their income, but that they *won't* make an effort to live on their income. Disciplined use of money and resources are the key. Without discipline and divine help, the best of plans fail. King Solomon wrote that in discipline *"there is hope"* (Proverbs 19:18).

We can maintain our spending plans each month by consistently 1) keeping expenses down, and 2) not taking on new debt. When we are tempted to drop our plans of action and return to our old ways of spending and living, we need to stop and think for a moment. We can reflect on seeing a better way of life for ourselves, as our financial obligations will be met, one at a time. We can reflect on the financial freedom we'll have as we learn to make better life choices.

> **We can maintain our spending plan each month by consistently 1) keeping expenses down, and 2) not taking on new debt.**

Spending Plan

DAY FOUR

> **With goals in mind, we learn to make reasonable decisions with the money entrusted to us.**

SEEK BALANCE

When we decide on a spending plan and consistently maintain it, we will get our finances and lifestyle back into balance. With goals in mind, we learn to make reasonable decisions with the money entrusted to us. We learn to carefully weigh our alternatives and choices, deciding on the ones that work best for us.

As we learn to seek balance in our finances, we need to believe that God will help us. This isn't something we can do of our own natural knowledge and strength. God will give us fortitude and strength in our daily choices. The Old Testament tells us of the prophet Habakkuk who felt helpless and called to God for help. We clearly see how Habakkuk was reassured with promise when he confidently stated, *"Yet I will rejoice in the LORD, I will be joyful in God my Savior. The Sovereign LORD is my strength"* (Habakkuk 3:18–19). Since it is in our sin nature to make selfish decisions, we need to put our hope and trust in God to help us. When we turn our finances over to Him, He can work in our lives and in our particular situations.

A first step is to aim to operate on a balanced budget every month. We should know what our net income is each month. We also need take the time to be more aware of our cash flow. Writing down all of our expenditures will be well worth the time. We will be able to observe our spending patterns more quickly and make better choices in the coming months.

A big way to balance budgets is to keep family expenses down by paying cash for consumables. This includes general living expenses, clothing, and entertainment. We need to avoid charging these items. "Cash transactions" can also take the form of a check or debit card purchase. Make it difficult to buy on impulse and keep credit cards at home. Our spending plans should allocate enough funds to be able to pay cash for our expenses.

Resist the sales hype for unnecessary purchases. When buying essentials (i.e., groceries, cleaning supplies, etc.), if we shop using a reasonable needs list, we can avoid the temptation to make impulsive and hasty purchases. We can leave the store satisfied that we stayed within our spending plan. Before making purchases, ask these questions: Do I need it? Is it the best buy? Will the upkeep be expensive? If the item is a luxury, is it a luxury I can afford?

Note: Parents may have different reasons for living beyond their means. Perhaps they are willing to overspend for their children, thinking this will make them feel loved. Spending led by emotions can hurt the family in the long run, bringing about even more stressful living.

 A simpler life can break the cycle of an unbalanced lifestyle. What are some factors that you personally need to keep in mind when making spending decisions? Are you more tempted to spend unwisely at certain stores or with particular friends or family members? List some steps below that you can take to be a wiser shopper and to maintain your spending plan.

1. _____

2. _____

3. _____

4. _____

5. _____

When we proactively look for workable ways to cut expenses, worthwhile results most likely will ensue. When funds are mishandled and poor decisions are made, families face frustration, stress, and worry. It becomes more difficult to pay essential bills and obligations such as utilities, auto insurance and maintenance, and healthcare expenses. Yet, payments must be made. Proverbs 3:28 advises us: *Do not say to your neighbor, 'Come back later; I'll give it tomorrow'—when you now have it with you.* We can make an effort to pay what is due, knowing we have the ability to make better choices.

We all know how learned behaviors are hard to overcome. Yet it is possible to live within our means. Reducing lifestyle consumption does not come easily. However, the money that is freed up from nonessential and unplanned purchases can help to balance our budget.

IMPULSE BUYING

If we shop using a reasonable list, we can avoid the temptation to make impulsive and hasty purchases. Before making purchases, ask these questions: Do I need it? Is it the best buy? Will the upkeep be expensive? If the item is a luxury, is it a luxury I can afford?

Consider the ways we can cut costs and create more cash flow. Then list some possible ways your family can cut expenses in these areas:

Housing (mortgage/rent, gas, heating, electricity, water, telephone, internet, maintenance/repairs, household furnishings)

_____

_____

_____

Transportation (auto loans, car insurance, gas)

_____

_____

_____

Food (groceries, school lunches)

_____

_____

_____

Clothing and shoes

_____

_____

_____

Health expenses (doctor, prescriptions, health club costs)

_____

_____

_____

Entertainment (eating out, movies, babysitting, club fees, vacations, magazines, newspapers, books, computer games and software)

_____

_____

_____

Miscellaneous (hair care, stamps, mailings, gifts, flowers, allowances, pet care, dry cleaning)

_____

_____

_____

Work-related expenses

_____

_____

_____

As we learn ways to balance our budgets and our lifestyles, we should stay away from taking on any new debt. Adding debt will only take us two steps back after taking steps in the right direction.

Look at Ephesians 5:15–18 (NASB) below on how we are to live.

verse 15 *Therefore be careful how you walk, not as unwise men, but as wise,*

verse 16 *making the most of your time, because the days are evil.*

verse 17 *So then do not be foolish, but understand what the will of the Lord is.*

verse 18 *And do not get drunk with wine, for that is dissipation, but be filled with the Spirit.*

According to Ephesians 5:15, how should we live?

_____

_____

How should we use our time (Ephesians 5:16)?

_____

_____

What are we to understand (Ephesians 5:17)?

_____

_____

With what must we be filled (Ephesians 5:18)?

_____

_____

> **"Be very careful, then, how you live—not as unwise but as wise."**
>
> **Ephesians 5:15**

In these verses Paul reminds us to be careful and wise in the way we conduct our lives. We should use our time wisely. In Ephesians 5:17, Paul tells us to *"understand what the will of the Lord is."* In this verse, the word *"understand"* in the original Greek denotes "moral reflection, pondering, or laying to heart."[4] In Ephesians 5:18 we read, *"Do not get drunk with wine, for that is dissipation."* The term *dissipation* is derived from the Greek *asotia,* specifically meaning "extravagant squandering on one extreme." Spiros Zodhiates explains that the Greek term *asotos* is "a prodigal . . . one who spends too much, who slides easily under the fatal influence of flatterers and the temptations with which he has surrounded himself into spending freely on his own lusts and appetites."[5] It is interesting to note that in this verse Paul contrasts two persons, a person with an extravagant manner of living and a person who is *"filled with the Spirit."*

Matthew Henry comments on Ephesians 5:18. He explains:

> Men should [have] a plentiful measure of the graces of the Holy Spirit, that would fill their souls with great joy, strength, and courage, which things sensual men expect their wine should inspire them with. . . . We [should not] be satisfied with a little of the Spirit, but to be aspiring after measures, so as to be filled with the Spirit. Now by this means we shall come to understand what the will of the Lord is; for the Spirit of God is given as a Spirit of wisdom and of understanding.[6]

The Spirit of God will teach us to be careful and wise as we strive for reasonable and well-balanced living. As we turn away from our natural sinful inclinations, we can aspire to have more of the "great joy, strength, and courage" the Holy Spirit provides for us. And the Holy Spirit *will* fill us with His extraordinary joy and peace!

GIVING AND SHARING

A biblical concept of stewardship isn't just about how wisely we spend our money, but about our giving, as well. Getting our finances in order also involves giving back that which has been given to us. Worldly motives often get in the way of our desire to give. We want to hold onto what is "ours," often forgetting that God is the source of all of our possessions and blessings.

When we have received the joy of salvation and God's favor in our lives, we want to give back to God. King Solomon wrote, *"Honor the LORD with your wealth, with the firstfruits of all your crops"* (Proverbs 3:9). We are motivated to give a part of what we have as an expression of our gratitude and our reverence and fear of Him. It is a part of our faith. *"But just as you excel in everything—in faith, in speech, in knowledge, in complete earnestness and in your love for us—see that you also excel in this grace of giving"* (2 Corinthians 8:7).

When we tithe or give offerings to the church we acknowledge God's ownership of our lives. We recognize that what we have comes from Him and all we have belongs to Him. We acknowledge that God is in control of every part of our life and that He will provide for us. *"Each man should give what he has decided in his heart to give, not reluctantly or under compulsion, for God loves a cheerful giver"* (2 Corinthians 9:7).

When we give, we think of others' needs as well as our own. We give out of our obedience, love, and abundance. We give out of the blessings that we have been blessed with. And God promises to supply our needs. As we step out in faith and give, God can make our money and resources go further. We can trust Him to care for us and our needs and thank Him for His goodness and generosity.

When making decisions on where and how we should give, we can ask God to help us in our giving decisions. We shouldn't neglect giving to the various ministries of our church where we worship. We know there are many charitable organizations. We need to be careful that the message of the "religious" organizations requesting funding is true to the gospel message and scriptural principles. Is it a ministry where the gospel is preached? We need to be cautious and check out how their funds are used, including the percentages going to fund-raising and the administration of the organization or ministry. Be knowledgeable about their accountability records and the leaders in the organization.

The Bible emphasizes the importance of sharing with others and showing kindness to others. Proverbs 19:17 tells us that *"He who is kind to the poor lends to the LORD, and he will reward him for what he has done."*

📖 What does Jesus say about giving as recorded in Acts 20:35?

_____

> "I have had many things in my hands, and I have lost them all; but whatever I have been able to place in God's hands I still possess."
>
> —Martin Luther

Jesus told the parable of a very wealthy man and a poor man named Lazarus. Read the account of these men in Luke 16:19–31.

Briefly describe the life of the rich man (verse 19).

_____

_____

Briefly describe how Lazarus lived (verse 20–21).

_____

_____

_____

This parable describes the rich man as one who wears expensive purple garments, feasts well, and lives well. He may have been a man of nobility and great influence. Yet he uses none of his influence to help a helpless man, Lazarus, who sits at the rich man's gate day after day, hoping for, at the very least, crumbs from his table. Even the dogs took pity on Lazarus.

The rich man is hard-hearted and shows no mercy to the poor man at his gate. When he dies, however, he no longer enjoys a life of luxury and earthly pleasures. Instead, he goes to a place of misery and agony. However, Lazarus experiences true comfort and consolation following his death and enjoys being at the side of Abraham in paradise. Jesus says in this parable that upon Lazarus' death, *"the angels carried him to Abraham's side"* (Luke 16:22). Lazarus is honored and looks forward to an eternity of heavenly joy and glory. This parable brings out the distinct contrasts between the conditions of people on earth and where they spend their lives for eternity.

Albert Barnes adds these notes about the parable:

> The design of the narrative is to be collected from the previous conversation. He [Jesus] had taught the danger of the love of money, the deceitful and treacherous nature of riches, that what was in high esteem on earth was hateful to God, that they ought to listen to Moses and the prophets, and that it was the duty of people to show kindness to the poor. The design of the parable was to impress all these truths more vividly on the mind, and to show the Pharisees that with all their boasted righteousness and their external correctness of character, they might be lost.[7]

When Jesus ministered here on earth, He didn't need to tell His disciples and the countless people He met that He loved them. For His deeds show that He loved them, as He gave of His love and helped people with their physical needs. By meeting their physical needs, Jesus also created the opportunity to relieve their spiritual needs and burdens.

Jesus not only offers His love and consolation to us, but He also desires our commitment. He promises: *"Come to me, all you who are weary and burdened, and I will give you rest. Take my yoke upon you and learn from me, for I am gentle and humble in heart, and you will find rest for your souls. For my yoke is easy and my burden is light"* (Matthew 11:28–30).

John, Jesus Christ's beloved apostle, explains that as children of God, our deeds will naturally display His love in us. He states, *"If anyone has material possessions and sees his brother in need but has no pity on him, how can the love of God be in him?* (1 John 3:17). We are to love *"with actions and in truth"* (1 John 3:18).

In his letter to Timothy, Paul gives definite directives for the wealthy. He says, *"Command them to do good, to be rich in good deeds, and to be generous and willing to share. In this way they will lay up treasure for themselves as a firm foundation for the coming age, so that they may take hold of the life that is truly life"* (1 Timothy 6:18–19).

Let's look at a paraphrase of 1 Timothy 6:17–19:

> *Tell those who are rich not to be proud and not to trust in their money, which will soon be gone, but their pride and trust should be in the living God who always richly gives us all we need for our enjoyment. Tell them to use their money to do good. They should be rich in good works and should give happily to those in need, always being ready to share with others whatever God has given them. By doing this they will be storing up real treasure for themselves in heaven—it is the only safe investment for eternity! And they will be living a fruitful Christian life down here as well.* (LB)

When Paul addresses the church at Philippi, he reminds them of their generosity to him from the time they had first heard the gospel (see Philippians 4:15). He thanks the church members there for constantly showering gifts upon him when he needed them the most (verse 16). He has not forgotten their kindness and concern for him. With gratefulness Paul responds, *"They [the gifts] are a fragrant offering, an acceptable sacrifice, pleasing to God. And my God will meet all your needs according to his glorious riches in Christ Jesus"* (verses 18–19). Paul doesn't say that he hopes or wishes that their needs will be met. He *knows* without a doubt that God will supply their needs. He knows that God multiplies the gifts of people who freely give.

Read Luke 6:38 on Jesus' words about giving, then fill in the blanks.

"Give, and it will be _____ to you. A _____ measure, pressed down, shaken together and _____

_____, will be _____ into your lap. For with the _____ you use, it will be _____ to you."

Although this verse comments on giving and receiving, we must remember that we do not give so we can receive. We do not give for the praise and attention of men or to impress people. When we give of our material possessions, we express our obedience and willingness to surrender our lives to God. We desire to please God with our gifts.

Write your own prayer in the space provided.

_____

_____

_____

_____

_____

_____

_____

_____

_____

_____

"They [the gifts] are a fragrant offering, an acceptable sacrifice, pleasing to God. And my God will meet all your needs according to his glorious riches in Christ Jesus."

Philippians 4:18–19

NOTES

1. Adam Clarke, *Adam Clarke's Commentary on the Bible*, "Hebrews 12:11 Commentary." In e-Sword Bible software database, 2005, Rick Meyers.

2. Matthew Henry, *Matthew Henry's Commentary on the Whole Bible,* "Proverbs 13:18 Commentary." In e-Sword Bible software database, 2005, Rick Meyers.

3. Spiros Zodhiates, *Hebrew-Greek Key Word Study Bible* (Chattanooga: AMG Publishers, 1990), 1738.

4. Ibid., 1878.

5. Ibid., 1813.

6. Henry, *Matthew Henry's Commentary on the Whole Bible,* "Ephesians 5:18 Commentary."

7. Albert Barnes, *Albert Barnes' Notes on the Bible*, "Luke 16:19 Commentary." In e-Sword Bible software database, 2005, Rick Meyers.

Notes

Borrowing and Credit: Understanding Biblical Principles

I n Week Eight we took a closer look at our lifestyle and the ways we could be wiser consumers. We benefit from examining our lifestyles, since we desire to manage our money in ways that work best for us. As parents, we also want to help our children learn the importance of using money wisely.

King Solomon states in Proverbs 22:7, *"The rich rule over the poor, and the borrower is servant to the lender."* Taking on debt leads to a relationship of dependence to the lender. This dependence is ongoing until the obligation is paid in full. Yet many families continue to take on more and more debt, many of them not fully aware of the consequences until it is too late.

Studies show that using credit cards will increase spending by 33–34 percent. This has proven to be true even among those who typically pay off their credit card balances at the end of the month.[1] When we pay with cash, we seem to be more aware of our money leaving our pocketbook. Consequently, by using cash we tend to be less impulsive in our buying habits.

The idea of buying things on credit has become commonplace in our culture. People have grown accustomed to borrowing for something they currently don't have the cash to buy. Obviously, we cannot indefinitely spend more than we earn. Such habits are bound to affect us negatively sooner or later.

PERILS OF CREDIT

Today, more than ever, it is easy to obtain credit. Consequently, many individuals and families get caught up in a continuous cycle of debt. Increasingly, they are becoming overextended financially. With each passing month they find themselves facing a growing mountain of debt, as they quickly learn that it is so much easier to get into debt than to get out.

When they make purchases on credit that they cannot afford, they simply delay the decision as to how they will pay it back. The delay factor snowballs and makes the money situation more difficult to handle later.

Some individuals do not mind having many debts. In fact, the heavy burden of debt is a way of life for them. They choose to live a life tied to debt. Yet, this should not be thought of as a normal way of life. Whether times are good or not so good, it is best to have as few creditors as possible.

Most of us probably have shelter, food, and clothing that is more than adequate. Yet the world's wisdom invites us to "enjoy" life to the fullest today. It tells us that we should not need to wait for what we want. The world says, "Why wait when we can have it now? Why not live like everyone else?"

Less contentment in life often leads to more debt. Excessive borrowing leads to more troubles than ever thought imaginable. Those who find it difficult to meet their obligations soon find they are making late payments. Late charges and bad credit soon follow. Money problems interfere with family relationships, causing family discord. Excessive borrowing cannot be ignored. It needs to be dealt with one creditor at a time.

Some people may think that their only temporary solution for paying revolving debts is to consolidate them. This enables them to pay the loan amount over a longer period of time. One popular option is to refinance mortgages to cash out home equity for the purpose of consolidating high-interest loans and credit cards. This option allows homeowners to absorb credit card debt into their mortgage payments, meaning their house payments will likely go up, but total monthly expenditures will still go down if all their separate minimum credit card payments are absorbed into one mortgage payment per month based on 15- or 30-year mortgage terms.

People using the refinance/debt consolidation option should weigh the benefits versus the drawbacks. Keep in mind that when using an option like this, your total debt is not eliminated; you are just stretching out the payments over a longer period of time, and it will likely take you longer to pay off your mortgage. This option is not likely to be helpful to homeowners who are considering selling their homes and relocating in the near future, as you could end up owing more on your home than what you could realistically sell it for.

Debt consolidation can help people better manage their monthly budgets. However, if poor money habits and management do not change, more ominous trouble could be just over the horizon. Those who do not change their habits could quickly find themselves maxed out once again in credit card debt with a higher mortgage payment to boot.

DEBT = DEPENDENCY

King Solomon stated in Proverbs 22:7, *"The rich rule over the poor, and the borrower is servant to the lender."* Taking on debt leads to a relationship of dependence to the lender.

Often the wants and desires for the nicer things in life are overrun by the realities of paying for them. The "good life" of frivolous spending and living by borrowing is overcome by money problems and family arguments. Proverbs 17:1 reminds us, *"Better a dry crust with peace and quiet than a house full of feasting, with strife."* Paraphrased, this verse says, *"A dry crust eaten in peace is better than steak every day along with argument and strife"* (LB).

Look up the verses of similar thought in Proverbs 15 and 16.

According to Proverbs 15:16, what is better than great wealth with turmoil?

_____

_____

In Proverbs 15:17, what is better than a fattened calf with hatred?

_____

_____

In Proverbs 16:8, what is better than much gain with injustice?

_____

_____

A lack of patience leads individuals to borrow unnecessarily. It may be best, in some instances, to delay a purchase. Many individuals are quick to borrow rather than wait for a provision that God may bring their way. God said that He will provide for our needs. We may need to slow down and wait on God for His provision for us. His timing is not our timing. Restlessness and hasty decisions often lead to poor results in the long run.

Second Peter 2:19 states, *"For a man is a slave to whatever has mastered him."* We can be bound or restrained by anything in life, and we find that money or possessions is no exception. What are some signs of being overcome by credit?

☞ Inability to pay monthly credit card balances in full

☞ Reaching credit limits

☞ Spending over half of the paycheck on debt

☞ Receiving past due notices or penalties from creditors

☞ Thinking of credit as money to spend, not cumbersome debt

☞ The number of creditors keeps growing

☞ Spouses are not honest with each other about their use of credit

☞ Items that were once paid with cash are now put on a charge account

It is important to maintain a good payment history and credit rating. Bills should be paid on time, every time. Whenever necessary, contact should be made with the creditor if there is no way possible to pay a bill in full by the due date (such as a utility bill). If you can at least make a partial payment, call the payee and ask for permission to pay what you can and promise to pay the rest as soon as possible.

A big peril of taking on credit obligations is the possible loss of future income. When families find that they are trapped with debt, loss of income makes the situation even harder to handle. Borrowing money against future income is a decision that needs to be made carefully. Families shouldn't presume that income and situations will remain the same as they are in the present. Changes are inevitable.

📖 Read James 4:13–15 about people who boast about tomorrow.

Why do you think we should be cautious about making boastful statements such as those found in James 4:13?

_____

_____

_____

What does James say to caution readers about this attitude (James 4:14)?

_____

_____

APPLY As we consider what James says, how can we make plans for the future (James 4:15)? How do these verses relate to taking on credit obligations?

_____

_____

_____

James reminds us we need to be careful not to boast and brag about our future plans. We may have the best of intentions when we make plans. However, only God knows for sure what will happen tomorrow. Realizing this, we can strive to limit our credit obligations.

In order for us to have a a balanced financial life, our old ways of thinking must change. We are reminded in Proverbs, *"For as he thinks in his heart, so is he"* (Proverbs 23:7, NKJV). If we think and say we can't help the way things are, we eventually reap what we sow. As we study the patterns in our own lives that limit us, we can look for ways to improve and change them.

LIFE IS BUT A MIST

"Now listen, you who say, 'Today or tomorrow we will go to this or that city, spend a year there, carry on business and make money.' Why, you do not even know what will happen tomorrow. What is your life? You are a mist that appears for a little while and then vanishes. Instead, you ought to say, "If it is the Lord's will, we will live and do this or that.' " (James 4:13–15)

Borrowing and Credit

DAY TWO

AVOID BORROWING

The Bible does not forbid borrowing money. But it does not encourage it either. The topic of borrowing and owing money to others is always discussed as a negative principle in the Bible. We find many warnings to avoid borrowing.

In the book of Deuteronomy, God promises many blessings to the people of Israel if they would obey His commandments and walk in His ways. Among these great blessings, God promises He will: *"bless all the work of [their] hands. [They] will lend to many nations but will borrow from none"* (Deuteronomy 28:12). Having their needs met, the people of Israel would not need to borrow. Instead, blessed with sufficient wealth, they would lend to other nations.

Credit itself is not a problem, but the misuse of credit is. When we find ourselves depending on credit for more and more of our expenses, we must uncover the causes of our financial difficulties. When we have few or no credit obligations, our family finances are on a solid foundation.

We find ourselves in a lot of red ink today because it is easier and faster to borrow than to save. It is easier to purchase an expensive item and charge it to our credit card than it is to wait until we are able to pay with cash. When more credit is available to us, as it is for many of us, we are tempted to use more of it. Remember that a credit limit is not a cash account. Impulsive and hasty decisions are usually not the best decisions. Proverbs 19:2 reminds us, *"It is not good to have zeal without knowledge, nor to be hasty and miss the way."*

When people have reached the point of serious financial difficulties, many of them often find themselves going to God for help and for answers. Learning to depend on God for their needs, they go directly to the Source of all knowledge and blessings.

King David is an example of someone who hit "rock bottom" several times for different reasons throughout his life. King David's prayer in Psalm 119 is one of real communion and honor to the Lord. He esteems God's word and writes of the benefits of following it. David desires understanding so he can live a life that pleases God.

📖 Read Psalm 119:33–40, observing what David longs for.

What are the first four words of Psalm 119:33?

_____

_____

According to Psalm 119:36, David wanted to turn his heart away from what?

_____

_____

In Psalm 119:37, from what did David want his eyes to turn away?

_____

_____

What kind of attitude does David display in verses 33–40?

_____

_____

In these verses we sense David's attitude of submission and dependence on God. Desiring to delight in the Lord and His laws, David wants to turn away from selfish gain (verse 36). David doesn't want his life to be overcome by worthless things that get in the way of the more important matters in life (verse 37).

As we gain insight into how we can improve our finances, it's essential to follow through with this knowledge. As we continue to work on being better managers of our financial resources, our financial situation will improve.

No longer confined by financial burdens, we gain enormous benefits. Some of these great advantages are:

Surplus Money—Paying off our debts allows us to have surplus money, increasing cash flow. This enables us to focus less on our bills, and on other

"The LORD will open the heavens, the storehouse of his bounty, to send rain on your land in season and to bless all the work of your hands. You will lend to many nations but will borrow from none."

Deuteronomy 28:12

things in life besides ourselves and our money problems. We can redirect our income and time to short-term and long-term goals.

Full Ownership—When we borrow money, even though we may be current on all our monthly payments, we are still under the lender's authority. However, we are less likely to lose our assets when our obligations are paid in full. We are the rightful owners and we retain full ownership.

A More Stable Financial Position—No doubt you've heard the Golden Rule: *"Do to others what you would have them do to you"* (Luke 7:12). However, there is another Golden Rule used by lenders that states: "Those with the gold make the rules." Those who do not have the "gold," or money, are dependent on those who have access to the gold. When we have a stable financial position, we gain more independence financially.

More Prepared for a Job Loss—In today's rapidly cycling business environment, we can no longer expect long-term security in our jobs. However, when we have few or no credit obligations, it is easier to handle the loss of a job. We can depend on the emergency and savings funds we set aside to get us through this time of transition.

Living More on Less—When we have fewer financial obligations, we are able to live on less income. By using cash for purchases, we eliminate interest payments, saving us thousands of dollars every year. People often comment that they don't know *why* they can't get ahead financially. A likely reason may be that a large percentage of their income is already spoken for with credit obligations. They have little financial leverage left to pay extra on their loans.

Psychological and Physiological Benefits—Kicking the credit habit allows us to truly enjoy life more. Cutting back on impulse spending and learning to be wise consumers leads to a more satisfying and sufficient way of life. As we free ourselves from our credit obligations, we find we gain these benefits:

Better Communication—When a tight budget and unpaid bills are no longer a preoccupation, communication improves between spouses and family members. Relationships at home and at work show improvement.

Contentment—Individuals who have good money habits and who plan well are more content in life. Our ability to handle money responsibly creates more contentment.

More Confidence in the Future—Having a debt-free lifestyle helps reduce the worries of tomorrow's uncertainties. We can plan for a comfortable future by how we live today. When we have little or no debt, a controlled lifestyle, and trust in God, we no longer need to be anxious about tomorrow.

A Simpler and Calmer Life—Life becomes freeing when we can cut back on all that overwhelms us. As we pay off our financial obligations, we realize we can slow down our pace in life. We are less rushed and more relaxed. We no longer feel like we are in a "rat race" and our lives become less demanding and complicated. As our financial obligations become more manageable, life is greatly simplified.

Less Stress—It seems our society today is dealing with more signs of stress than ever before. Less stress and worry lead to better health. Living with many credit obligations easily multiplies stress and anxiety. Individuals find that symptoms from health problems improve when financial matters are dealt with.

More Focused on Others—Being free of credit obligations enables us to better help others as we become aware of their needs. We are no longer caught up in our own world of worries and natural indifference to others. We find we are better able to use our gifts and abilities to help people and worthy organizations.

Kicking the credit habit allows us to truly enjoy life more. Cutting back on impulse spending and learning to be wise consumers leads to a more satisfying and sufficient way of life.

Freedom to Change Careers—When job satisfaction polls are taken, a surprisingly large number of workers are dissatisfied with their jobs. When we are no longer dependent on every dollar of income to pay our current bills, there is more freedom to change jobs or careers. With proper planning, we can take the opportunity to pursue other career and work interests.

 Take a few moments to reflect on how your personal or family life would be different today if you had fewer or even no debt obligations. How would you spend your time differently? How might your relationships be different? Consider your reasons and use these as a catalyst for creating your financial freedom.

Earlier in our Bible study you listed your life goals. Listing your goals brings you one step closer to completing them. The good news is that positive action leads to a disciplined lifestyle. And a disciplined lifestyle opens up options and choices you may never have imagined.

While achieving our goals, we have a clear vision of what we want and the confidence to carry out goals. We have a structured plan, and yet remain flexible for God's direction in our lives. The Book of Proverbs reassures us with these words, *"We can make our plans, but the final outcome is in God's hands. . . . Commit your work to the Lord, then it will succeed"* (Proverbs 16:1, 3, LB).

REPAY YOUR OBLIGATIONS

When a person borrows money, he promises to pay the lender according to the terms agreed upon. The promise is a solemn vow that is not to be taken lightly. The agreement is to be carried out as promised. The rights belong to the lender, not the borrower. Proverbs 22:7 states, *"The rich rule over the poor, and the borrower is servant to the lender."*

We are obligated to pay what is owed when we borrow from a friend or relative, use our credit cards for purchases, or take out a loan. As Christians we are held even more accountable, for we are expected to have a higher standard of conduct. Psalm 37:21 says, *"The wicked borrow and do not repay."* The godly, however, conduct business fairly, knowing that the actions of the righteous should honor the Lord. Desiring to live with integrity, we must avoid being stumbling blocks for others. Paul wrote the believers, *"We put no stumbling block in anyone's path, so that our ministry will not be discredited"* (2 Corinthians 6:3).

The Bible teaches many principles concerning borrowing. Scripture does not discuss borrowing and lending in glowing terms. We are reminded throughout the Bible to think carefully about our actions and plans, for we will be responsible for the outcome. If we choose to borrow, we should be well aware of the consequences. The author of Ecclesiastes claimed, *"It is better not to vow than to make a vow and not fulfill it. Do not let your mouth lead you into sin. And do not protest to the temple messenger, 'My vow was a mistake' "* (Ecclesiastes 5:5–6). We are told to keep our word once a vow is made. Consequently, we should guard our steps and carefully make our decisions. Yet it seems we find an increasing number of people coming up with excuses as to why they should *not* have to pay their debts, as opposed to why they

The book of Proverbs reassures us with these words, "We can make our plans, but the final outcome is in God's hands. . . . Commit your work to the Lord, then it will succeed."

Proverbs 16:1, 3 (LB)

Borrowing and Credit
DAY THREE

Psalms 37:21 says, "The wicked borrow and do not repay." The godly, however, conduct business fairly, knowing that the actions of the righteous should honor the Lord.

should pay them. Although incomes have steadily increased, bankruptcies have become more prevalent. People are taking back their vows of repayment to their lenders. By their words and actions, those in default on loans and credit cards or who have filed for bankruptcy are not known for being reliable. God looks for people who will follow through with their promises. He blesses them and their children. *"Many a man proclaims his own loyalty, but who can find a trustworthy man? A righteous man who walks in his integrity—How blessed are his sons after him"* (Proverbs 20:6–7, NASB).

Contrast the wonderful picture of God blessing righteous people and their children with another image of children growing up with the same attitude as their parents: that of disregard for authority and failure to fulfill their promises. In the latter picture, parents do not instill values of honesty and patience to save or pay back a lender. They act as though *their* rights come first. They live with little regard for the lender, thinking of themselves as victims when they are asked to pay what they promised to pay.

📖 Paul emphasizes the importance of obeying and giving honor to those in authority. (He is a great example of one who submitted to the Roman soldiers and authorities as a prisoner in Rome). In Romans 13, Paul writes concerning having a proper attitude toward those in authority and how to live with our neighbors. Read Romans 13:1–10 about directives for us to follow.

What two reasons does Paul give for submitting to authorities (Romans 13:5)?

_____

_____

Write Romans 13:7, noting the directive for what is owed.

_____

_____

_____

_____

According to Romans 13:8, what should not remain outstanding?

_____

_____

Describe love, according to Romans 13:10.

_____

_____

Some families make excuses why they *can't* repay a lender, when in reality, they have the ability to repay. They have decided, for whatever reason, they *won't* pay back what they borrowed. We are reminded again, *"Do not withhold good from those who deserve it, when it is in your power to act"* (Proverbs 3:27).

Other families believe that living on credit is a kind of financial planning. They have no intention of ever getting out of debt and have become addicted to living life "on the edge" through credit. The lifestyle they've become accustomed to "lends itself" to remaining in debt.

"Let no debt remain outstanding, except the continuing debt to love one another, for he who loves his fellow man has fulfilled the law."

Romans 13:8

Too many families have learned to depend on credit cards to get through crunch times. This has led to unmanageable bills for families already on tight budgets. Since credit cards have higher interest rates, it's important to begin paying down the credit cards first.

Some families have turned to bill consolidation loans for a temporary solution. Yet, the loan isn't the solution to financial problems if the root of the problem is not resolved first. The loan won't change one's spending habits.

One drawback of consolidation loans is that people tend to stop worrying about their bills and spend even more. Studies show that many people make more purchases immediately after consolidating. They mistakenly think that with the financial pressure off them, they can be more at ease and let up their guard. Another drawback is the consolidation loan's presence on their credit record.

📖 There's a story in the Old Testament of a widow who owed money to her creditors, but all she had in her possession was a jar of oil. The creditor was ready to take her two children as slaves. Read about the miracle in 2 Kings 4:1–7 that turned this woman's life around.

Write your insights found in this story.

_____

_____

_____

_____

It's important to remember that we can trust God to work in our lives and perform both little and big financial miracles. We must never give up hope on the One who has always been loyal to His children. *"Being confident of this, that he who began a good work in you will carry it on to completion until the day of Christ Jesus"* (Philippians 1:6).

As we finish today's lesson, we are reminded that if we obey God and desire to please Him, we *can* receive what we ask of Him. Our prayers will be answered. John encourages us with these words, *"Dear friends, if our hearts do not condemn us, we have confidence before God and receive from him anything we ask, because we obey his commands and do what pleases him"* (1 John 3:21–22).

COSIGNING, OR SURETY

Borrowing and Credit

DAY FOUR

This week we have been looking at the Bible's emphasis that borrowing should be done wisely and sparingly. Today we will examine what the Bible says about cosigning on a loan, or being surety for another.

The Bible talks about *surety*, defined as "one who agrees to be responsible for the debt or default of another."[2] By agreeing to becoming surety, you are liable for another person's debt. Scripture warns against surety as a principle; however, it does not condemn it. Consenting to be surety for another is presuming upon your friend or family member's future and your own future. Someone who puts up surety is *not* staying out of harm's way, since the outcome is unknown.

The Bible talks about surety, defined as "one who agrees to be responsible for the debt or default of another." By agreeing to becoming surety, you are liable for another person's debt.

We will look at Proverbs 6:1–5 as we learn more about surety. Proverbs 6:1 begins with a warning to those who *"have become surety for your neighbor, have given a pledge for a stranger"* (NASB). The word *neighbor* is derived from the Hebrew noun *rea* and can have several meanings. It can mean "a close friend, an acquaintance, someone who is part of the family."[3] Verse one also specifies the action of giving *"a pledge for a stranger."* Continuing in verse one, the words *given a pledge* mean "becoming a guarantor, like shaking hands on an agreement."[4]

📖 Note what the Bible says about surety in Proverbs 6:1–5. Solomon's words of counsel are intended for the son *after* he has already pledged to be surety for someone.

Proverbs 6:2 says one who has given a pledge to surety has done two things. What are they?

_____

_____

What clear directive does Proverbs 6:3 make for one who has pledged surety?

_____

_____

Solomon compares freeing oneself from surety to what actions (Proverbs 6:5)?

_____

_____

Proverbs 6:3 states, *"Go and humble yourself; press your plea with your neighbor!"* Adam Clarke explains, "Continue to press him . . . to pay his creditor; give him no rest till he does it, or you may expect to be left to pay the debt").[5]

Matthew Henry, writes,

"It is every man's wisdom to keep out of debt as much as [possible], for it is an encumbrance upon him, entangles him in the world, puts him in danger of doing wrong or suffering wrong. It is a great folly to entangle ourselves with [needy] people, and to become bound for their debts. . . . A man ought never to be bound as surety for more than he is both able and willing to pay, and can afford to pay without wronging his family, in case the principal fail, for he ought to look upon it as his own debt."[6]

Let's look at other warnings in Proverbs on surety:

11:15—*"He who puts up security for another will surely suffer, but whoever refuses to strike hands in pledge is safe."*

20:16—*Take the garment of one who puts up security for a stranger; hold it in pledge if he does it for a wayward woman."*

22:26–27—*"Do not be a man who strikes hands in pledge or puts up security for debts; if you lack the means to pay, your very bed will be snatched from under you."*

The Bible is very clear on the dangers of offering surety or collateral for someone else. People often think that by providing surety for a friend or family member they are merely doing a favor for that person. They believe it will only involve the inconvenience of the time it takes to sign the loan papers. The cosigner probably signs fully expecting the initial borrower to make the monthly payments.

In general, business transactions today require a cosigner for a loan when the borrower is a high-risk case for a professional lender. The cosigner makes the loan possible.

When you agree to cosign, in reality, you are a co-borrower. You agree to take on another person's debt. However, should the initial borrower default on the payments, your assets, possessions, and good name may be in jeopardy to cover that debt. You can expect the lender to use typical procedures for debt collection such as adding legal and collection fees. If necessary, the lender may also garnish your wages.

If the initial borrower misses several payments, expect to get a phone call asking you to immediately make up for the late payments, and bring the account up-to-date. This is "business as usual" for the lender. After all, in order for the loan to be possible, lenders needed your credit record and debt ratio information. It is your signature that secures the loan. Be ready and expect to step in if needed.

Anyone who cosigns a loan is equally responsible with the initial borrower for the loan made. Both the borrower and the cosigner owe from the time the loan is signed. The initial borrower's pay record in essence becomes the cosigner's pay record.

Even though the loan may be paid in full by the initial borrower, the new loan affects the cosigner's credit. Credit agencies receive the loan information, whether you are an initial borrower or not. Professional lenders consider the loans made through cosigning as additional liability on their records. This can keep the cosigner from getting other personal credit in the future.

If the borrower falls behind on payments, there is no guarantee that the cosigner will know what is going on. The lenders consider the secondary borrowers equally responsible for the payments. Depending on the system of the lender, the cosigner will be contacted about late payments. The unsettling part is that personal credit rating and the good name of the cosigner are affected negatively.

When asked to be a cosigner, think about the facts and consequences. Many friendships have been hurt or lost by the good intentions of cosigning for a friend or relative. You may have heard of someone who encountered troubles as a result of being a co-borrower. What were some of the consequences?

_____

_____

_____

The Bible is clear concerning signing for others' loans. Proverbs 17:18 states, *"It is poor judgment to countersign another's note, to become responsible for his debts"* (LB).

> **"It is poor judgment to countersign another's note, to become responsible for his debts."**
>
> **Proverbs 17:18 (LB)**

REDUCE CREDIT OBLIGATIONS

In Week Eight we began tracking our spending and decided on a manageable spending plan. We carefully looked at our spending habits and ways we could create more cash flow in our budget and calculated what we need to live on. As unnecessary spending is eliminated, we can take that money and apply it to our credit card bills and other higher interest bills.

One of the best "investments" we can make is to pay off our high interest debt. In most cases, credit card balances should be paid off first. If all we do is make the minimum payments each month, expect to make payments for years to come. Look for ways that other money sources can be freed up so the credit card balances can be paid down even more quickly. Consider selling assets no longer needed or used. Search the closets, bookshelves, and garage for items that can be sold.

As you pay each credit card off, celebrate that you are becoming debt-free. Do not hinder your progress by applying for new credit cards. Make it a habit to pay with cash, not credit. Consider only using credit cards for purchases that lend themselves to a credit card transaction (reserving and renting a vehicle, reserving a hotel room, or purchasing plane tickets). However, as soon as the monthly statement arrives, set aside money to pay the card's balance in full to avoid paying interest. If you are still carrying revolving debt on the card, at least pay the total amount of your purchases for that month along with a minimum payment on the revolving portion of the debt. (This way you are not adding to your revolving debt load.)

Tackle those credit obligations. As each loan is paid in full, take the amount of money that was going toward the first loan and put it toward the next loan. Plan to reduce your credit obligations more quickly with a rapid debt-reduction plan. Plan by setting a date when you will become debt-free.

Once we have all of our credit balances paid off and we're operating on a cash basis, we won't need to concern ourselves with the interest rates that take more of our hard-earned money. As we pay down the balance on each loan, we'll be even more motivated and excited to keep at it.

It serves no benefit to develop a plan to tackle credit obligations if we don't put it into action. If we find ourselves taking a detour from our spending plan and financial goals, we need to immediately ask ourselves *why* and quickly correct course. Could it be that we have taken on more debt because we have easily become conformed to this world? *"Don't copy the behavior and customs of this world, but be a new and different person with a fresh newness in all you do and think. Then you will learn from your own experience how his ways will really satisfy you"* (Romans 12:2, LB). We can have success in paying off our debts as we think more of our eternal and kingdom rewards as believers and less of our earthly treasures.

📖 Read about the natural battle between God and money in Matthew 6:19–24.

What happens to earthly treasures (verse 19)?

_____

_____

"Don't copy the behavior and customs of this world, but be a new and different person with a fresh newness in all you do and think. Then you will learn from your own experience how his ways will really satisfy you."

Romans 12:2 (LB)

Where are we to "store up" our treasures (verse 20)?

_____

_____

Finish this verse found in Matthew 6:21: *"For where your treasure is _____ _____ ____ _____."*

Write Matthew 6:24 in your own words.

_____

_____

After Jesus spoke these words, the book of Luke records what happened next. *"The Pharisees, who loved money, heard all this and were sneering at Jesus. He said to them, 'You are the ones who justify yourselves in the eyes of men, but God knows your hearts. What is highly valued among men is detestable in God's sight'"* (Luke 16:14–15).

Matthew 6:24 states, *"You cannot serve God and mammon"* (NASB). *Barnes Notes on the Bible* states:

> Mammon is a Syriac word, a name given to an idol worshipped as a god or riches. The Jews used this word to denote wealth. The meaning is, you cannot serve the true God, and at the same time be supremely engaged in obtaining the riches of this world. One must interfere with the other.[7]

Clarke's Commentary on the Bible comments,

> He who gives his heart to the world robs God of it, and, in snatching at the shadow of earthly good, loses substantial and eternal blessedness. How dangerous it is to set our heart on riches, seeing it is so easy to make them our God![8]

📖 Read Proverbs 21:29.

What does a wicked man do? How does an upright man live?

_____

_____

📖 Read Proverbs 27:12 on how the wise live.

What does the prudent person do? What happens to the "simple" who don't change their ways?

_____

_____

_____

_____

_____

_____

If we don't reduce our credit obligations in a timely manner, we are endangering our future and our family's future. Just as the weather can be unpredictable, our tomorrow is also unpredictable. We can be better prepared for the uncertain future.

"The prudent see danger and take refuge, but the simple keep going and suffer for it."

Proverbs 27:12

 Look more objectively at your lifestyle and find ways to cut down on non-essential costs. Consider how you might be able to adjust spending even more, so that you can immediately take action with a rapid debt-reduction plan. Talk with other family members, if necessary, and decide how expenses can be reduced even more in the following areas: home expenses, utilities, transportation, food, clothing, and entertainment. What are these new cost-cutting plans? List them here.

Home expenses

_____
_____
_____
_____

Utilities

_____
_____
_____
_____

Transportation

_____
_____
_____
_____

Food

_____
_____
_____
_____

Clothing

_____
_____
_____
_____

Entertainment

_____
_____
_____
_____

Work to pay off debts early. The advantages certainly outweigh the disadvantages. Make the decision to be debt-free! And believe that God will help you make it happen. Honor Him with your choices and your decisions.

Write a prayer to the Lord, or make a journal entry in the space provided.

_____

_____

_____

_____

_____

_____

_____

_____

_____

_____

_____

_____

Work to pay off debts early. The advantages certainly outweigh the disadvantages.

NOTES

1. Ron Blue, *Master Your Money* (Nashville, TN: Thomas Nelson, Inc., 1991), 113.

2. *Funk & Wagnalls Standard Desk Dictionary*, Vol. 2, (USA: Harper & Row Publishers, Inc. 1984), 680.

3. Spiros Zodhiates, *Hebrew-Greek Key Word Study Bible* (Chattanooga, TN: AMG Publishers, 1990), 1776.

4. Ibid., 1793.

5. Adam Clarke, *Adam Clarke's Commentary on the Bible*, "Proverbs 6:3 Commentary." In e-Sword Bible software database, 2005, Rick Meyers.

6. Matthew Henry, *Matthew Henry's Commentary on the Whole Bible,* "Proverbs 6:3 Commentary." In e–Sword software database, 2005, Rick Meyers.

7. Albert Barnes, *Albert Barnes' Notes on the Bible*, "Matthew 6:24 Commentary." In e-Sword software database, 2005, Rick Meyers.

8. Clarke, *Adam Clarke's Commentary on the Bible*, "Matthew 6:24 Commentary."

Notes

Saving and Planning
For Future Needs

While we work to pay off our financial obligations, we must not neglect to prepare and save for future needs. The Bible talks about the importance of saving our resources for a later time. As we become more prepared for the future, our hope and outlook on life will be renewed.

There are several examples in the Old Testament of people who strategically saved their resources for a time they would be needed. We will take a brief look at the lives of two men who walked with God (Noah and Joseph) and were used for His purposes. Then we will look some more into what Scripture has to say about saving for the future. And along the way we will offer practical suggestions for saving for an emergency fund, investing money for retirement, and protecting your family with life insurance.

Saving for Short-term Goals

When God saw man's wickedness on the earth, Noah was found to have favor in God's eyes. *"Noah was a righteous man, blameless among the people of his time, and he walked with God"* (Genesis 6:9). God told Noah that, though He would bring floodwaters on the earth and everything on the earth would perish, he would save Noah and his family. Noah did what God commanded, building an ark according to His

Saving and Planning

DAY ONE

plans, and bringing into the ark two of every living creature, male and female (Genesis 6:17–19).

Noah was also told *"to take every kind of food that is to be eaten and store it away as food for you and for them"* (Genesis 6:21). Imagine the enormity of the tasks of rounding up all the animals, then gathering and storing enough food for them. This was no small feat. Yet Noah was faithful in obeying God. The verse following the directive for Noah to store the food says, *"Noah did everything just as God commanded him"* (Genesis 6:22). Noah, his family, and all of the animals walked safely onto dry ground after having lived for over a year in the ark. God blessed Noah and his sons, Shem, Ham, and Japheth. They were the fathers of *"the people who were scattered over the earth"* (Genesis 9:18–19).

Joseph, Jacob's son, carefully managed and saved the resources of the land of Egypt. Pharaoh recognized that Joseph was a man of godly wisdom and put him in charge of overseeing the entire nation of Egypt (Genesis 41:41). Joseph was thirty years old when he began traveling throughout Egypt. He oversaw the collection of grain and food for seven years, storing it in the cities near the locations where the food was grown (Genesis 41:46–48). *"During the seven years of abundance the land produced plentifully"* (verse 47).

Joseph was prepared for the seven years of famine that came later. When the Egyptians began begging for food, Pharaoh told them go to Joseph for assistance. Having wisely planned ahead, Joseph sold the grain to the Egyptians that had been set-aside in the storehouses. And there was enough grain left over to supply other needy countries with food (Genesis 41:55–57). God used the extra supplies of food to preserve Jacob's family who was living in Canaan at the time of the severe famine. Jacob's son Judah was part of Jesus' royal line. He was the ancestor *"of Joseph, the husband of Mary, of whom was born Jesus, who is called Christ"* (Matthew 1:2, 16).

Scripture encourages us to prepare for the future. In fact, it tells us to look at the ants who are *"extremely wise"* because *"they store up their food in the summer"* (Proverbs 30:24–25). We are told to learn a practical lesson from the ant, a small creature of God's creation.

📖 A warning against the folly of being surety for a neighbor (Proverbs 6:1–5) is followed by a warning against a person's inaction to be prepared. Read Proverbs 6:6–11, about how Solomon observed the small ant and its wisdom.

Why should we consider the ant's ways (Proverbs 6:6)?

_____

_____

What does the ant do (Proverbs 6:8)?

_____

According to Proverbs 6:9–10, what does Solomon call someone who does not store provisions for the future?

_____

What are the consequences of *not* storing provisions (Proverbs 6:11)?

_____

_____

> **"A man who loves pleasure becomes poor; wine and luxury are not the way to riches!"**
>
> **Proverbs 21:17 (LB)**

The wise ant plans ahead by storing for future needs. Matthew Henry adds,

> We must prepare for [tomorrow] and not mind the present time only, not eat up all, and lay up nothing, but in gathering time treasure up for a spending time. Thus provident we must be . . . not with anxious care, but with a prudent foresight.[1]

What keeps people from saving for the future? For some individuals it is their overindulgent lifestyle. They think only of the present. They focus on themselves and the pleasures of life. Paul warns Timothy of this group of people:

> *"In the last days it is going to be very difficult to be a Christian. For people will love only themselves and their money; they will be proud and boastful, sneering at God, disobedient to their parents, ungrateful to them, and thoroughly bad. They will be hardheaded and never give in to others; they will be constant liars and troublemakers and will think nothing of immorality. They will be rough and cruel, and sneer at those who try to be good. They will betray their friends; they will be hotheaded, puffed up with pride, and prefer good times to worshiping God. They will go to church, yes, but they won't really believe anything they hear. Don't be taken in by people like that"* (2 Timothy 3:1–5, LB).

We read in Proverbs of the results of this pleasure-seeking lifestyle. *"A man who loves pleasure becomes poor; wine and luxury are not the way to riches!"* (Proverbs 21:17, LB).

Another reason individuals do not save is that they are so overwhelmed with all their bills and obligations; they feel there is nothing left to save. Yet, all they need to do is just begin saving with small dollar amounts and remember to do it regularly.

Still another reason is that people may feel it is the duty of others to take care of them when needs arise. They expect the government, their family members, or other Christians to help them out. Although at times some families receive help in these ways, it's foolish to expect that these means of assistance will always be guaranteed. God will sustain us, but we must also do our part.

Just as we can learn to master our money by budgeting, we can learn to master our money by saving on a regular basis. Even though all we may be able to set aside is a small amount of money, it's a beginning. Saving consistently will be rewarded.

Save for current needs and unexpected expenses. Be prepared for a possible loss of income. Have an emergency fund and maintain it. Be able to have access to the cash quickly, if necessary. Cash reserves are most commonly kept in checking accounts, savings accounts, short-term Certificates of Deposit, or money market funds. Consider having your accounts at a credit union. Credit unions are nonprofit organizations that typically offer higher rates on checking and savings accounts.

Make savings automatic. Take advantage of automatic payroll for savings. Save "extra" money from bonuses, tax refunds, a second job, and gifts. Watch the amount of money grow as you stay focused on building an emergency fund and other savings funds!

Just as we can learn to master our money by budgeting, we can learn to master our money by saving on a regular basis.

SAVING FOR INTERMEDIATE AND LONG-TERM GOALS

As we work on reducing our debts, we should increase our savings. Family members need to work together on planning for their intermediate and long-term goals.

Intermediate financial goals are made with the intent of accomplishing them within one to five years. These goals may be paying off all credit card or installment debt. It could include saving to buy a new vehicle with cash, saving money for major home improvements, (such as exterior siding, new plumbing, new flooring, updated kitchens and bathrooms, etc.).

Long-term financial goals are made with a time frame of five years, fifteen years, and even longer. This could include saving for our children's college education, a new home, or starting a business. Saving for retirement is probably the most important of long-term goals. One of the best ways to save for retirement is to have an automatic payroll withdrawal into your employer's defined contribution plan. The most common tax-deferred plans are the 401(k) or the 403(b). (The 403[b] plans are available to nonprofit institutions.) If your employer matches the funds you contribute or a percentage of the contribution, you can save even more in your pretax plan. Dollar amounts can also be regularly set aside into other retirement vehicles such as Individual Retirement Accounts (IRAs) and Roth accounts.

We must be intentional about planning and saving adequately for a long-term horizon. *"A sluggard does not plow in season; so at harvest time he looks but finds nothing"* (Proverbs 20:4). A sluggard is "a person habitually lazy or idle."[2] A paraphrase of this verse says, *"If you won't plow in the cold, you won't eat at the harvest"* (LB). Even when circumstances are not always favorable, by persevering we will be able to enjoy life more in the harvest, or during the latter years of our lives.

We know it's not always easy to set aside money for future needs and goals. It is often tempting to spend our money as we're overcome by today's wants. We are reminded that, *"A man's life does not consist in the abundance of his possessions"* (Luke 12:15). As we plan for our future, we must carefully consider what we are able to save today.

📖 Before we set out to do something, it is important to count the cost. Read Luke 14:28–30 on saving adequately for our needs.

Have you known anyone who began a project and then had to bail out because of the lack of money or resources?

_____

_____

Jesus uses this analogy to explain the importance of counting the cost of being His disciple.

 Think about your financial goals.

> **"A man's life does not consist in the abundance of his possessions."**
>
> **Luke 12:15**

Briefly list your intermediate financial goals:

_____

_____

_____

_____

_____

Will you be able to accomplish them, at the rate you're going? If so, keep it up!

_____

_____

Briefly list your long-term financial goals:

_____

_____

_____

_____

_____

Luke 14:29 gives the illustration of a builder laying the foundation of a tower, then not being able to complete it. Consider your lifestyle today. Will you be able to maintain your lifestyle during your retirement years, or will you need to cut back on living expenses and make some changes?

Read Proverbs 21:20 about saving.

What is found in the house of the wise?

_____

_____

What does the foolish person do (Proverbs 21:20)?

_____

_____

The New American Standard Bible states, *"There is precious treasure and oil in the dwelling of the wise, but a foolish man swallows it up"* (Proverbs 21:20). *Barnes' Notes on the Bible* comments, "The wise man keeps a store in reserve. He gains uprightly, spends moderately, never exhausts himself."[3] According to Matthew Henry,

> *"Those that are wise will increase what they have. Their wisdom will teach them to proportion their expenses to their income and to lay up for [tomorrow]. There is a treasure of things . . . laid up in season, and particularly of oil, one of the staples commodities of Canaan."*

How can we best learn "to proportion" our expenses today and at the same time save for the future? We can discuss our expenses with our spouse and other family members and look for workable ways to save. We can meet with reputable financial advisors who will objectively assess our financial stand-

> *"The wise man keeps a store in reserve. He gains uprightly, spends moderately, never exhausts himself."*
>
> **—Albert Barnes**

ing.

While saving what we can, we must not neglect to take our matters of concern to God, our Provider. Paul encourages us to *"be strong in the Lord, and in His mighty power"* (Ephesians 6:10). *"With all prayer and petition pray at all times in the Spirit"* (Ephesians 6:18, NASB). The word *petition* refers to "supplication or prayer for particular benefits."[5] Philippians 4:6 says, *"Be anxious for nothing, but in everything by prayer and supplication with thanksgiving let your requests be made known to God."* When we ask for God's wisdom and help, He will provide in ways we couldn't have imagined. Let's believe that He will answer us and provide for our specific requests.

Why pray? Part of praying is asking God for wisdom, provision, His compassion, and mercy. We can pray even when we are going through difficult times. When the prophet Jeremiah wrote the book of Lamentations, he was in a somber mood. He was overwhelmed with the destruction of Jerusalem and the suffering it had caused. Yet it was during this time that he penned these beautiful words of hope and trust:

> *Because of the LORD's great love we are not consumed,*
> *for his compassions never fail.*
> *They are new every morning; great is your faithfulness.*
> *I say to myself, 'The LORD is my portion; therefore I will wait for him.'*
> *The LORD is good to those whose hope is in him, to the one who seeks him;*
> *It is good to wait quietly for the salvation of the LORD."* (Lamentations 3:22–26)

Having lived a long life, King David could confidently say, *"I was young and now I am old, yet I have never seen the righteous forsaken or their children begging bread"* (Psalms 37:25). He was reassured that the righteous won't be forgotten or abandoned. David knew without a doubt that he could trust God to be faithful. As people who want to obey and serve God, we can trust Him with that same resolve. *"For the LORD loves the just and will not forsake his faithful ones"* (Psalms 37:28).

Saving and Planning

DAY THREE

INVESTING

As we work to meet our family's needs throughout the year, we can invest the surplus. Our goal is to grow and multiply our assets for tomorrow's needs (Matthew 25:20). In order for our money to maintain its value, we need to invest it.

As we look at Jesus' parable of the servants and the ten minas (Luke 19:11–26), we are reminded that investing is another way to show our stewardship. (A mina was about three months' wages.) Jesus told this parable while traveling to Jerusalem, where He would spend His final days on earth. He told the story to help His disciples understand the kingdom of heaven.

📖 Read Luke 19:11–26, considering what the passage reveals about the present responsibility of the servants.

According to Luke 19:13, what did the nobleman tell his ten servants after giving each of them a mina?

_____

What was the first servant's reward for earning ten more minas (Luke 19:16–17)?

_____

_____

How was the second servant rewarded for earning five more minas (Luke 19:18–19)?

_____

_____

What was done with the mina that another servant did not use (Luke 19:24)?

_____

_____

According to Luke 19:26, what is a principle we learn from this parable?

_____

_____

_____

"Why then didn't you put my money on deposit, so that when I came back, I could have collected it with interest?"

Luke 19:23

From this story, we learn that before the nobleman goes to another country, he gives one mina to each servant. The servants are given the same opportunity to increase their money. The master looks for servants who would be faithful with what they have been given. The results show different degrees of improvement. By investing, one servant multiplies his mina by ten. Another produces five more minas with the one he is entrusted. The servant who neglected to invest his share of his gift was left with only the one mina the nobleman had given him earlier.

God has given resources to each of us. We cannot say that we haven't received anything of significance. To the ones who increase their resources, God will give more. Those who neglect their responsibility to increase what they've been given will not be profitable. This parable teaches us that God expects his children to use their resources well. It also shows us that faithful servants will be rewarded according to their degrees of faithfulness.

APPLY List some resources and abilities that God has given you.

_____

_____

_____

_____

Have you ever thought about your money as being loaned to you from God? If Jesus returned today, would you be able to say you were faithful in investing your money and resources?

_____

_____

This parable speaks about our present responsibility as Christ's servants and our future judgment in heaven. When Christ returns in His glory, we will be asked to show how well we managed and invested our resources. As we strive to live faithfully, we will also be rewarded here on earth. *"Love the LORD, all his saints! The LORD preserves the faithful"* (Psalms 31:23).

Investing for Our Future

As we find workable ways to save for our present needs, we must also consider ways to wisely invest for our retirement years. Just as it is important to consult with our spouses concerning spending plans or budgets, it is just as important to consult with them about long-term savings and investments. Husbands and wives need to be accountable to each other for financial decisions affecting them and other family members. Opinions need to be exchanged freely and honestly, and investment options should be considered carefully.

Our spouses can help us decide among our investing options; they provide another cushion of protection against poor decisions. When a spouse doesn't have a peace about an investment option, that needs to be taken into consideration. Couples who are willing to listen and respect each other will benefit greatly from this. They can put their pride and ego aside and desire to make the best decisions possible for their family. Single adults can consult with trusted friends and advisors on the best options for them. *"Humility and the fear of the LORD bring wealth and honor and life"* (Proverbs 22:4).

When planning and saving for the future, don't limit your funds to one type of investment. Diversification reduces the risk of a catastrophic loss. Study all your options available and look for investments where time is "on your side" and working for you.

Be willing to weigh all counsel and advice. *"Where there is no counsel, the people fall; but in the multitude of counselors there is safety"* (Proverbs 11:14, NKJV). Work with a financial advisor, if necessary. Get references. What is the philosophy of the investment advisor? Does he or she have a good track record?

You may be approached by a promoter or friend to "invest" in a great moneymaking deal. He may put pressure on you to act quickly, desiring to collect your money as soon as possible. He may say that there are other potential investors lined up to participate, such as your friends and acquaintances. Don't be pressured to make a quick decision.

The investment idea may sound like a "deal of a lifetime," a great deal that cannot be passed up. However, it's important to remember the good advice of sticking with what you know. It is best to stay within your areas of expertise, the areas where you have the most experience and training.

Be careful with the desire to speculate with your money. Solomon, in all his wisdom, warned about "get-rich-quick" schemes:

> *"There is another serious problem I have seen everywhere—savings are put into risky investments that turn sour, and soon there is nothing left to pass on to one's son. The man who speculates is soon back to where he began—with nothing. This, as I said, is a very serious problem, for all his hard work has been for nothing; he has been working for the wind. It is swept away. All the rest of his life he is under a cloud—gloomy, discouraged, frustrated, and angry."* (Ecclesiastes 5:13–17, LB)

Some people are tempted to act dishonestly in their investments because of their strong desire to attain wealth. They may rationalize their questionable behavior by calling their actions "insignificant" or "harmless." They may

Our spouses can help us decide among our investing options; they provide another cushion of protection against poor decisions.

say that since other people are doing it, it must be all right. Proverbs 16:8 tells us, *"A little, gained honestly, is better that great wealth gotten by dishonest means"* (LB). People acting dishonestly are soon found out. *"The man who wants to do right will get a rich reward. But the man who wants to get rich quick will quickly fail"* (Proverbs 28:20, LB).

Solomon has an antidote for people who deliberate on how they can quickly accumulate riches. He wrote about the virtues of saving one's money steadily. *"Steady plodding brings prosperity; hasty speculation brings poverty"* (Proverbs 21:5, LB).

Saving and Planning

INSURANCE AND WILLS

Paul advises us to provide for family members in our household (1 Timothy 5:8). Having adequate health insurance is one way to provide for our families. Today, we are more dependent upon insurance coverage for good health care. Health costs have seen a staggering increase in recent years; the rate of medical inflation is growing faster than general inflation. A costly illness, medical emergency, or hospital stay could easily set us back financially. Most employers offer health insurance with group rates, which are less expensive than when purchased individually. One way to save on health insurance premiums is to have a plan with a higher deductible.

Health and Life Insurance

Life insurance benefits family members who cannot provide adequately for themselves. It helps protect the family income in the event a working parent dies. It also helps prevent the loss of the family estate through estate taxes, so the estate can be passed on to the next generation.

Life insurance premiums differ according to one's ideal level of protection, level of comfort, or minimal level of provision. A person can purchase temporary or permanent insurance. Temporary insurance is better known as "term life" and permanent insurance covers the policyholder for a lifetime. Remember that the purpose of life insurance is to help maintain our loved ones' lifestyles, not necessarily increase them. The amount of insurance that a family needs (or can afford) is generally determined by these factors: the adult's age, income, health, expenses, and the number of dependent family members.

APPLY

Briefly list the life insurance provider or providers for your family.

1) Life Insurance Company: _____

Value of Policy: $ _____

Person Insured: _____

2) Life Insurance Company: _____

Value of Policy: $ _____

Person Insured: _____

The Bible talks about the importance of leaving an inheritance for our children. There are over two hundred references for the word inheritance throughout the Bible.

3) Life Insurance Company: _____

Value of Policy: $ _____

Person Insured: _____

4) Life Insurance Company: _____

Value of Policy: $ _____

Person Insured: _____

Keep all insurance policies together for easy access. See that the insurance policy information is kept up-to-date, including beneficiaries. Keep the address and phone number of your life insurance agent current.

Providing Through a Will or Trust

Every adult should consider having a will. This prevents the state from making decisions concerning one's assets and children at the time of one's death. We can legally declare our wishes and intentions concerning the assets we leave. If we have underage children, we can designate guardians for them. A will enables us to plan ahead for charitable giving, allowing us to allocate funds to the organizations of our preference. Too many people underestimate the importance of drawing up a will.

When consulting with an attorney about a will, the attorney may suggest having a "trust" to better manage one's assets. Among other advantages, a trust helps to reduce estate expenses and to save taxes. Since there are a variety of trusts, your attorney can discuss with you the best option for your family situation.

Having a will is important, but we must realize that it's just as important to title one's assets carefully. The "Operation of Law" applies to assets where beneficiaries are named, including retirement accounts, IRA accounts, trusts, and life insurance policies. When obtaining these assets, whomever you name on the form as beneficiary will receive the assets at the time of your death. The "Operation of Law" also applies to accounts owned with another person for savings or investment. These are also known as "joint accounts."

 Do you have a will or a trust? If not, are you willing to let the state's laws decide the fate of your estate? Do you know how your assets are "titled"? Have you thought carefully about the beneficiaries of your assets? Relationships and circumstances may change. Estate and relationship problems can be prevented with open communication with family members and proper estate planning.

The Bible talks about the importance of leaving an inheritance for our children. There are over two hundred references for the word *inheritance* throughout the Bible. It was customary for a father to leave an inheritance to his children. When Rachel and Leah left their father's household, they inquired about their inheritance from their father (see Genesis 31:14). In the book of Ruth we read that Naomi sold the land she had inherited to Boaz. (see Ruth 4: 9–10). The Lord gave the people of Israel legal requirements on the matters of inheritance (Numbers 27:5–11).

📖 Read what the following verses say about inheritance.

"Wisdom, like an inheritance, is a good thing."

Ecclesiastes 7:11

According to Proverbs 13:22, who leaves an inheritance for his children's children?

_____

What is inherited from parents (Proverbs 19:14)?

_____

According to Psalms 37:18, whose inheritance will endure forever?

_____

Solomon compared an inheritance to wisdom. He stated, *"Wisdom, like an inheritance, is a good thing and benefits those who see the sun. Wisdom is a shelter as money is a shelter"* (Ecclesiastes 7:11–12).

As we close Day Four, let's remember the wonderful inheritance God our Father has left for us:

> *"Giving thanks to the Father, who has qualified you to share in the inheritance of the saints in the kingdom of light."* (Colossians 1:12)

> *"Praise be to the God and Father of our Lord Jesus Christ. In his great mercy he has given us new birth into a living hope through the resurrection of Jesus Christ from the dead, and into an inheritance that can never perish, spoil or fade—kept in heaven for you."* (1 Peter 1:3–4)

MAINTAIN FINANCIAL FREEDOM

Saving and Planning

DAY FIVE

Why do so many individuals delay saving? It may be that they find the cost of living unmanageable, and the thought of saving overwhelms them. Yet, when they don't save, they place themselves in a corner of less preparedness for life's certainties and uncertainties.

We can begin to attain financial freedom by trimming unnecessary spending and paying off debts. As we cut our spending and pay down our debts, we will generate additional funds to save.

We can maintain our financial freedom by preparing adequately for our future needs. To do this we must save a portion of our earnings on a regular basis. Here are some ways to help our payment and savings systems run more smoothly:

Set aside money into savings accounts before paying the bills. If your employer offers a 401(k) savings plan, use payroll deduction to automatically deduct an amount that works for you. (The IRS does have limits in how much you can contribute.) Also if your workplace offers "Cafeteria Plan" benefits, any amount you have payroll-deducted can be taken out of your check before withholding taxes are calculated, saving you a considerable amount in tax dollars.

Pay insurance premiums using an automatic checking withdrawal system.

We can maintain our financial freedom by preparing adequately for our future needs. To do this, we must save a portion of our earnings on a regular basis.

Have a direct deposit system set up through your workplace with a credit union or bank. This is a great tool for keeping your finances under control and for making savings automatic. Regular and preplanned amounts can be allocated for deposit directly into checking accounts, loan accounts, or savings. Savings funds can include funds for emergencies, property taxes, or education. Save time by not waiting in line to cash your paycheck.

If we find ourselves dipping into savings accounts intended for other expenses, **it is important to pay back those withdrawals as soon as possible.**

By following through with our savings goals, we are more prepared for unplanned expenses such as loss of income, unexpected medical expenses, and vehicle repairs. Financial advisors recommend setting aside three to six months' salary for an emergency fund. This may mean giving up some of our wants and desires so we can be more prepared financially for the future.

Put your savings into secure investments. To eliminate risk, go to a credit union or bank with FDIC insurance. Start saving with:

>   **A money market account**—You typically earn higher interest on these accounts than with a traditional savings account.
>
>   **A certificate of deposit, or CD**—A CD allows you to have a set interest rate for a predetermined period of time. The longer you lock in the interest rate, the higher the rate. There are penalties for early withdrawal.
>
>   **A money market mutual fund**—An investment in short-term bonds that provides a cash reserve for investors. It pays one to two percent more than a bank money market account but is not insured.

If you find it difficult to save, think about this: by saving just $50 a week, after one year those small weekly savings add up to $2,600. Better yet, if $150 a week is saved, it will have grown to $7,800.

Spend less than you make and save the rest. Establish a maximum standard of living. Decide where the surplus will go, along with the amounts.

Establish an earning plan for your retirement years. If you haven't started saving for retirement, there is no better time to begin than the present. Perhaps your employer offers 401(k) plans that you can contribute to on a regular basis. Your employer may even match what you regularly put into your account, up to a certain percentage. If your employer does not offer a 401(k) plan, open an IRA (Individual Retirement Account) and start saving. You can open an IRA at a number of banks and credit unions. Shop around for the best dividend rates.

Remember that you can get interest to work for you by saving as *much* as you can as *early* as possible. By doing so, you will have time and interest working on your side.

 During Lesson 6 of this Bible study we took a brief look at our financial goals. We listed three goals with a beginning plan of action. Today we will divide our financial goals into two groups. What changes will we need to make to be more prepared for the future?

List your financial goals and prioritize them according to their importance. Write financial goals for each category with a plan of action.

Short-Term Financial Goals	Plan of Action

Intermediate and Long-Term Financial Goals	Plan of Action

This is the time to make a better future for you and your family. Ask God for wisdom and direction as you make these important decisions and follow through with them. *"The blessing of the LORD brings wealth, and he adds no trouble to it"* (Proverbs 10:22). Talk things over with your family members and financial advisors. Then make wise decisions.

📖 Solomon acknowledges that the good things in life are a gift of God. Read Ecclesiastes 5:18–20. Write Ecclesiastes 5:18 in your own words.

_____

_____

_____

Identify the gift of God mentioned in Ecclesiastes 5:19.

_____

_____

With what does God fill our heart (Ecclesiastes 5:20)?

_____

_____

"If the LORD delights in a man's way, he makes his steps firm; though he stumble, he will not fall, for the LORD upholds him with his hand."

Psalms 37:23–24

Albert Barnes explains the last verse of this passage. He states, "The days [of a person] pass smoothly and pleasantly, while he lives in the consciousness of God's favor."[6] King David wrote, *"If the LORD delights in a man's way, he makes his steps firm; though he stumble, he will not fall, for the LORD upholds him with his hand"* (Psalms 37:23–24).

The pursuit of God's will for our lives brings enjoyment and contentment. *"He who pursues righteousness and love finds life, prosperity and honor"* (Proverbs 21:21). What a wonderful promise that God blesses people who obey and love Him!

Lord, thank You that You love and care for me. Thank You for the resources You have given to my family and me. Help me not to take them for granted. I pray for Your wisdom as I seek to use these resources sensibly. I pray that my financial decisions would be pleasing to You. In Jesus' name, I pray. Amen.

Write your own prayer or a journal entry in the space provided.

_____

_____

_____

_____

_____

_____

_____

_____

_____

Notes

1. Matthew Henry, *Matthew Henry's Commentary on the Whole Bible,* "Proverbs 6:6-11 Commentary." In e-Sword Bible software database, © 2005, Rick Meyers.

2. *Funk & Wagnalls Standard Desk Dictionary,* Vol. 2 (USA: Harper & Row Publishers, Inc., 1984), 634.

3. Albert Barnes, *Albert Barnes' Notes on the Bible,* "Proverbs 21:20 Commentary." In e-Sword Bible software database, 2005, Rick Meyers.

4. Henry, *Matthew Henry's Commentary on the Whole Bible,* "Proverbs 21:20 Commentary."

5. Spiros Zodhiates, *Hebrew-Greek Key Word Study Bible* (Chattanooga: AMG Publishers, 1990), 1819.

6. Barnes, *Albert Barnes' Notes on the Bible,* "Ecclesiastes 5:20 Commentary."

Notes

Notes

BEING CONTENT
WITH GOD'S PROVISION

Last week we looked at the importance of financial planning for the future. As we save and invest, we can be more prepared for the needs that arise in both the near and distant future stages of life. We can plan as best we can. As we learn to manage our income well, we get the most from what we have, making the best use of the resources God gives us. And we can be content knowing that no matter what happens, God will be there for us. In Lesson 11, we'll examine what it means to be satisfied with what we have, knowing that God cares for us. We can be satisfied with all that He provides for us day by day and year by year.

God has promised in His Word that He will make provision for us. Consider His words: *"Even to your old age and gray hairs I am he, I am he who will sustain you. I have made you and I will carry you; I will sustain you and I will rescue you. To whom will you compare me or count me equal? To whom will you liken me that we may be compared?"* (Isaiah 46:4–5).

What a wonderful promise that God will sustain us and carry us! No one knows us and loves us better than the One who made us. We can know without a doubt there is nothing today or in the future that *"will be able to separate us from the love of God that is in Christ Jesus our Lord"* (Romans 8:39).

> *As we save and invest, we can be more prepared for the needs that arise in both the near and distant future stages of life.*

GOD PROVIDES FOR US

As Scripture proclaims, God truly does provide for us and wants us to live by faith, depending on Him for provision. This is not easy for us to do; faith of this type doesn't come naturally. It was not easy for David, a man who had gone from being a shepherd to a great and privileged king. Yet we sense in David's psalms his strong desire to be closer to God and to find his joy in God. As we read David's psalms, we become aware that he finds his security and strength in God Himself. His joy and security are not found in his present circumstances, but in God alone.

📖 Read Psalm 145:1–21, one of David's psalms of praise. It is originally an acrostic poem, beginning with the letters of the Hebrew alphabet. Note the many ways David beautifully expressed God's greatness.

📖 Our Father cares for His creation. How much more will He care for His people. Read Psalm 34:8–10. These verses show that David wanted others to experience God's goodness and provision. He wanted others to know they could find their satisfaction in God alone. Fill in the blanks to complete these verses:

"Taste and see that _____; blessed is the man who _____. Fear the LORD, you his saints, for those who fear him_____. The lions may grow weak and hungry, but those who _____ lack no good thing." (Psalms 34:8–10)

Psalm 34:9 tells us, *"fear the LORD, you his saints."* When we fear God, we show reverence to God and honor Him. We recognize Him as being all-powerful and show that we are in awe of Him. *"The fear of the LORD is the beginning of wisdom"* (Psalms 111:10). *"The fear of the LORD teaches a man wisdom, and humility comes before honor"* (Proverbs 15:33). Does our daily life show that we honor God? Do we approach our Father God with an attitude of reverence? Psalm 34:9 tells us the result of our choice to fear the Lord: *"For those who fear him lack nothing."* Our sense of reverence for God leads us to a place of rest and security in Him. We have a deep sense of His protection and watchfulness over us.

Most little children know that they can be protected, loved, and provided for by their parents. They put their full trust in their parents, believing their mother and father will do what is best for them. They feel safe knowing their parents will provide for them and will give things that are good for them. In the same way, we also can know that our Heavenly Father will provide for us. We can approach our merciful and loving God humbly and with a sense of reliance.

Before David's son Solomon became king, David praised God before the people for making provision for the new temple in Jerusalem. For years he wanted to build a temple where his people could worship God. The time had come for the temple to be built. His son Solomon would be the one to carry out the enormous task of building this holy place of worship.

📖 Read David's prayer in 1 Chronicles 29:10–19.

According to verse 11, what belongs to the Lord?

What comes from the Lord (verse 12)?

Referring to verses 10–13, what was David's attitude toward God?

APPLY As you go about your day, how often do you honor God with praises to Him? Do you tell others of God's blessings and provision? How have you been learning to depend on God's goodness and grace? Throughout your day, you can ask God to make you more aware of the many ways He provides for us. You can also thank Him for bringing these matters to your attention.

Putting the Giver before the Material Blessings

When Moses gave his talks to the people of Israel, he told them they must not forget where their material blessings came from. He reminded them that during their forty years in the desert, God had provided them with manna to eat (Deuteronomy 8:3–4). Moses reminded them that after they entered the Promised Land, they must not forget their God. He appealed to them saying, *"You may say to yourself, 'My power and the strength of my hands have produced this wealth for me.' But remember the LORD your God, for it is he who gives you the ability to produce wealth"* (Deuteronomy 8:17–18).

If we're not careful, our wealth and possessions can get in the way of our relationships with God. It can become the central part of our life, turning our hearts from Him. In the book of Jeremiah we read: *"Let not . . . the rich man boast of his riches, but let him who boasts boast about this: that he understands and knows me, that I am the LORD, who exercises kindness, justice and righteousness on earth, for in these I delight"* (Jeremiah 9:23–24).

In the New Testament, apostle Paul wrote to a young man, Timothy, warning him to "fight the good fight of faith." He knew of the challenges and

THE LORD IS GOOD!

"They will celebrate your abundant goodness and joyfully sing of your righteousness. The Lord is gracious and compassionate, slow to anger and rich in love. The Lord is good to all; he has compassion on all he has made." (Psalms 145:7–9)

pressures Timothy would face as a pastor and leader of the converts in the early church at Ephesus. Paul thought highly of Timothy and counseled him to be loyal to God's work. His charge to Timothy to live an exemplary life also applies us today.

In 1 Timothy 6:17–19, Paul warns the people of Ephesus against trusting more in their wealth than in God. He wrote: *"Command those who are rich in this present world not to be arrogant nor to put their hope in wealth, which is so uncertain, but to put their hope in God, who richly provides us with everything for our enjoyment"* (1 Timothy 6:17). The word *wealth* in this verse literally means "money" or "possessions." Therefore, Paul tells Timothy to transmit the message to wealthy people that they should not be arrogant, nor put their hope in their money or possessions.

In the words of *The Living Bible*, 1 Timothy 6:17 states: *"Tell those who are rich not to be proud and not to trust in their money, which will soon be gone, but their pride and trust should be in the living God who always richly gives us all we need for our enjoyment."*

During Jesus' ministry on earth, most of His warnings were not directed to the poor, but to the rich. He taught many lessons on the perils of abundance and riches. He stated, *"It is hard for a rich man to enter the kingdom of heaven."* He added, *"Again I tell you, it is easier for a camel to go through the eye of a needle than for a rich man to enter the kingdom of God"* (Matthew 19:23–24). Jesus knew that in the hearts of people there was a strong affection for the things of this world.

Jesus traveled from one village to another, teaching about the kingdom of God. One day He told the parable of the sower to a large crowd that had gathered. As you read this parable, think about where the seeds fell and what happened to them. The seed is the word of God. Read the parable of the sower in Luke 8:5–15.

What grew along with the seeds and choked the plants (Luke 8:7)?

_____

What strangled or choked the hearers of the word of God and what was the result (Luke 8:14)?

_____

_____

_____

According to Luke 8:15, what act or habit helps produce a crop (Luke 8:15)?

_____

_____

_____

Believers may find that their zeal for the things of God has diminished as they've become distracted by their possessions. The distractions of this world have robbed them of an abundant life in Christ.

Not only can our possessions and wealth keep us from having a growing relationship with the Savior, but a strong desire for wealth and riches can as well. A desire for wealth can get in the way of a fulfilling and close relationship with our Lord, and the author of Hebrews tells us to eliminate the distractions that keep us from the perfecting of our faith.

> *"Let us throw off everything that hinders and the sin that so easily entangles, and let us run with perseverance the race marked out for us. Let us fix our eyes on Jesus, the author and perfecter of our faith, who for the joy set before him endured the cross, scorning its shame, and sat down at the right hand of the throne of God."* (Hebrews 12:1–2)

> *"Keep your lives free from the love of money."* (Hebrews 13:5)

 Take a moment to reflect whether your possessions or desire for riches may be causing you to take your eyes off Jesus, the perfecter of our faith. Is the love of money or possessions a barrier to your full and complete devotion to Christ? May we not be overcome by life's riches and pleasures, but may we keep our focus on the One who is our Provider.

TRUSTING IN GOD FOR OUR NEEDS

Being Content

DAY THREE

How content are we in God's care? Do we actively trust God for our needs and concerns? When we find ourselves worrying about our needs of life, we can turn our worries into a strong trust that God will provide for us. We can take all of our needs to God, without reservation.

The psalmist wrote, *"Cast your cares on the LORD and he will sustain you; he will never let the righteous fall"* (Psalms 55:22). In another psalm of praise, David said, *"You who fear him, trust in the LORD—he is their help and shield. The LORD remembers us and will bless us: He will bless the house of Israel, he will bless the house of Aaron, he will bless those who fear the LORD—small and great alike"* (Psalms 115:11–13).

When Jesus was on the mountainside teaching to the crowds, He reminded the people of our heavenly Father's care. Jesus told the crowds their heavenly Father knew of their needs and He was watchful over them. He told them they did not need to worry about the necessities of their life and told them of the cure for worry.

📖 Read the words of Jesus in Matthew 6:25–34.

Summarize verses 25–30 in a few sentences.

_____

_____

_____

_____

According to Matthew 6:30, when we worry, what is insufficient in our lives?

_____

"Cast your cares on the Lord and he will sustain you; he will never let the righteous fall."

Psalm 55:22

What directive did Jesus give in Matthew 6:33?

_____

_____

Let's look at a paraphrase of Matthew 6:31–33:

> *So don't worry at all about having enough food and clothing. Why be like the heathen? For they take pride in all these things and are deeply concerned about them. But your heavenly Father already knows perfectly well that you need them, and he will give them to you if you give him first place in your life and live as he wants you to.* (Matthew 6:31–33, LB)

Chapter 11 of Hebrews is known as the "faith chapter," and it lists names of people who displayed faith that pleased God. Beginning with Abel, the list of commendation includes biographical models who boldly persevered throughout their lives.

How is faith biblically defined? Faith is defined as *"being sure of what we hope for and certain of what we do not see"* (Hebrews 11:1). The writer of Hebrews boldly states, *"Without faith it is impossible to please God, because anyone who comes to him must believe that he exists and that he rewards those who earnestly seek him"* (Hebrews 11:6). Having faith, we can give our worries to God and believe He will keep us in His care. Faith is relying on God and putting our trust in Him.

As the apostle Peter makes his closing remarks in his first epistle, he addresses the issue of being humble and giving our worries to God. To the younger believers of the church he states, *"God opposes the proud but gives grace to the humble. Humble yourselves, therefore, under God's mighty hand, that he may lift you up in due time"* (1 Peter 5:5–6). Humbling ourselves before God, we yield our desires to Him, no longer with the attitude of desiring to hold onto what we want. Instead we surrender our will to Him, realizing, after all, that we're not completely self-sufficient.

God knows of our worries and needs, and He wants to take that burden off our shoulders and our hearts. Peter's next directive after emphasizing our need to be humble is, *"Cast all your anxiety on him because he cares for you"* (1 Peter 5:7).

The correlation of living a righteous life and having our prayers answered is very evident. As we remain in Him and obey His commands, He will be attentive to us. In John 15:7, Jesus has a promise: *"If you remain in me and my words remain in you, ask whatever you wish, and it will be given you."* In First Peter we read: *"For the eyes of the Lord are on the righteous and his ears are attentive to their prayer, but the face of the Lord is against those who do evil"* (1 Peter 3:12).

In James 4:1–4, James addresses the state of people's hearts. He chastises those who quarrel and covet because of the strong desires within them. James stated, *"When you ask, you do not receive, because you ask with wrong motives, that you may spend what you get on your pleasures"* (James 4:3). He warns that *"friendship with the world"* is not conducive to those who are friends of God (James 4:4).

Jesus reassures us that our Father knows what our needs are before we ask Him (Matthew 6:8). Yet we are told to pray for our needs. Praying to our heavenly Father should be as natural as breathing. To experience a growing relationship

"Without faith it is impossible to please God, because anyone who comes to him must believe that he exists and that he rewards those who earnestly seek him."

Hebrews 11:6

with God, we need to talk with Him daily. Praying confidently and diligently, we should be able to talk freely to God about everything that concerns us. If there comes a time when we don't want to talk to God about certain things, that may be a warning that we're not committing all of ourselves to Him. God wants all of us. Prayer keeps us in constant communion with our Lord.

📖 Jesus wants our prayers to be given with right motives and clean hearts. He gave us "The Lord's Prayer" as a model prayer. Read the prayer found in Matthew 6:9–13.

The Lord's Prayer is structured according to different areas of focus. Write the words of this prayer as they relate to adoration, intercession, petition, forgiveness, and guidance. The first part is completed as an example.

ADORATION: *"Our Father in heaven, hallowed be your name."*

INTERCESSION:

PETITION:

FORGIVENESS:

GUIDANCE:

Let us not only pray for our own needs, but let's remember to intercede for other people's needs, as well. James writes, *"pray for each another"* (James 5:16). Paul prayed consistently for the believers. *"Since the day we heard about you, we have not stopped praying for you and asking God to fill you with the knowledge of his will through all spiritual wisdom and understanding"* (Colossians 1:9). Paul prayed that they might become mature in their faith and that their love would *"increase and overflow for each other and for everyone else"* (1 Thessalonians 3:12).

We must continue to pray that the unsaved would come to know Jesus as Redeemer and Lord. In his letters to various churches, Paul requests that the believers pray for them and their ministry. He states, *"Pray for us that the message of the Lord may spread rapidly and be honored, just as it was with you"* (2 Thessalonians 3:1). Praying for the needs of our country and of the world, we're to *"carry each other's burdens"* (Galatians 6:2).

We can show our concern and care for others through our words and actions. *"An anxious heart weighs a man down, but a kind word cheers him up"* (Proverbs 12:25). Unbelievers can be more receptive to the things of God through the actions of caring Christians. The church of believers can encourage and help each other. Paul wrote to the church of the Thessalonians saying, *"Encourage one another and build each other up, just as in fact you are doing"* (1 Thessalonians 5:11).

At times we may feel that we don't know how to pray about our concerns. Even so, there is the wonderful promise that the Holy Spirit intercedes for us.

> *"The Spirit helps us in our weakness. We do not know what we ought to pray for, but the Spirit himself intercedes for us with groans that words cannot express. And he who searches our hearts knows the mind of the Spirit, because the Spirit intercedes for the saints in accordance with God's will."* (Romans 8:26–27)

How reassuring to know that we always have an intercessor for us!

God invites us to share our needs and concerns with Him and encourages us to depend on Him, not on our human and insufficient ways. As God's children, we know that He loves us, hears us, and knows what is best for us. He is greater than we can ever imagine. And He can do greater things than we can imagine!

Being Content

DAY FOUR

LEARNING TO ACCEPT OUR CIRCUMSTANCES

We all face challenges and difficult circumstances in life. To expect otherwise would be ludicrous. When sin entered this world through Adam, the human race inherited a sinful nature. The enemy came in the form of a serpent into the beautiful Garden of Eden, bringing deception, lies, and evil to Adam and Eve and all of mankind and spawning a corrupting influence the world has seen throughout the ages.

Jesus' words remind us of man's sinfulness: *"Flesh gives birth to flesh, but the Spirit gives birth to spirit. . . . Men loved darkness instead of light because their deeds were evil"* (John 3:6, 19). As Jesus taught the Jews, He reminded them of their enslavement to sin. *"They* [the Jews] *answered him, 'We are Abraham's descendants and have never been slaves of anyone. How can you say that we shall be set free?' Jesus replied, 'I tell you the truth, everyone who sins is a slave to sin' "* (John 8:33–34). The good news is that we have victory over sin and our sinful nature. God has made us *"alive with Christ."* When we received Him, *"He forgave us all our sins"* (Colossians 2:13). Jesus triumphed at the cross when He *"disarmed the powers and authorities"* of the enemy (Colossians 2:15). We have extraordinary victory through the cross.

We can hope and plan for today and the future as best as we can, yet we know we face obstacles in life. Having financial plans is a great idea, yet things may not always work out as we planned. We may be in a job or career that we think will always be there; however, we need to be ready for changes that will inevitably come about. There may be difficult relationships to deal with. We may feel overwhelmed with what's happening in our lives. But there is great news. Jesus said, *"In this world you will have trouble. But take heart! I have overcome the world"* (John 16:33).

We may find ourselves powerless in different situations, yet God is in control. Nothing can happen to us except what He allows to happen.

At times we may wonder why we face trying circumstances. Some problems may be brought on by our own disobedience to God's laws. There are natural consequences for a life lived for one's selfish desires. On the other hand, it may be difficult to understand how we can have serious illnesses or losses in our lives, when we have lived a life pleasing to God. This was the case of Job in the Old Testament. Sometimes God puts us in a place where all we can do is listen to Him and learn from Him. Maybe we need to slow down and wait upon the Lord, understanding that we may not know or understand why things happen until we see our Savior face to face.

As we continue in our walk with God, we can think back to what He has taught us in the past through our experiences and trials. We can also learn to be aware of what He desires to teach us through our present circumstances. He wants us to be His holy people, a group of people dedicated to Him. *"I will put my laws in their minds and write them on their hearts. I will be their God, and they will be my people"* (Hebrews 8:10). He will show us where we have strayed from His ways. His divine influence and strength will help us overcome our sinful ways.

We can trust God in the good times and through the difficult times. Knowing God is with us gives us the confidence we need when we face hard times. We can believe His promise that He will always be with us when we put our hope in Him.

Jeremiah is an Old Testament example of a man who lived in difficult times. Yet his belief in God made him strong enough to face the political unrest of his day. At the age of thirteen, Jeremiah was appointed to be a prophet and speak to the nations as God's messenger. Feeling insecure and frightened at times, Jeremiah's desire was that Judah would renew an alliance with God. For forty years he didn't stop preaching his warnings that the kingdom of Babylon would take over the land of Judah, causing the destruction of Jerusalem and the other towns.

Jeremiah warned the people of Judah that God would be judging them because of their wickedness in forsaking Him. *"Your wickedness will punish you, your backsliding will rebuke you. Consider then and realize how evil and bitter it is for you when you forsake the LORD your God and have no awe of me"* (Jeremiah 2:19).

During Jeremiah's last years, there was already a group of Jews taken captive by King Nebuchadnezzar. They were taken from Jerusalem and were living in Babylon. Jeremiah sent a letter to the exiles, many of whom were priests, prophets, craftsmen, artisans. At the time, Daniel was among the other captives there.

Jeremiah was rejected by others, including his own brothers, and he often feared for his life. He was imprisoned several times by top officials and nearly killed. Yet, even to the very end of his life, he did not forsake God. He continued to preach about God's eternal faithfulness to His people.

📖 Jeremiah sent a letter to the Jews in Babylon, offering them promise and hope. Read Jeremiah 29:4–14, the Lord's words for His people.

Although the Jews were captives in Babylon, were they to live feeling sorry for themselves (see Jeremiah 29:4–7)? What were they told to do?

_____

_____

_____

_____

According to Jeremiah 29:11, what plans does God have for us?

_____

_____

_____

> *As we continue in our walk with God, we can think back to what He has taught us in the past through our experiences and trials. We can also learn to be aware of what He desires to teach us through our present circumstances.*

> *"For I know the plans I have for you, . . . plans to prosper you and not to harm you, plans to give you hope and a future. . . . You will seek me and find me when you seek me with all your heart."*
>
> *Jeremiah 29:11, 13*

God's people will show their desire to follow God with their actions. List the action words mentioned in Jeremiah 29:12–13.

_____

_____

When the Jews were living as exiles, the message God gave them was to accept the increases and decreases in their lives. Although they were no longer living in the land of their fathers, they were to make the best of the situation. They were encouraged to look for the peace and prosperity their new land had to offer.

Our circumstances may overwhelm us. Yet we can be encouraged that God is in charge, no matter how things may look. Each of us has a purpose and a role in God's plan. God wants us to trust Him, even when we don't understand His ways.

Our circumstances can be used to help us find God's direction for our lives. We can use the experiences to help us put our faith into action. Paul wrote with certainty, *"And we know that in all things God works for the good of those who love him, who have been called according to his purpose"* (Romans 8:28). Paul discovered that his contentment was not found in circumstances or things, but in his relationship with Christ.

📖 Read what Paul said about contentment in Philippians 4:11–13. What did Paul say he learned (verse 11)?

_____

What extremes had Paul experienced in his life (verse 12)?

_____

_____

What was Paul's secret for contentment (verse 13)?

_____

_____

📖 Look at 1 Timothy 6:6–8 for more verses on the topic of contentment. What quality along with godliness is a valuable combination (1 Timothy 6:6)?

_____

Summarize 1 Timothy 6:7–8.

_____

_____

_____

Paul understood how the things of this earth are temporal but that which lasts is eternal. He encouraged the believers with these words:

> *"We do not lose heart. . . . For our light and momentary troubles are achieving for us an eternal glory that far outweighs them all. So we fix our eyes not on what is seen, but on what is unseen. For what is seen in temporary, but what is unseen is eternal."* (2 Corinthians 4:16–18)

We can have peace from God's person, power, and grace. *"You will keep in perfect peace him whose mind is steadfast, because he trusts in you"* (Isaiah 26:3). As we entrust our lives to the Lord, we'll learn to abide in Him and to grow more content in our circumstances. Thankful for God's provision, we'll find contentedness in what we have and in what comes our way.

 Heavenly Father, thank You for Your providence throughout my life. I praise you for your unending love and grace to all. I am learning to be content in You and Your provision. Help me to grow in wisdom as You show Your eternal ways to me. Forgive me for my lack of faith at times. I entrust my life into Your care. I entrust my possessions into your care. I give You my concerns and burdens right now. Thank you for Your presence in my life. In Jesus' name I pray. Amen.

BEING GRATEFUL FOR WHAT WE HAVE

How grateful are we for what we have? Do we feel thankful for the many things God provides for us? Are we thankful for what people give us and the kindness people show us? As believers, we are to be grateful. We must not neglect to express our thanks.

We please God when we show gratitude in our lives. I am reminded of the story in the Old Testament of how the people of Israel escaped a life of hardship under Pharaoh's rule. They followed Moses out of Egypt and miraculously crossed the Red Sea, walking on dry ground to the other side. The book of Exodus 14:31 says, *"And when the Israelites saw the great power of the LORD displayed against the Egyptians, the people feared the LORD and put their trust in him and in Moses his servant."* God had delivered them when they saw no way of escape from the Egyptian army. They praised God for His intervention.

Not long after this great victory, the Israelites began complaining and feeling sorry for themselves. *"In the desert the whole community grumbled against Moses and Aaron. The Israelites said to them, 'If only we had died by the LORD's hand in Egypt! There we sat around pots of meat and ate all the food we wanted, but you have brought us out into this desert to starve this entire assembly to death' "* (Exodus 16:2–3). Moses responded by telling the people God had heard their grumbling and he said, *"You are not grumbling against us, but against the LORD"* (Exodus 16:8).

Moses instructed the people that God would supply them with bread in the morning and meat in the evening (Exodus 16:8). Daily God sent them manna, which was *"white like coriander seed and tasted like wafers made with honey"* (Exodus 16:31) and quail. They would learn to be dependent on God for their nourishment. This is one of many occasions when the people of Israel complained about the circumstances they found themselves in as they wandered and lived in the desert for forty years. Rather than giving thanks for what they had, they showed ingratitude through their constant complaining.

The New Testament presents a story with a lesson on the importance of being thankful. From the beginning of Jesus' ministry, He healed the sick and taught the message of salvation. Jesus sent this message to John the Baptist:

> **"Alas, how many, even among those who are called believers, have plenty of all the necessities of life, and yet complain of poverty!"**
>
> **—John Wesley**

"The blind receive sight, the lame walk, those who have leprosy are cured, the deaf hear, the dead are raised and the good news is preached to the poor" (Luke 7:22). Jesus healed leprosy and many other diseases. Leprosy is an infectious skin disease that was painful and ugly. In that day, lepers were quarantined and shunned from society. (It is believed that Job had leprosy, and Naaman the Syrian was healed of leprosy when he washed himself in the Jordan River). The book of Luke describes an occasion when Jesus healed ten lepers at one time. Their lives changed completely They were healed of the awful skin disease and were no longer shunned from society. How many thanked Jesus?

📖 Read Luke 17:11–19 on the healing of ten lepers.

As the lepers stood at a distance, what did they yell out to Jesus (Luke 17:13)?

_____

_____

As you observe these words, what emotions do you think they were feeling?

_____

_____

_____

When Jesus saw them He said, *"Show yourselves to the priests."* Earlier in Jesus' ministry, when He healed a man with leprosy (Luke 5:12–14), He gave the man the exact same instructions. Keep in mind that the ceremonial law of the Old Testament was still in force. The priests were judges of whether one was ceremonially clean. As these lepers were walking in the direction of the priests, they were cleansed from their disease.

According to Luke 17:15, what did one healed leper do?

_____

_____

_____

The Samaritan returned to give thanks, not the Jews who were knowledgeable of the laws of Moses. The lone Samaritan thanked God, while the nine Jews either forgot, neglected, or refused to give God the glory. Jesus used this incident to point out the ingratitude of the others.

What were Jesus' words to the grateful leper (Luke 17:19)?

_____

_____

Matthew Henry comments on these final words of Jesus to the leper:

> The rest [of the lepers] were made whole by the power of Christ, in compassion to their distress, and in answer to their prayer; but he was made whole by his faith, by which Christ saw him distinguished from the rest. Note that temporal mercies are then doubled and sweetened to us when they are fetched in by the prayers of faith, and returned by the praises of faith.[i]

When the people of Israel recalled the day they had been delivered from slavery in Egypt, they praised and thanked God. But when they began complaining, they showed a lack of trust in God's ability to provide. They chose to forget their God of provision and instead focused on themselves and their problems.

In the same way, we who are children of God have been delivered from sin through the victory on the Cross. God has provided a way of escape from death to eternal life. At the time of Christ's death, the veil in the temple of Jerusalem was divided and torn in two, signifying a new covenant. We must not forget the day we made a decision to put our complete trust in our Savior and Redeemer or fail to appreciate what He has done for us.

Philippians 2:14–15 gives us instructions for daily living. *"Do everything without complaining or arguing, so that you may become blameless and pure, children of God without fault in a crooked and depraved generation, in which you shine like the stars in the universe."* We can find ways to be thankful, rather than complain. Ephesians 5:20 says, *"Always giving thanks to God the Father for everything, in the name of our Lord Jesus Christ."*

📖 Read Psalm 100, a psalm for giving thanks. What insights do you gain from this psalm?

_____

_____

_____

📖 Look at 1 Thessalonians 5:16–18. According to this passage, what is God's will for us?

_____

_____

_____

How well are you learning to follow God without complaining? Do you remember to thank God for the gifts you receive from Him? He not only wants us to be satisfied with His gifts to us, but to praise and thank Him often for them.

_____

_____

_____

"Let them give thanks to the LORD for his unfailing love and his wonderful deeds for men, for he satisfies the thirsty and fills the hungry with good things." (Psalms 107:8–9)

🙇 Thank the Lord for the blessings you have.

_____

_____

_____

_____

> **"Enter into his gates with thanksgiving and his courts with praise; give thanks to him and praise his name."**
>
> **Psalm 100:4**

_____

_____

_____

_____

_____

_____

_____

_____

NOTES

1. Matthew Henry, *Matthew Henry's Commentary on the Whole Bible,* "Luke 17:19 Commentary." In e-Sword Bible software database, © 2005, Rick Meyers.

Notes

Notes

EXPLORING OUR RICHES AS BELIEVERS

Last week we looked at the importance of learning to be content with all God gives to us. We can learn to be good stewards of the resources we have by choosing to get our personal finances in order and eliminating debt and the unending hassles and problems that come with it. Planning for our future as best as we know how may prove to be a meaningful exercise, yet we must still continue to depend on God for sustenance. Sometimes it becomes easy to think that all we have attained or acquired is of our own doing, but in reality, every breath we take comes from God.

This week we'll explore our riches we have as believers. We won't focus specifically on temporal or earthly riches, such as lands, houses, or gold. We won't be referring to the word *riches* in the context of currency or stocks and bonds. Instead, our focus will be on the spiritual riches and blessings that are ours to enjoy.

This week we'll explore the riches we have as believers.

THE RICHES OF GOD'S GRACE

Believer's Riches

DAY ONE

As we consider the immeasurable riches God bestows upon us, what could we say is our richest gain? The greatest gift we will ever receive through God's grace is our personal redemption. This is our richest gain. He has made His grace known to us through his beloved Son, Jesus Christ. *"In him we have redemption through his blood, the forgiveness of sins, in accordance with the riches of God's grace"* (Ephesians 1:7). The word *redemption* means, "ransom, a price paid." Born in sin, we were captives and slaves of sin. Through Christ's death on the cross, He paid a ransom for us. He paid such an enormous price that we no longer need to be slaves to sin. Instead, we can have *"forgiveness of sins."* Forgiveness is the act of releasing or sending away one's sins from the sinner. God canceled the debts of all of our faults, guilt, and transgressions through His Son. We have once and for all been pardoned and delivered from the power of sin. The death and resurrection of Christ have disarmed the enemy.

The forgiveness of sins is an act of God's grace. All we need to do is accept and receive this wonderful gift of redemption. When we do, we are set free. *"For all have sinned and fall short of the glory of God, and are justified freely by his grace through the redemption that came by Christ Jesus"* (Romans 3:23–24). Grace is the source of justification. *"It is for freedom that Christ has set us free. Stand firm, then, and do not let yourselves be burdened again by a yoke of slavery"* (Galatians 5:1). We are no longer creatures of bondage to corruption and the things of this world. Sin is no longer our master.

When we allow Jesus to enter our lives as our Savior and Lord, He transforms our lives. *"And we, who with unveiled faces all reflect the Lord's glory, are being transformed into his likeness with ever-increasing glory, which comes from the Lord, who is the Spirit"* (2 Corinthians 3:18). When Jesus walked on this earth and lived among His disciples, He told them He was the "gate" through whom people would be saved. Jesus said, *"I have come that they may have life, and have it to the full"* (John 10:10). Trusting Christ brings a new life with a new purpose for living. We become spiritually rich.

Read Ephesians 2:1–10, on how we are made alive in Christ.

Name two characteristics of God (verse 4).

_____

_____

Even when we were dead in our transgressions, what saves us (verse 5)?

_____

What does God express in His kindness to us through Christ Jesus (verse 7)?

_____

_____

What does not save us? Why (verses 8–9)?

_____

_____

As you look over this passage, write down new insights you've gained.

_____

_____

_____

_____

"It is because of [God] that you are in Christ Jesus, who has become for us wisdom from God— that is, our righteousness, holiness and redemption."

I Corinthians 1:30

All of us who put our faith in Christ Jesus are *"sons of God"* (Galatians 3:26). Whatever our background or family history may be, God is *"rich in mercy"* toward all of us (Ephesians 2:4). He desires *"to make the riches of his glory known"* not only to the Jews but also to the Gentiles" (Romans 9:23–24). *"For there is no difference between Jew and Gentile—the same Lord is Lord of all and richly blesses all who call on him"* (Romans 10:12). All who trust in the Lord can participate in God's riches.

Through God's favor toward us, we have been offered the gift of salvation and a new life in a new family. As Christians, God has lovingly adopted us into the family of God. As members of His family, we receive the blessings and love He lavishes upon us. As our heavenly Father, He shows undeserved kindness to us. Colossians 1:12–13 reminds us of our awesome inheritance: *"Giving thanks to the Father, who has qualified you to share in the inheritance of the saints in the kingdom of light. . . . For he has rescued us from the dominion of darkness and brought us into the kingdom of the Son he loves."* Through God's favor and benevolence, we receive His unconditional love and care. He gives us direction and guidance in our Christian walk and provides us with the strength we need to get through difficult situations.

📖 Let's find out more about God's incomparable grace. What do the following verses say about grace?

2 Thessalonians 2:16—What has God given us by His grace?

_____

1 Timothy 1:13—14—In what manner was grace given to Paul?

_____

James 4:6—To whom is grace promised?

_____

_____

1 Peter 4:10—How do we administer God's grace?

_____

_____

How amazing that we have access to God's immeasurable grace through His Son. We are introduced to this unmerited favor and acceptance the instant we are declared guiltless. *"Therefore, since we have been justified through faith, we have peace with God through our Lord Jesus Christ, through whom we have gained access by faith into this grace in which we now stand; and we rejoice in the hope of the glory of God"* (Romans 5:1–2). Just as the sun's rays shine down upon us, God's grace falls upon us; His love surrounds us.

In his letter to the Ephesians, Paul wrote a prayer for the young Christians in Ephesus. His deepest desire was that they would come to know and experience their heavenly Father's love, and the riches of His grace. These are the words of his prayer:

> *I kneel before the Father, from whom his whole family in heaven and on earth derives its name. I pray that out of his glorious riches, he may strengthen you with power through his Spirit in your inner being, so that Christ may dwell in your hearts through faith. And I pray that you, being rooted and established in love, may have power, together with all the saints, to grasp how wide and long and high and deep is the love of Christ, and to know this love that surpasses knowledge—that you may be filled to the measure of all the fullness of God.*

PSALM 84:11–12

"For the LORD God is a sun and shield; The LORD bestows favor and honor; No good thing does he withhold from those whose walk is blameless. O LORD Almighty, Blessed is the man who trusts in you." (Psalm 84:11–12)

Now to him who is able to do immeasurably more than all we ask or imagine, according to his power that is at work within us, to him be glory in the church and in Christ Jesus throughout all generations, for ever and ever! Amen. (Ephesians 3:14–21)

THE VALUE OF WISDOM

"Get wisdom, get understanding; do not forget my words or swerve from them. Do not forsake wisdom, and she will protect you; love her, and she will watch over you. Wisdom is supreme; therefore get wisdom. Though it cost all you have, get understanding. Esteem her, and she will exalt you; embrace her, and she will honor you. She will set a garland of grace on your head and present you with a crown of splendor." (Proverbs 4:5–9)

THE RICHES OF GOD'S WISDOM

Wisdom is the key to living a life of purpose and fulfillment. To begin enjoying the riches of God's wisdom, people must first listen to the voice of wisdom. Those who refuse to listen to the call of wisdom will continue in simple and naïve ways, suffering the consequences of foolish actions. Their minds remain closed to a more rewarding and fulfilling way of life. *"The simple inherit folly, but the prudent are crowned with knowledge"* (Proverbs 14:18). Foolish people do not know God and walk in darkness (see Ecclesiastes 2:14).

Scripture tells us to go a different way. Proverbs 9:6 tells us, *"Forsake foolishness and live, and go in the way of understanding"* (NKJV). We are to *"forsake,"* abandon, or leave behind our old life of foolishness. By doing so, we will live. In this verse, the Hebrew word translated *live* literally means "to make alive, to refresh, to rebuild, to restore to life."[1] Spiros Zodhiates comments:

> Life comes from a right relationship with God. The choice between life and death is ours. Life is completely related to the Word of God. As Jesus points out, we gain our very life from God's words and not merely from bread.[2]

How do we attain true wisdom? When we make the decision to "fear God" and to have the proper regard for God, the door to wisdom will open up to us. *"The fear of the LORD is the beginning of knowledge, but fools despise wisdom and discipline"* (Proverbs 1:7). Having a right relationship with God enables us to have a better understanding of the ways of God. As we seek to know God better, He will make Himself known to us. *"The fear of the LORD is the beginning of wisdom, and knowledge of the Holy One is understanding. For through me your days will be many, and years will be added to your life. If you are wise, your wisdom will reward you"* (Proverbs 9:10–12).

Joseph, the young man who was sold by his brothers into slavery in Egypt, was blessed with great wisdom. Potiphar, one of Pharaoh's top officials, bought Joseph and allowed him to live in his own house. *"The LORD was with Joseph and he prospered"* (Genesis 39:1–2). Acts 7:10 states, *"[God] gave Joseph wisdom and enabled him to gain the goodwill of Pharaoh king of Egypt; so he made him ruler over Egypt and all his palace."* The King of Egypt recognized Joseph's wisdom and said, *"Since God has made all this known to you, there is no one so discerning and wise as you"* (Genesis 41:39). God used Joseph to preserve his family and the descendants of Abraham. This was one way God fulfilled his promise to Abraham that he would have many descendants.

God used Moses, another man of great wisdom, to protect and lead His people out of slavery in Egypt. Pharaoh's daughter saw three–month old baby Moses crying in a wicker basket in the Nile River. She took pity on the baby boy and adopted him, protecting him from Pharaoh's order to have all the

Hebrew babies killed. Moses grew up in the palace, privileged to receive a classical education. *"Moses was educated in all the wisdom of the Egyptians and was powerful in speech and action"* (Acts 7:22). God entrusted Moses with His laws, the Ten Commandments. Moses led His people and judged them with extraordinary understanding.

We are well aware of Solomon's proverbs, or wise sayings. Shortly after Solomon became king, the Lord spoke to him in a dream. He told this young man he could have anything he wanted. When given the choice, Solomon humbly answered, *"Give your servant a discerning heart to govern your people and to distinguish between right and wrong"* (1 Kings 3:9). The Lord was pleased with his request and responded:

> *I will give you a wise and discerning heart, so that there will never have been anyone like you, nor will there ever be. Moreover, I will give you what you have not asked for—both riches and honor—so that in your lifetime you will have no equal among kings. And if you walk in my ways and obey my statutes and commands as David your father did, I will give you a long life.* (1 Kings 3:12–14)

Solomon chose wisely and was given unusual wisdom. He had a

> *"very great insight, and a breadth of understanding as measureless as the sand on the seashore. . . . He spoke three thousand proverbs and his songs numbered a thousand and five. He described plant life, from the cedar of Lebanon to the hyssop that grows out of walls. He also taught about animals and birds, reptiles and fish."* (1 Kings 4:29, 32–33)

Solomon led in the construction of Israel's grand temple and palace and judged wisely as king. All of the nations came to know of his splendid kingdom, wisdom, and riches.

When Jesus lived on earth, the people He met and those who heard of Him were amazed at His great wisdom. When He was a young boy of twelve, Jesus sat in the temple courts, listening to the teachers and having dialogue with them. *"Everyone who heard him was amazed at his understanding and his answers"* (Luke 2:47). As Jesus grew, His level of wisdom grew. *"And Jesus grew in wisdom and stature, and in favor with God and men"* (Luke 2:52). When Jesus returned to His hometown, He taught the worshipers in the synagogue, astonishing them with His great understanding of God and the Scriptures (Matthew 13:54). John, the beloved disciple, wrote these powerful words: *"The Word became flesh and made his dwelling among us. We have seen his glory, the glory of the One and Only, who came from the Father, full of grace and truth"* (John 1:14).

Having reverence for God and a right relationship with Him is the first step in attaining wisdom. Secondly, we must learn and study the Word of God to gain wisdom for life.

It is natural to be lax and inactive in our growth of spiritual knowledge. We are so easily influenced by this world's temporal value system. Yet, we must not neglect access to the treasure of wisdom by studying God's Word for us. King David writes, *"The law of the LORD is perfect, reviving the soul. The statutes of the LORD are trustworthy, making wise the simple"* (Psalms 19:7). David also states, *"The unfolding of your words gives light; it gives understanding to the simple"* (Psalms 119:130). When we read God's Word, we gain a whole new facet of understanding and wisdom. We learn more of Scripture's eternal value system.

HOLD ON TO SOUND WISDOM

"By wisdom the LORD laid the earth's foundations, by understanding he set the heavens in place; by his knowledge the deeps were divided, and the clouds let drop the dew. My son, preserve sound judgment and discernment, do not let them out of your sight; they will be life for you, an ornament to grace your neck. Then you will go on your way in safety, and your foot will not stumble." (Proverbs 3:19–23)

PROVERBS 8:17–21

"I [wisdom] love those who love me, and those who seek me find me. With me are riches and honor, enduring wealth and prosperity. My fruit is better than fine gold; what I yield surpasses choice silver. I walk in the way of righteousness, along the paths of justice, bestowing wealth on those who love me and making their treasuries full."

GODLY WISDOM PRODUCES GOOD FRUIT

"Who is wise and understanding among you? Let him show it by his good life, by deeds done in the humility that comes from wisdom.... The wisdom that comes from heaven is first of all pure; then peace-loving, considerate, submissive, full of mercy and good fruit, impartial and sincere. Peacemakers who sow in peace raise a harvest of righteousness." (James 3:13, 17–18)

What are the rewards of wisdom?

☞ An understanding of what is right, just, and fair (Proverbs 2:9)

☞ Happiness and joy (Proverbs 2:10)

☞ Security and protection from the ways of devious people (Proverbs 2:11–12).

☞ A long and good life, riches and honor (Proverbs 3:16)

☞ Pleasant ways and peace (Proverbs 3:17)

☞ Life and blessings (Proverbs 3:18)

📖 Read 1 Corinthians 2:6–16 on wisdom.

According to 1 Corinthians 2:6, who speaks the message of wisdom?

_____

How is God's wisdom revealed to us (1 Corinthians 2:10)?

_____

_____

Record any new insights you've gained from these verses in 1 Corinthians.

_____

_____

📖 Look at Ephesians 1:17–21.

Why did Paul ask God to give the Ephesians wisdom and revelation (verse 17)?

_____

_____

Why did Paul pray that the eyes of their heart be enlightened? List the three reasons (verses 18–19).

_____

_____

 When you mature as a Christian, you will grow with the understanding you need to make the right decisions. You will learn to recognize what God would have you to do in your daily life. This will affect many different areas of life, including the decisions you make that affect personal finances. Are you willing to seek God's help for personal finances? Are you open to asking Him for wisdom in the changes you may need to make in this area? He can help you become wiser and show you better ways to handle your money and resources, bringing more peace to your life.

Who can imagine the extent of God's wisdom? He is all-powerful and all knowing. Read the following verses as a prayer, with praise and thanksgiving:

Oh, the depth of the riches of the wisdom and knowledge of God! How unsearchable his judgments, and his paths beyond tracing out! 'Who has known the mind of the LORD? Or who has been his counselor? Who has ever given to God, that God should repay him?' For from him and through him and to him are all things. To him be the glory forever! Amen. (Romans 11:33–36)

TRUE PROSPERITY IS IN RIGHT LIVING

How can we be blessed and have a life that prospers? Wisdom is the key to living a life of fulfillment. We gain wisdom through our reverence for God, seeking Him, and learning more of His Word. Getting understanding in the ways of God is important. Even more important is obedience to God's Word. When we apply godly wisdom to our lives, our right living leads to prosperity. King David joyfully exclaimed, *"Let the LORD be magnified, Who has pleasure in the prosperity of His servant"* (Psalms 35:27, NKJV). God delights in our well-being as we learn to trust and obey Him.

Genesis 12 records that God told Abraham to leave his country, the land of Haran, and go to another land. God promised to make him into a great nation and to bless him. *"I will bless those who bless you . . . and all the peoples on earth will be blessed through you"* (Genesis 12:3). Abraham trusted God as he left his homeland to find a new land for his family. Although he wasn't perfect, Abraham listened to God and by faith obeyed Him. God blessed Abraham *"abundantly"* giving him *"sheep and cattle, silver and gold, menservants and maidservants, and camels and donkeys. [His] wife Sarah has borne him a son in her old age, and he has given him everything he owns"* (Genesis 24:34–36). God wants to bless people, families, and nations today just as He desired to do in Abraham's time.

📖 Fill in the chart with examples of people in the Old Testament who obeyed God and prospered.

Scripture	Who Prospered	How He Prospered
Genesis 26:1, 12–14		
Genesis 32:1–5, 10; 33:11		
Genesis 39:1–4		

Prosperity is not just related to money and possessions, but to the wholeness and well–being of our lives. When we have a right relationship with God and with others, God will bless us. He will honor our desire to be faithful to Him, and we will be rewarded accordingly. The prophet Isaiah wrote, *"Tell the righteous it will be well with them, for they will enjoy the fruit of their deeds"* (Isaiah 3:10). Another prophet, Jeremiah, warned the people of Judah that they should not forget the Almighty God of Israel. Jeremiah told them to remember the command God gave their fathers, *"Obey me, and I will be your God and you will be my people. Walk in all the ways I command you, that it may go well with you"* (Jeremiah 7:23). Jeremiah continued speaking to the people of Judah, telling them what their forefathers did. Instead of listening to God, *"they followed the stubborn inclinations of their evil hearts. They went backward and not forward"* (Jeremiah 7:24). The disobedience of the people led to harsh discipline.

Solomon, in all his wisdom, states,

> *"He who conceals his sins does not prosper, but whoever confesses and renounces them finds mercy. Blessed is the man who always fears the LORD, but he who hardens his heart falls into trouble."* (Proverbs 28:13–14)

"Blessings on all who reverence and trust the Lord—on all who obey Him! Their reward shall be prosperity and happiness."

Psalm 128:1–2, LB

Solomon also comments, *"Because the wicked do not fear God, it will not go well with them, and their days will not lengthen like a shadow"* (Ecclesiastes 8:13).

📖 What does God's Word say about prosperity? Read these verses and summarize what brings prosperity and success.

Joshua 1:8

_____

_____

_____

2 Chronicles 26:3–5

_____

_____

Job 36:11

_____

_____

_____

Psalm 128:1–2

_____

_____

_____

TRUE PROSPERITY

Prosperity is not just related to money and possessions, but to the wholeness and well-being of our lives. When we have a right relationship with God and with others, God will bless us. He will honor our desire to be faithful to Him, and we will be rewarded accordingly.

> *"Whoever trusts in his riches will fall, but the righteous will thrive like a green leaf."*
>
> **Proverbs 11:28**

The psalmist David contrasts the unrighteous and the righteous in Psalm 1. He uses poetry and figurative language in his prayers. He compares the righteous, the person who trusts in God, with the unrighteous.

📖 Read the first of David's prayers or psalms (Psalms 1:1–6).

What is the righteous person compared to (Psalms 1:3)?

_____

_____

What is the result of righteous living (Psalms 1:3)?

_____

_____

According to Psalms 1:6, what does the Lord watch over?

_____

God is the Rewarder of those who diligently seek Him (Hebrews 11:6). The ones who love God have favor with Him and walk in His favor. He looks for people who will live wholeheartedly for Him. *"For the eyes of the LORD range throughout the earth to strengthen those whose hearts are fully committed to him"* (2 Chronicles 16:9). How reassuring to know that the Lord will supply us with the courage and strength needed to withstand life's challenges.

As we draw closer to God, there is a new awareness of His provision and of the blessings He brings into our lives. Our faith in God and in His Son Christ Jesus is a great treasure to possess. We can always hold onto that. We can have victorious lives as we know God's Word and obey it. God has a wonderful promise for those who are faithful to Him. He *"loves the just and will not forsake his faithful ones"* (Psalms 37:28).

In closing, read the encouraging words of the apostle John: *"Dear friend, I pray that you may enjoy good health and that all may go well with you, even as your soul is getting along well. . . . I have no greater joy than to hear that my children are walking in the truth"* (3 John 1:2, 4).

THE BLESSINGS OF OUR FELLOWSHIP WITH CHRIST

ROMANS 14:17–19

"For the kingdom of God is . . . of righteousness, peace and joy in the Holy Spirit, because anyone who serves Christ in this way is pleasing to God and approved by men. Let us therefore make every effort to do what leads to peace and to mutual edification."

Are we sharing in the joys that fellowship with Jesus Christ brings? When we turn away from the life of spiritual darkness and sin, we make a commitment to walk in the light of God's presence. We make a decision to please our Savior and have fellowship with Him. *"For you were once darkness, but now you are light in the Lord. Live as children of light (for the fruit of the light consists in all goodness, righteousness and truth) and find out what pleases the Lord. Have nothing to do with the fruitless deeds of darkness"* (Ephesians 5:8–11). If we desire to have fellowship with Jesus, we turn our backs completely on the foolish ways of sin. We must be born again to have fellowship, or communion, with Him.

God has made it possible for us to have fellowship with His Son. *"He will keep you strong to the end, so that you will be blameless on the day of our Lord Jesus Christ. God, who has called you into fellowship with his Son Jesus Christ our Lord, is faithful"* (1 Corinthians 1:8–9). When we desire to have a close relationship with Jesus, we receive Him and abide in Him. We practice "right living," or righteousness.

Our salvation offers so much more than a future reward of a home in heaven with our Redeemer. God wants to restore to us what we lost when sin entered the world. Through His Son we can experience His never-ending love and a growing relationship with Him.

Nicodemus, an honored member of the Jewish Sanhedrin, was an interpreter of the law. He recognized that there was something different about this man Jesus. Nicodemus observed Jesus' teachings and signs and knew He had *"come from God"* (John 3:2). The religious teacher desired to know more of God and His power. Jesus responded by saying he needed to be born again. *"I tell you the truth, no one can enter the kingdom of God unless he is born of water and the Spirit. Flesh gives birth to flesh, but the Spirit gives birth to spirit"* (John 3:5–6). When we are born again, we receive the Holy Spirit.

During Jesus' last days on earth, He told His disciples He would be leaving them. But Jesus also comforted them with a promise. He said, *"I will ask the*

> *"God, who has called you into fellowship with his Son Jesus Christ our Lord, is faithful."*
>
> *1 Corinthians 1:9*

Father, and He will give you another Counselor to be with you forever—the Spirit of truth. . . . You know him, for He lives with you and will be in you. I will not leave you as orphans; I will come to you" (John 14:16–18). The Holy Spirit is our promised Helper. He lives and works within us, providing the help and strength we need to overcome sin and to follow God.

📖 When we receive Christ, we inherit a new identity. Read about this new identity in Romans 8:13–17.

According to Romans 8:13, who enables us to win over the old sin nature and live an abundant life in Christ?

_____

Who are the sons of God (verse 14)?

_____

Paul wrote about *"the riches of [God's] kindness, tolerance and patience"* and how we are led to repentance by God's kindness (Romans 2:4). He explains that *"we are God's workmanship"* (Ephesians 2:10), and whatever our age may be, God is continually in the process of building Christian character in us. As holy temples of the Lord, we are in the process of being built *"to become a dwelling in which God lives by his Spirit"* (Ephesians 2:22). Our lives are changed by the work of the indwelling Holy Spirit, not by our own efforts.

📖 How does the Holy Spirit work? Look at the following verses and summarize your answers.

John 14:26

_____

_____

_____

John 16:7–8

_____

_____

_____

John 16:13

_____

_____

_____

Acts 1:8

_____

_____

_____

Romans 5:5

_____

_____

_____

Romans 8:26–27

_____

_____

_____

Ephesians 3:16

_____

_____

_____

The Holy Spirit also enables the believer to have the fruit of holy living. He produces the fruit with these characteristics: *"But the fruit of the Spirit is love, joy, peace, patience, kindness, goodness, faithfulness, gentleness and self-control. Against such things there is no law"* (Galatians 5:22–23). How have we seen God work in our lives in these areas?

Christ invites us into a deeper relationship with Him. Paul warns us that in the last days people will be *"lovers of pleasure rather than lovers of God—having a form of godliness but denying its power"* (2 Timothy 3:1, 4–5). What can we do to strengthen our commitment to Him? Let's not miss out on the blessings that Christ has for us.

 When we enjoy close fellowship with Christ our Redeemer, we learn more of what it means to *"have the mind of Christ"* (1 Corinthians 2:16). He builds Christian character in us and the fruit of holy living is seen in us. We grow more attuned to His thoughts, understanding, and will for us. As we gain spiritual knowledge, we became less self-centered and more Christ-centered. How do you think this affects our beliefs and decisions as we manage our resources, including our money?

Our Rewards in Heaven

In this final lesson we have been studying how we are rewarded for right living. Although we may live in a world of sin, we can receive the unending riches of God's grace and His wisdom and experience the spiritual riches and blessings of God. We can enjoy the fellowship we have in Christ, growing and maturing as Christians, and experience joy and peace that only come from God. However, we will experience joy, peace, and God's glory on a grander scale when we get to heaven. *"Only those whose names are written in the Lamb's book of life"* will enter heaven (Revelation 21:27). When we are welcomed by our Savior face to face, we'll be trans-

I CORINTHIANS 2:9–10

"As it is written: 'No eye has seen, no ear has heard, no mind has conceived, what God has prepared for those who love him'—but God has revealed it to us by his Spirit."

"His divine power has given us everything we need for life and godliness through our knowledge of him who called us by his own glory and goodness.

2 Peter 1:3

formed by His power, and be *"like his glorious body"* (Philippians 3:21). Our eternity in heaven is better than we can ever imagine!

At the Last Supper, Jesus told His twelve disciples He would soon be leaving them. When Simon Peter asked where He was going, Jesus responded, *"Where I am going, you cannot follow now, but you will follow later"* (John 13:36). His disciples had left everything and learned from their Master for three years; they could not comprehend why He would leave them. Jesus comforted them saying, *"Trust in God; trust also in me. In my Father's house are many rooms; if it were not so, I would have told you. I am going there to prepare a place for you"* (John 14:1–2). Jesus was going to heaven, the eternal home of God, His Father.

In a spiritual sense, we have an inheritance as children of God. God is keeping an inheritance in heaven for those who have a *"new birth."* This is *"an inheritance that can never perish, spoil, or fade"* (1 Peter 1:3–4). Paul states, *"Having believed, you were marked in him with a seal, the promised Holy Spirit, who is a deposit guaranteeing our inheritance until the redemption of those who are God's possession"* (Ephesians 1:13–14).

The best way to be prepared to meet our Lord is to faithfully do His will. We can trust God to produce a godly life in us. And one day we'll be called to heaven; *"our citizenship is in heaven"* (Philippians 3:20). It is a place of great beauty and joy. We will inherit our eternal home, *"the city with foundations, whose architect and builder is God"* (Hebrews 11:10). The apostle John received a revelation of heaven, the Holy City. He wrote that it is God's shining brightness, or His glory, which lights heaven (Revelation 21:23). There is no need for the sun. This is how he described the New Jerusalem, descending out of heaven:

> *It shone with the glory of God, and its brilliance was like that of a very precious jewel, like a jasper, clear as crystal. It had a great, high wall with twelve gates, and with twelve angels at the gates. On the gates were written the names of the twelve tribes of Israel. . . . The wall of the city had twelve foundations, and on them were the names of the twelve apostles of the Lamb. . . The wall was made of jasper, and the city of pure gold, as pure as glass. The foundations of the city walls were decorated with every kind of precious stone. . . . The twelve gates were twelve pearls, each gate made of a single pearl. The great street of the city was of pure gold, like transparent glass.* (Revelation 21:11–14; 18–19, 21)

Once we enter heaven's gates, we will no longer have the worries, struggles, and pain we experience on earth. There will be no more sadness, crying, or death. We won't suffer from the effects of sin since there is no sin in heaven. Everything will be made new (Revelation 21:4). As servants of God, we will serve Him with work we will enjoy (Revelation 22:3), and we will dwell in a perfect place where God and His angels live.

Although we presently reside here on earth, our hope is in heaven. Just as an engaged couple makes preparations for their future wedding and life together, Christians also live in anticipation of seeing their Redeemer, Jesus Christ. We look forward to the day we will meet Him. As we practice right living, we *"will receive a rich welcome into the eternal kingdom of our Lord and Savior Jesus Christ"* (2 Peter 1:11).

Peter stated that we have what we need to practice right living:

"His divine power has given us everything we need for life and godliness through our knowledge of him who called us by his own glory and goodness. . . . For this very reason, make every effort to add to your faith goodness; and to goodness, knowledge; and to knowledge, self-control; and to self-control, perseverance; and to perseverance, godliness; and to godliness, brotherly kindness; and to brotherly kindness, love. For if you possess these qualities in increasing measure, they will keep you from being ineffective and unproductive in your knowledge of our Lord Jesus Christ." (2 Peter 1:3, 5–8)

Not only will we enjoy the rewards of our inheritance of heaven. Jesus promised His disciples that *"when the Son of Man sits on his glorious throne,"* He will reward His followers for their service (Matthew 19:28–30). Everyone who reveres Him, great and small, will be commended and receive recognition (Revelation 11:18). People who have been persecuted for their faith will also be greatly rewarded in heaven (Matthew 5:11–12).

📖 Read about a promised reward mentioned in 2 Timothy 4:7–8 .

What three things did Paul say he had done (verse 7)?

_____

_____

_____

According to 2 Timothy 4:8, what will the Righteous Judge award those who eagerly look forward to His return?

_____

_____

_____

📖 There are other crowns mentioned that the Righteous Judge will award to His followers. They are:

☞ Incorruptible Crown (1 Corinthians 9:25)

☞ Crown of Life (James 1:12; Revelation 2:10)

☞ Crown of Glory (1 Peter 5:1–4)

As our hearts are drawn to matters of eternal value, things of this earth seem less important to us (Matthew 6:21). A.W. Tozer, 20th century Christian author and pastor, wrote these words in a prayer: "O God, be Thou exalted over my possessions. Nothing of earth's treasures shall seem dear unto me if only Thou art glorified in my life."[3]

 As you complete this Bible study, consider whether you have placed possessions in the proper perspective of God's economy. Do you aspire to be wise stewards of your resources, eliminating financial hardship and debt as much as possible? Do you desire to be financially prepared as much as possible for future needs? Trust God to help you make the right decisions and provide for your needs.

Write down any new insights you've gained from today's lesson.

_____

_____

_____

"Every good and perfect gift is from above, coming down from the Father of the heavenly lights, who does not change like shifting shadows."

James 1:17

_____

_____

_____

In his desire to follow God, A. W. Tozer prayed:

> *O Lord, I have heard a good word inviting me to look away to Thee and be satisfied. My heart longs to respond, but sin has clouded my vision till I see Thee but dimly. Be pleased to cleanse me in Thine own precious blood, and make me inwardly pure, so that I may with unveiled eyes gaze upon Thee all the days of my earthly pilgrimage. Then shall I be prepared to behold Thee in full splendor in the day when Thou shalt appear to be glorified in Thy saints and admired in all them that believe. Amen.*[4]

NOTES

1. Spiros Zodhiates, *Hebrew-Greek Key Word Study Bible* (Chattanooga, TN: AMG Publishers, 1990), 1725.

2. Ibid.

3. A. W. Tozer, *The Pursuit of God* (Camp Hill, PA: Christian Publications, 1993), 101.

4. Ibid., 91.

Notes

Appendix 1: Monthly Expenses Worksheet (Page 1)

Income	Giving	Home Mtg./ Ins.	Repairs Maint. Furniture	Property Taxes	Water	Sanitation	Electric	Gas	Cable	Phone Cell Internet	Groceries School Lunches	School Tuition Daycare	Misc.	Entertainment Eating Out	Total

Appendix 1: Monthly Expenses Worksheet (Page 2)

Total Pg. 2	Total Pg. 1	Credit Obligations	Vacation	Life Insurance	Savings Investment	Emergency Fund	Clothes	Assoc.&. Clubs	Medical Insurance	Prescriptions	Doctors Dentist	Insurance Plates.	Car Repairs	Car Loans	Gas

Notes

Notes

Notes

Notes

Notes

Notes

Notes